REDISCOVERING
THE AMERICAN
COVENANT

ROADMAP TO RESTORE AMERICA

MARK BURRELL

Ballast Books, LLC
Washington, DC
www.ballastbooks.com

ISBN: 978-1955026147

Library of Congress Control Number has been applied for

Printed in Hong Kong

Published by Ballast Books
www.ballastbooks.com

For more information, bulk orders, appearances or speaking requests,
please email info@ballastbooks.com

ACKNOWLEDGEMENTS

To my family, who was never quite sure I would ever finish this but encouraged me nonetheless!!!

To my spiritual mentor, Dave Stuckey, who gave me a critical grounding in theology.

To Bill Federer for his extensive research and encouragement in the completion of this book.

To Hillsdale College, which provided much-needed guidance on my outline and writing style.

To my illustrator, Tom Post, who has brought this topic to life in a fresh way.

To my dear wife, Charlene, who never hesitated in supporting this effort.

And lastly,

To ALL American patriots, past and present, who, through their speeches and writings, have provided critical insight into the most unlikely event in human history: the drafting and adoption of the American Covenant—the Declaration of Independence.

CONTENTS

Introduction 1

Chapter 1: The State of The Union 11

Chapter 2: The Source of Civil Government 39

Chapter 3: Learning From Israel 69

Chapter 4: Evangelism Through Justice 109

Chapter 5: Starting a Nation 137

Chapter 6: The Formula for Freedom 171

Chapter 7: The Pursuit of Happiness 199

Chapter 8: The Progressive Blueprint for Civil Government . . 219

Chapter 9: Christian Citizenship 259

Chapter 10: The Role of The Church 293

Chapter 11: Roadmap to Restore America 329

Appendix 342

Selective Bibliography 372

Endnotes 375

MUHLENBERG

REDISCOVERING THE AMERICAN COVENANT

> Strive for full restoration, encourage one another, be of one mind, live in peace.
>
> —2 Corinthians 13:11

For many of us these days, it feels as if the United States has never been less united. The nation, it seems, has become irrevocably fractured along political and ideological lines—Republican/Democrat, liberal/conservative, red/blue, etc. Sitting down for Thanksgiving dinner with family has never been more uncomfortable and the admonition to avoid discussing religion or politics in polite company has never been more apropos. What has happened to America? And how can we reverse the trend?

> —Joe Pierre

REDISCOVERING THE AMERICAN COVENANT

> Strive for full restoration, encourage one another, be of one mind, live in peace.
>
> —2 Corinthians 13:11

> For many of us these days, it feels as if the United States has never been less united. The nation, it seems, has become irrevocably fractured along political and ideological lines—Republican/Democrat, liberal/conservative, red/blue, etc. Sitting down for Thanksgiving dinner with family has never been more uncomfortable and the admonition to avoid discussing religion or politics in polite company has never been more apropos. What has happened to America? And how can we reverse the trend?
>
> —Joe Pierre*
> September 5, 2018[1]

I grew up in Bucks County, Pennsylvania, with strong Christian parents who were active in church and believed in America. I was the youngest of four, all of whom played instruments and participated in school band. I enjoyed playing patriotic songs on my trumpet and remember playing Sousa marches in Memorial Day parades. History was one of my favorite subjects, and living just outside Philadelphia, I was exposed to an abundance of colonial history. School field trips included visits to Valley Forge, Betsy Ross's house,

---

* Joseph M. Pierre, MD, is a health sciences clinical professor in the Department of Psychiatry and Biobehavioral Sciences, David Geffen School of Medicine at UCLA, and the acting chief of Mental Health Community Care Systems at the VA Greater Los Angeles Healthcare System. I do not follow him; I just happened to see his article and completely identify with this opening in this online article from *Psychology Today*.

2

the Liberty Bell, and Independence Hall. One of my favorite places was the Franklin Institute, a science and history museum that fueled my mechanical interests. I graduated from Penn State in 1984 with an engineering degree and have worked in the private sector for more than thirty-five years in manufacturing, process development, and program management roles.

Along the way, I married, had four children, and now have a growing number of grandchildren. I also was fortunate to find a spiritual mentor in my twenties who helped me work through a myriad of questions I had with my faith. Given the doctrinal questions I had, he took me through systematic theology,* an approach to studying the Bible that parallels the scientific method. I found this liberating, given my science and engineering background—not that I had all the answers, but I learned how to study the Bible in a logical, methodical way. I see the Bible as a big database available to all to understand what God wants us to know about ourselves, how we can be reconciled to Him, and how to live. Since then, my wife and I have helped to start several churches, and I have had a teaching ministry for more than thirty years.

I recognize I had a very pro-America experience growing up compared to others, but I started to hear a different narrative about America in the 1980s. I heard the founders were not genuine Christians but deists, who rejected the idea that God intervenes in the affairs of mankind. I also heard they were at fault for not abolishing slavery during the founding era and that the US Constitution said they thought slaves were worth only three-fifths of a person. Then there is Thomas Jefferson, who, I had heard, denied the Trinity and wrote his own Bible, pulling out important details he did not agree with or believe.

Worse, I then stumbled upon another big problem with the founding: How could the Revolution have been biblically justifiable with Romans 13 saying we should submit to our civil leaders? From a Christian perspective, these were all serious charges against

---

* My spiritual mentor gave me a list of numerous books on systematic theology to read, including Enns, Ryrie, Thiessen, Moody, and Chafer (fortunately the condensed two-volume set!).

the American founding that appeared to have no reasonable defense. I decided I needed to study this further.

Curious about how much God cares about civil government and what responsibility I had to support my own government, I started picking up books on the subject in the 1990s. I soon realized I needed to go back to the Bible to see what it said about justice, rights, and governing, using the systematic theology approach I had been taught. When searching for verses, I quickly realized there are thousands of passages on the topic; it was just that no one pointed them out to me and so I *did not see them*. I started to arrange verses to identify principles around governing like any other area of theology. Then I looked at the Reformation to see how the theology around civil government evolved leading up to the American founding. I felt like I was discovering puzzle pieces and slowly putting them together to answer three questions—who are we as Americans, what do we as a nation believe about civil government, and what is supposed to bind us together?

My journey caused me to rethink civil government and my citizenship role as a Christian. I soon realized I did not fully understand the American Revolution and the importance of the primary founding document, the Declaration of Independence. I discovered there was a lot of theology informing not only the Declaration itself but also the process the founders took to establish a new nation. I realized that I was uncovering not a mere side topic but instead a significant new dimension to the Bible that elevated my faith to a new level. Along the way I gained a far greater appreciation for the faith of the founders and what they accomplished. It is this merging of the biblical underpinnings and historical narrative on the American founding and our citizenship duty I wish to pass on to the Christian community and my fellow Americans.

QUESTIONS THIS BOOK ANSWERS

This book is intended to address several critical questions in America today:

1. What ideas truly informed the American founding, specifically captured in the Declaration of Independence?
2. What is the responsibility of every American, especially Christians, regarding the maintenance of civil government to provide equal and impartial justice for all?
3. What forces are dividing America and driving our cultural and national decline?
4. What must happen to restore America to the vision captured in the Declaration of Independence to protect everyone's God-given rights to life, liberty, and the pursuit of happiness?

In *Rediscovering the American Covenant,* I illuminate *the principles and promises of governance that bind all Christians universally and that bind Americans in particular,* as captured in the Declaration of Independence. In each chapter, I walk through the Bible, examining verses pertaining to liberty, justice, rights, and governance that are largely ignored by the modern church. I show where God ordained the institution of civil government—with universal expectations binding on mankind across all nations and all eras. I demonstrate how God relayed to the nation of Israel key principles to establish and run a just civil authority, and how he blessed Israel when they followed his plan and judged them when they did not. From these verses I summarize the governing principles God has provided for all nations, so they may govern in a way that honors him and thereby experience His blessing. I also summarize resulting citizenship responsibilities individuals have, especially Christians, to help establish and maintain justice in the communities and nations in which they live.

Given the growing division across America, I contrast the progressive* worldview challenging the American experiment with our founding covenant and the ideology that informed it. It is important that all Americans understand these two worldviews and the conflicting ideas driving the division we are seeing across the country. Lastly, using

---

* Throughout the book, when referring to the early Progressive movement, I capitalize *Progressive*. I do not capitalize modern progressivism.

biblical principles, I propose a path forward to restore America to the vision captured in our national founding covenant.

Along the way I address many questions surrounding the American founding and how to harmonize the Christian faith with historical events from the founding to today:

- Was the founding biblically justifiable or did it violate Romans 13?
- Was America founded as a Christian nation?
- Does focusing on politics hamper evangelism?
- Were the founders deists?
- Did the founders support the modern definition of "separation of church and state"?
- Why didn't the founders abolish slavery?
- Did the founders believe slaves were worth three-fifths of a person?
- Shouldn't Christians be concerned with God's heavenly kingdom versus politics?
- If Jesus did not talk about politics, why should Christians worry about politics?

TARGET AUDIENCE FOR THIS BOOK

This book is for all Americans seeking to better understand why political dynamics in America have become so contentious over the last few decades. As Joe Pierre states in his article from September 5, 2018, the division we are seeing in America has become increasingly uncomfortable, and more people are trying to understand why this is happening. To get to the root cause of the problem in America today one must first understand the true biblical and historical origins of our founding. One must also understand how the founding worldview compares to the progressive worldview. The Far Left now driving this worldview has become increasingly and openly Marxist, seeking to cut all ties to our founding and fundamentally transform America into something much different than our founding vision of liberty and justice for all.

We are rapidly approaching a point where all Americans will be forced to declare what position they embrace. This book is intended to help inform all Americans to make this decision.

More directly, this book is targeted towards Christians, especially church leaders, who are open to a thoughtful and thorough analysis of what the Bible teaches in this area and how these concepts informed the American founding. My claim is that all Christians have citizenship responsibilities in the communities and nations in which they live. In this book I show how this topic is vital to ensuring the peace and safety required for every individual to go on his or her own personal faith journey, which the Bible speaks to:

> Strive for full restoration, encourage one another, be of one mind, live in peace. (2 Cor. 13:11)

I also address the assertion that the church must avoid politics because it hampers evangelism. Lastly, I lay out the roadmap to restore America to a God-honoring nation.

GETTING THE MOST FROM THIS BOOK

I acknowledge that the content is a bit advanced and assumes a basic knowledge of history and the Bible. To get the most from this book, I have included several things to help the reader internalize and apply key principles:

- Numerous illustrations throughout from my good friend Tom Post. These illustrations help transport the reader back to key historical events in the life of Israel and America and convey the key meaning of citizenship principles put into practice.
- A biblical timeline showing key principles of civil government expressed in the Old Testament and affirmed in the New Testament.
- A summary of key governing principles to aid in putting citizenship duty into practice. This includes biblical references,

and I encourage the reader to read through these periodically to help internalize them and then put them into practice.

• Lastly, there is a summary of typical objections from Christians on this topic in the Appendix. These objections are summarized in the chapter where they naturally arise and are more fully explained in the Appendix.

My challenge to the reader is to use this book as a starting point to understand what the Bible has to say about civil government and the responsibility Christians have to help establish liberty and justice for all, no matter where they live. My hope is that in reading this book you will rediscover the American covenant and commit yourself to it as so many Americans have since the founding era.

For those who do not have a personal faith in Jesus Christ, I hope this book will help show God's love for mankind and his provision for our being restored to him. This restoration can happen only by acknowledging the sin in your life, repenting of it, and accepting Jesus as having paid your sin debt by dying on the cross. Each person's faith journey is made possible by having religious liberty which the civil authority is to provide. This gospel message is woven throughout the book and is actually the intent of the colonial phrase "pursuit of Happiness," further explained in chapter 7.

For Christians already engaged or serving in the public square, this book will affirm the great sacrifices many of you are making and will strengthen your convictions in continuing to strive to protect our founding principles. For those of you not engaged, my assertion is that this study will build your faith in new and unforeseen ways. It will help you appreciate what some of your fellow believers are doing as they battle it out in the political arena— often without much support from fellow Christians. It will help you see the connection between providing justice and protecting the ability of every individual to go on his or her own personal faith journey—choosing to follow God or not.

Ultimately, this book is a call to action to those not engaged, whether Christian or not. America has been the beacon of hope for the oppressed around the world for many years, but we are now at a tipping point. We must first understand who we are as Americans, how we got to be where we are today, and then how to restore America as a God-honoring nation. My hope and prayer is that Christians will rediscover the American covenant and lead the way—not only because America is worth restoring, but because this is an important part of honoring God as we live out our faith.

— Mark Burrell
June 2022

Chapter 1

The State of the Union

Forgetting Our National Covenant

Therefore, you kings, be wise; be warned, you rulers of the earth.
Serve the LORD with fear and celebrate his rule with trembling.
—Psalm 2:10–11

Four score and seven years ago our fathers brought forth on this
continent, a new nation, conceived in Liberty, and dedicated to the
proposition that all men are created equal. Now we are engaged
in a great civil war, testing whether that nation, or any nation so
conceived and so dedicated, can long endure.
—Abraham Lincoln
November 19, 1863

CHAPTER 1

THE STATE OF THE UNION

Forgetting Our National Covenant

Therefore, you kings, be wise; be warned, you rulers of the earth.
Serve the LORD with fear and celebrate his rule with trembling.
—Psalm 2:10–11

Four score and seven years ago our fathers brought forth on this
continent, a new nation, conceived in Liberty, and dedicated to the
proposition that all men are created equal. Now we are engaged
in a great civil war, testing whether that nation, or any nation so
conceived and so dedicated, can long endure.
—Abraham Lincoln
November 19, 1863

America is fractured and at a constitutional crossroads—
and we have been here before. The American Civil War
was the bloodiest war fought on American soil. The
Southern states seceded from the Union, wanting to
preserve their right to maintain the institution of slavery. The main
issue was the assertion that Blacks were not entitled to the unalienable, God-given rights captured in the Declaration of Independence: a
right to manage one's own life, exercise one's own liberty, and pursue
happiness according to one's own conscience. Just prior to the Civil
War, the Supreme Court ruling in the 1857 case *Dred Scott v. Sandford*
stated slaves' rights were not included in the Constitution. The question before the country was, Did this vision of human rights captured
in the Declaration apply to slaves, or was the Dred Scott decision correct in saying it did not?

In July 1863, the Union army won the pivotal Battle of Gettysburg, which was a turning point in the war. In November, President Lincoln and other dignitaries gathered in Gettysburg to pay tribute to the 160,000 soldiers who fought and the 7,000 who died there. In what became one of the most quotable presidential speeches in American history, Lincoln summarized the essential element that made the American founding unique—that it was *conceived in liberty*.* He also stated the cold reality of what was taking place: a test to determine whether self-government initiated by people with a common vision would prevail, or if the Union would dissolve because of a fundamental disagreement on the true meaning and scope of the vision. In the end, the Union was preserved—and yet, the struggle for civil rights continues to this day.

As we now march headlong into the twenty-first century, America is at a new crossroads. The decision before the American people today is whether we still believe in and will collectively defend our national founding covenant—the Declaration of Independence. Today's disagreement, however, is different from that of the Civil War. Today the debate is whether there is an objective moral standard—what the Declaration calls "the Law of Nature and of Nature's God"—to which all Americans must turn to guide personal behavior *and civil lawmaking*.† The rejection of an objective moral truth central to the Judeo-Christian worldview has led to the rise of a secular humanistic worldview. This godless worldview is based on a subjective, ever-changing truth and has led to the redefinition of the most iconic phrase in all our founding documents: the right of every individual to *life, liberty, and the pursuit of happiness.*

---

* Lincoln's Gettysburg address is inscribed in the Lincoln Memorial in Washington, DC, and is visited by thousands of people each year. The introduction states, "Four score and seven years ago…," identifying the nation's founding with the signing of the Declaration of Independence in 1776.

† This will be explored further in later chapters. The quick explanation is that the "Law of Nature" is a reference to what mankind generally acknowledges as morally true (general revelation based on one's conscience and what can be seen in nature), and the phrase "of Nature's God" is a reference to the moral law in the Bible summarized by the Ten Commandments. The use of this statement in the first paragraph in the Declaration asserts the founders were making a biblical moral argument to separate from England instead of a self-serving rationale, as was normally the case in revolutions.

This means our national vision for a just civil government has changed since the founding in the minds of many fellow Americans, and with that change, the boundaries of the Constitution have also changed. Many Americans still believing in our national founding covenant and the moral law that justified it have been focusing on trying to get back to the Constitution, but abuses to the Constitution are merely a symptom of the actual root problem—*a fundamental rejection of our national founding covenant.* If we hope to get back to the faithful application of the Constitution as originally ratified to promote our core founding principles, we must rediscover, understand, and recommit ourselves to our national founding covenant—the Declaration of Independence.

In this chapter I will explain the American founding covenant, summarize the events leading to our current *state of the union*, and describe the resulting problem we face today.

THE AMERICAN COVENANT

It is common for nations to draft a document or some kind of manifesto explaining their philosophy for governing and what they hope to achieve. America's founders followed this same path in June of 1776, debating and finally approving the Declaration on July 4. I will unpack the biblical origins of the Declaration in the next few chapters but will summarize key principles informing America's founding covenant here:

1. A divine moral law permeates and sustains the universe and operates as the standard by which all laws and conduct of governing leadership should be measured.*
2. God has bestowed certain unalienable rights on all individuals that cannot be taken away.
3. The purpose of government is to secure these unalienable rights by providing justice to all citizens and providing for the common defense against foreign and domestic enemies.

---

* The divine law, specifically the moral law, is also the standard for people realizing they are sinners in need of a Savior. This means the law used as the standard for governing is the same as for evangelism.

4. The role of government is to pass laws for the better ordering of the citizenry, recognizing these laws must be in harmony with the moral law.
5. Lawmakers maintain their authority based on a social contract: the consent of the people they are governing.
6. When a government violates these rights over a long period with no response to petitions by the citizens, that government forfeits its God-given ruling authority.
7. The citizens in such circumstances have the right to throw off the abusive government and to form a new government to provide for their safety, prosperity, and happiness.

These principles—concisely captured in the Declaration of Independence—are the bedrock foundation of who we are as Americans. Let's unpack them.

The starting point, and perhaps the most important principle, is recognizing there is a divine law communicated to mankind through reason and conscience, commonly referred to as the moral law. This moral law is summarized by the Ten Commandments, which were posted in schools and courtrooms across colonial America. The moral law was instrumental in establishing the rule of law that has permeated countless civilizations over the past 3,500 years. The opening paragraph of the Declaration of Independence refers to moral laws as the "Laws of Nature and of Nature's God." Natural law serves as the foundation for America's separation from England because the king had forfeited his God-given authority due to many unjust and immoral actions over a long period of time. In the founders' judgment, the king's ongoing immoral actions against the colonists left them no choice but to separate and establish a new government.

The second principle recognizes that certain unalienable rights come from God and cannot be taken away. How does one identify legitimate individual rights? Legitimate rights must be in harmony with the moral law. For instance, "Thou shalt not murder" implies the unalienable right to one's own life. "Thou shalt not steal" implies the unalienable right to accumulate and manage personal property without its being vandalized, defaced, or stolen. "Thou shalt not bear false witness" implies the unalienable right to be dealt with honestly. The Bible elevates individual rights, asserting that even society's most marginal people have them: the poor, the destitute, widows, and orphans.

The third principle reveals the narrow scope of civil government—that the *civil authority* is to ensure the individual rights of all. The Declaration puts it this way: "That to secure these rights, Governments are instituted among men." The civil authority is responsible to address threats to these rights whether they be internal or external threats. To defend against external threats to individual rights is commonly referred to as "providing for the common defense" of a community or nation.

The fourth principle is that the civil authority should pass laws to address issues creating confusion or disparities in the rights of everyone, regardless of class, race, or gender. Importantly, as with legitimate rights, man-made laws must be in harmony with the moral law to be legitimate and enforceable.

The fifth principle is that those passing laws do so with the understanding they are serving the citizenry that elected them. These elected officials derive "their just powers from the consent of the governed," according to the Declaration. This means there is a social contract between the ones governing and those governed: those governing will govern in accordance to the moral law.

The sixth principle is that if the civil authority governs in a way that violates the moral law, or laws legitimately passed, the citizenry will have the authority to remove those lawmakers. This is the basic principle the founders used in the Declaration to justify separation: the right to reject and replace an immoral civil authority. This principle could be applied only after a "long train of abuses" over many years, with no possible recourse. This is precisely what happened in colonial America—the founders felt the king was governing immorally with no possible chance to reconcile. Because of this, he forfeited his God-given responsibility to rule over the colonies.

The seventh principle is that if a group of people find themselves in this situation, where their God-given rights are being infringed upon with no potential for redress, they have a right to form a new government. This new government must be established through a covenant where they explain their rationale for separation, recognize the supremacy of the moral law as guiding their actions, and declare their trust in God as they form a new nation.*

THE JUDEO-CHRISTIAN WORLDVIEW INFORMED THIS VISION

Growing up I was taught that America was founded as a Christian nation. Christianity was unquestionably the established and accepted religion in colonial America. Just prior to the founding era, the colonies experienced the first Great Awakening, fueling a wave of revival. Key phrases in the Declaration certainly affirm this complete reliance on God:

> •*endowed by their Creator with certain unalienable Rights...*
> •*appealing to the Supreme Judge of the World...*
> •*with a firm Reliance on the Protection of the divine Providence...*

After the Declaration was adopted, each of the colonies—now officially recognized as separate states—drafted its own constitutions. Most of these made direct and indirect references to the Christian faith and the duty each citizen had to contribute to a just and fair society.

Virginia led the way, becoming the first state to ratify the Articles of Confederation, on December 16, 1777. At that time, Virginia's Declaration of Rights, adopted in 1776, stated:

---

* The fundamental difference between the American and French Revolutions was the obedience and reverence the Americans had for the moral law and divine Providence to bless their effort. It takes a principled group of leaders to operate this way and is critical for the long-term viability of a nation. The French Revolution saw the beheadings of thousands due to renegade civil leaders who did not respect these basic biblical principles for governing, primarily the moral law as the rule of law and the need for the blessing of divine Providence.

That religion, or the duty which we owe to our Creator, and the manner of discharging it, can be directed only by reason and conviction, not by force or violence; and therefore all men are equally entitled to the free exercise of religion, according to the dictates of conscience; and that it is the mutual duty of all to practise Christian forbearance, love, and charity toward each other.[2]

South Carolina followed Virginia's lead, becoming the second state to ratify the Articles, on February 5, 1778. That same year, South Carolina adopted its Constitution, which stated:

No person shall be eligible to sit in the house of representatives unless he be of the Protestant religion.... All persons and religious societies who acknowledge that there is one God, and a future state of rewards and punishments, and that God is publicly to be worshipped, shall be freely tolerated. The Christian Protestant religion shall be deemed, and is hereby constituted and declared to be, the established religion of this State.[3]

Rhode Island was the fourth state to ratify the Articles, on February 9, 1778. At that time, Rhode Island was continuing to use its 1663 Charter, which stated:

That they, pursuing, with peaceable and loyal minds, their sober, serious, and religious intentions, of Godly edifying themselves, and one another, in the Holy Christian faith and worship, as they were persuaded; together with the gaining over and conversion of the poor ignorant Indian natives, in those parts of America, to the sincere profession and obedience of the same faith and worship ... by the good Providence of God ... there may, in time, by the blessing of God upon their endeavors be laid a sure foundation of happiness to all America ... and to preserve unto them that liberty, in the true Christian faith and worship of God.[4]

Connecticut was the fifth state to ratify, on February 12, 1778. At that time, Connecticut was continuing to use its 1662 Charter, which stated:

> Our said People Inhabitants there, may be so religiously, peaceably and civilly governed, as their good Life and orderly Conversation may win and invite the Natives of the Country to the Knowledge and Obedience of the only true GOD, and He Saviour of Mankind, and the Christian Faith, which in Our Royal Intentions, and the adventurers free Possession, is the only and principal End of this Plantation.[5]

New Hampshire was the seventh state to ratify, on March 4, 1778. New Hampshire's Constitution, adopted in 1784 stated:

> As morality and piety, rightly grounded on evangelical principles, will give the best and greatest security to government … the people of this state have a right to impower, and do hereby fully impower the legislature to … make adequate provision … for the support and maintenance of public protestant teachers of piety, religion and morality…. And every denomination of Christians demeaning themselves quietly, and as good subjects of the state, shall be equally under the protection of the law.[6]

These are but a sampling of founding documents clearly showing the impact of the Christian faith on the American founding.

The enduring impact of the Judeo-Christian worldview is also seen in buildings in our nation's capital. In the Capitol rotunda, there are eight different historical paintings, including *The Landing of Columbus*, *The Embarkation of the Pilgrims*, and *The Baptism of Pocahontas.** "In

---

* Columbus has become a controversial figure, now thought of as a conqueror with little regard for God's law, but he believed he was called to carry the light of Christ to undiscovered lands (Peter Marshall and David Manuel, *The Light and the Glory: Did God have a plan for America?* (Grand Rapids: Revell, 1980), 31). This calling is a clear directive in the Christian faith (Matt. 28). While a brilliant navigator and explorer, accounts of brutality show he was ill-equipped to govern the natives under his care. This further shows how important it is for civil leaders to govern God's way and how tyranny is the inevitable result when unqualified rulers are in charge.

God We Trust" is inscribed above the House chamber, and a marble relief of Moses rests above the gallery door.[7]

At the top of the Washington Monument (1884) is an aluminum capstone with the Latin phrase *Laus Deo*, which means "Praise be to God." Inside the monument are tribute blocks that say: "Holiness to the Lord"; "Search the Scriptures"; "The memory of the just is blessed"; "May Heaven to this union continue its beneficence"; "In God We Trust"; and "Train up a child in the way he should go, and when he is old, he will not depart from it."[8]*

Ironically, the Supreme Court Building (built in 1935), where key aspects of America's Christian founding have been deemed unconstitutional, also has many Christian references.† Images of Moses with the Ten Commandments are carved at the center of the sculpture over the east portico of the building[9] and on the bronze doors of the Supreme Court itself. In addition, all sessions of the court begin with the court's marshal announcing, "God save the United States and this honorable court."[10]

These references in founding documents and physical buildings leave a clear and lasting testimony to the Christian origins of America. They show that our civil leaders believed the admonition of Psalm 2:

Therefore, you kings, be wise; be warned, you rulers of the earth.
Serve the LORD with fear and celebrate his rule with trembling.
(Ps. 2:10–11)

Belief in and obedience to principles generates blessings or consequences in accordance with those principles, as America soon experienced.

---

* When George Washington took the oath of office on April 30, 1789, he asked that the Bible be opened to Deuteronomy 28. "Immediately following the oath, Washington added, 'So help me God,' and bent forward and kissed the Bible before him." (Newt Gingrich, *Rediscovering God in America*, 10).

† SCOTUS has declared displays of the Ten Commandments and prayer and Bible reading in public schools unconstitutional.

LIVING OUT THE NATIONAL COVENANT

America was poised to prosper after the adoption of the US Constitution except for one big problem: slavery. Slavery has existed in one form or another for thousands of years and was not new or unique in America. What *was* unique were the efforts started during the founding era to abolish slavery as America separated and started as a new nation. The founders put measures in place to restrain and eventually eradicate slavery, but Southern Democrats refused to let this institution end.* Eighty-five years after America's founding, the South seceded from the Union, ushering in the Civil War. This led to America's first constitutional crisis. President Lincoln correctly observed this as a test to see whether "any nation so conceived and so dedicated, can long endure." In the end, abolition won the day and the Union survived—though America was on an arduous path to provide "liberty and justice to all."†

In the eight decades that followed the Civil War, two world wars and the Great Depression forged a unified nation, effectively answering President Lincoln's question about national viability. The American experiment of self-government was working as long as the Judeo-Christian framework put in place at the founding was followed. Along the path, presidents encouraged citizens to embrace the Christian faith to keep America strong during challenging times:

> A God-fearing nation, like ours, owes it to its inborn and sincere sense of moral duty to testify its devout gratitude to the All-Giver for the countless benefits it has enjoyed. For many years it has been customary at the close of the year for the national Executive to call upon his fellow countrymen to offer praise and thanks to God for the manifold blessings vouchsafed to them … I, William Howard Taft, President of the United States of America, in pursuance of long-established usage and in response to the wish of the American people, invite my countrymen … to join … in appropriate

---

* A more detailed explanation of these measures is presented in the Appendix.

† In both England and America, Christians led the abolitionist movements that eventually ended slavery.

ascription of praise and thanks to God for the good gifts that have been our portion, and in humble prayer that His great mercies toward us may endure.[11]

—President William H. Taft

Our government rests upon religion. It is from that source that we derive our reverence for truth and justice, for equality and liberty, and for the rights of mankind. Unless the people believe in these principles they cannot believe in our government…The history of government on this earth has been almost entirely a history of the rule of force held in the hands of a few. Under our Constitution, America committed itself to ... the power held in the hands of the people.[12]

—President Calvin Coolidge

The fundamental basis of this nation's laws was given to Moses on the Mount. The fundamental basis of our Bill of Rights comes from the teachings we get from Exodus and St. Matthew, from Isaiah and St. Paul. I don't think we emphasize that enough these days. If we don't have a proper fundamental moral background, we will finally end up with a totalitarian government which does not believe in rights for anybody except the State![13]

—President Harry S. Truman

President Ronald Reagan's Christian worldview was evident in many of his documents, proclamations, and speeches:

I have seen the rise of fascism and communism. Both philosophies glorify the arbitrary power of the state ... but both theories fail. Both deny those God-given liberties that are the inalienable right of each person on this planet, indeed, they deny the existence of God.[14]

Our liberty springs from and depends upon an abiding faith in God.[15]

In fact, Reagan even proclaimed 1983 as the Year of the Bible:

By the President of the United States of America: A Proclamation Of the many influences that have shaped the United States of America into a distinctive Nation and people, none may be said to be more fundamental and enduring than the Bible. Deep religious beliefs stemming from the Old and New Testaments of the Bible inspired many of the early settlers of our country, providing them with the strength, character, convictions, and faith necessary to withstand great hardship and danger in this new and rugged land. These shared beliefs helped forge a sense of common purpose among the widely dispersed colonies—a sense of community which laid the foundation for the spirit of nationhood that was to develop in later decades. The Bible and its teachings helped form the basis for the Founding Fathers' abiding belief in the inalienable rights of the individual, rights which they found implicit in the Bible's teachings of the inherent worth and dignity of each individual. This same sense of man patterned the convictions of those who framed the English system of law inherited by our own Nation, as well as the ideals set forth in the Declaration of Independence and the Constitution…. Now, therefore, I, Ronald Reagan, President of the United States of America, in recognition of the contributions and influence of the Bible on our Republic and our people, do hereby proclaim 1983 the Year of the Bible in the United States.[16]

—President Ronald Reagan

These presidential quotes were revered through most of the twentieth century. They acknowledge the pervasive understanding that the Christian worldview informed the principles and vision for the American founding covenant and that the long-term health of the nation depended on their continued application.

Despite all the progress America has made and the evidence that Judeo-Christian principles informed the American founding, there are still those who insist Christianity was not the primary philosophical bulwark behind the American founding. They embrace the secular humanist worldview and believe Christianity should be banished from the public square.

AN ALTERNATE GOVERNING PHILOSOPHY

In the mid-nineteenth century, a different governing philosophy gained a political foothold. It was triggered by a series of individuals embracing a different explanation for the origins of mankind, why we behave the way we do, how we should be educated, and how we should govern ourselves. These individuals included people like Charles Darwin, Karl Marx, Sigmund Freud, and John Dewey. They advanced new ideas based on a secular (godless) worldview that evolved into the progressive movement we have in America today. It happened over a period of about 150 years and is now firmly entrenched in most of America's most important institutions.

The catalyst for this change was Charles Darwin's theory of evolution. Darwin articulated his theory of evolution in *On the Origins of Species* (1859), in which he asserted mankind evolved over time as opposed to being created by God.* This concept inspired a nineteenth-century political theorist named Herbert Spencer to suggest that laws could evolve as well.† Spencer's theory "influenced Harvard Law Dean Christopher Columbus Langdell (1826–1906) to develop the case precedent method of practicing law."[17] Rather than emphasizing what the law actually stated, Langdell taught his students to focus on how the law might be applied in a specific case based on previous rulings.

Previous to Langdell's theory, lawyers studied William Blackstone's *Commentaries on the Laws of England.*‡ Blackstone's philosophy was

---

* The full title was *On the Origin of Species by Means of Natural Selection, or the Preservation of Favoured Races in the Struggle for Life.* In this work Darwin presented the idea that populations evolve over the course of generations through a process of natural selection. Others had previously proposed evolutionary processes, but this book helped advance the theory.

† Herbert Spencer came up with the term "survival of the fittest" after reading Darwin.

‡ William Blackstone was an eighteenth-century jurist who wrote the *Commentaries on the Laws of England,* which became a key resource for lawyers for the next century. This book not only influenced the founders but also Charles Finney, who helped usher in the Second Great Awakening. While studying to be a lawyer, Finney read Blackstone and became a Christian because of it.

the law was given by God Himself, and the source of all law was the moral law found in the Bible. He believed the law was unchanging, and that the role of judges was to look for relevant biblical principles that would help decide a specific case. This was the legal theory the founders embraced and was universally accepted until Oliver Wendell Holmes Jr. embraced Langdell's theory of evolving law. Holmes was Langdell's student and later a justice on the Supreme Court of the United States.[18]

This new theory was called Legal Realism—a term that washed out the boundaries of moral absolutes. Legal realism gained traction as the Industrial Revolution drove social and economic changes.[19] In time, this philosophical evolution impacted the judicial system, and judges began to believe they should look to where society was headed and render their opinions to advance that evolution rather than focus on the documents and legal doctrines of the past.[20] The case precedent method enabled judges to view the Constitution as a living, evolving document, thus changing it forever. Consequently, social (and legal) evolution occurred through judicial activist judges instead of the Constitution's amendment process, which requires approval from a majority of the states.

As the movement spread in the early twentieth century, Progressives sought to use this approach to reshape America's legal landscape by taking advantage of the new case-precedent approach to change the meaning of the Constitution.[21] One of the most pivotal SCOTUS decisions that enabled Progressives to accomplish this was *Everson v. Board of Education* (1947).* This was the decision that claimed a constitutional principle of "separation of church and state," saying the church must not directly influence matters related to civil government. This phrase is nowhere found in the Declaration or US Constitution. Though contrary to 150 years of government practice and judicial

---

While working as a shopkeeper, Abraham Lincoln read Blackstone, which prepared him to become a lawyer and eventually a US representative and later, the president.

* SCOTUS – Supreme Court of the United States.

precedent, Justice Hugo Black stated,*

> In the words of Jefferson, the clause against establishment of religion by law was intended to erect "a wall of separation between Church and State"... [that] must be kept high and impregnable. We could not approve the slightest breach.

This ruling opened the door to deem unconstitutional any activity in public life remotely connected to Christianity. The effect was profound: within fifteen years, school prayer (1962) and Bible readings in public schools (1963) were deemed unconstitutional. Fifty years later, many public displays of the Ten Commandments have been removed. What provided the rationale for the Declaration of Independence, the violation of the Law of Nature and of Nature's God, is now foreign to many Americans.

As the memory of the Ten Commandments slowly recedes from the minds of many Americans, the Progressive mindset has crept into many media outlets and local, state, and national government office holders. Without the idea of an objective truth to search for, individuals in these institutions instead push narratives that suggest the American founding is horribly flawed and desperately needs to be fundamentally transformed. They cite numerous past civil rights violations as reasons the American system of government must be torn down and rebuilt (slavery as America's original sin, Indian relocation, segregation, etc.). But are these past violations, which most Americans condemn, examples of inequities due to the principles of liberty and freedom in America's founding documents, or are they examples where some civil leaders abused their authority and governed immorally? Is it reasonable to assume that giving up on the concept of self-government, scrapping liberty and justice for all, and electing political leaders motivated by

---

* Justice Black was a senator and active supporter of FDR. Other than a one-year stint as a police court judge in 1911, he had no experience as a judge. He was also a member of the KKK for several years, resigning from it in 1925. The 1947 ruling on *Everson v. Board of Education* did not deal with the Ten Commandments, but it implanted the phrase "separation of church and state" firmly in the minds of Americans and laid significant groundwork for many later cases. I discuss Jefferson's use of this phrase in its proper context in chapter 10.

a secular humanistic worldview will prevent these injustices from ever happening again? This is what contemporary progressives are proposing as they accuse America of institutional racism throughout its history and claim its need for fundamental transformation.

As contemporary progressivism spreads, it is becoming clearer that this new worldview is fundamentally at odds with America's national founding covenant. In this sense, our current crisis is similar to that of the Civil War era, in which Lincoln declared America to be a house divided with an important choice before it:

> A house divided against itself cannot stand. I believe this government cannot endure permanently half-slave and half-free. I do not expect the Union to be dissolved—I do not expect the house to fall—but I do expect it will cease to be divided. It will become all one thing or all the other.[22]

Just as Lincoln stated these two points of view regarding slavery could not co-exist, neither can progressivism and the principles in the Declaration truly coexist across America. Just as Americans had to choose to maintain slavery or abolish it, Americans today will need to choose which worldview they wish to support to inform the nature of their civil government and the future of America. Will they be a patriot or a progressive? Choosing will be difficult, given how little many Americans know about the founding. Unfortunately, this includes many Christians who do not understand how their faith actually informed all aspects of the American founding, including the creation of a new platform for global evangelism.

CHRISTIANS ARE ASKING QUESTIONS

As the confusion in the public square grows, many Christians are asking questions about this new progressive narrative. How should they process all these historical events and accusations against America through the prism of their faith? While sincere church leaders continue to push evangelism as the most important part of living the Christian life, many Christians want to know what their biblical responsibilities are toward civil government. Are we just to pray for our leaders and hope God will handle things, or is there more? Many sense something is amiss and are seeking biblical guidance on how they should be living out their faith in the civic arena while still sharing the gospel.

A 2015 Barna poll showed the broad interest Christians have in topics relating to governance and related social issues.* When asked about interest in these topics, a clear majority of Christians expressed a desire to learn more:[23]

Abortion—91%
–beginning of life, right to life, contraception, adoption,
   unwed mothers

Religious persecution/liberty—86%
–personal duty vs. government duty, church response,
   global conditions

Poverty—85%
–personal duty vs. government role, church response,
   homelessness, hunger, dependency

Cultural restoration—83%
–appropriate morals, law and order, defensible values and norms,
   self-government

Sexual identity—82%
–same-sex marriage, transgenderism, marriage, LGBT

Israel—80%
–role in the world, Christian responsibility to Israel,
   US foreign policy toward Israel and her enemies

---

* George Barna leads the Barna Research Group and is a well-known and respected pollster. The poll cited is from September 27, 2015, entitled "What Would People Like to Hear About in Church Sermons?"

Christian Heritage—79%
–role of Christian faith in American history, Church's role in
US development, modern-day relevance

Role of Government—76%
–biblical view, church-state relationship, personal
responsibility, limitations

Bioethics—76%
–cloning, euthanasia, genetic engineering, cryogenics,
organ donation, surrogacy

Self-governance—75%
–biblical support, personal conduct, impact on freedom,
national sovereignty

Church in politics/government—73%
–separation of church and state, legal boundaries, church
resistance to government

Islam—72%
–core beliefs, response to Islamic aggression, threat to
US peace and domestic tranquility

As part of Barna's survey, pastors were asked if they had plans to
discuss these topics from the pulpit. Only 14% answered "Yes." In my
discussions with pastors on this topic, the common response is, "We
don't talk about politics here, because we want to focus on sharing the
gospel." They view politics as too divisive, putting evangelism at risk.*
Yet their congregations are asking for biblical leadership—to understand what the word of God says about these things. Unfortunately,
most pulpits in America remain silent.

As a result, many Christians are conflicted about their personal
priorities. Many gifted and even called to serve in civil government
are not energized to engage. No one has taught or encouraged them
that civic engagement is a high calling from God and a legitimate and

---

* I address the claim that engagement in politics hampers evangelism in chapter 4.

necessary personal ministry. Many Christians who are engaged feel unsupported by the church and are left to serve in the political arena alone. Too many Christians do not see the duty they have and the value of establishing and maintaining liberty and justice for all. As a result, many Christians are on the sidelines and not engaged. Many churches recommend praying for civil leaders but focusing on evangelism and other tangible ministry needs—but the Bible has much more to say about citizenship, which we will see in the next few chapters.

THE STATE OF THE UNION

Every January, presidents deliver a "State of the Union" address to a joint session of Congress and the American people. The address usually includes a list of problems followed by programs they feel will make things better. The prognosis is almost always bright with a promise of prosperity—but only if their agenda is fully adopted.

Today, the true state of the union is even more precarious than during the Civil War:

- Over the last 150 years, the progressive worldview has gained a foothold in many of America's revered institutions. This includes many civil government offices (elected and appointed), TV, movies, news media, social media, public schools, most universities, big corporations, and many churches.
- The constant barrage of anti-American sentiments is driving division and anger. The year 2020 saw weeks of rioting across many major cities, leading to property destruction and loss of life.
- The idea that we were originally bound together through a mutual covenant has been all but forgotten by the average American. Rather than seeing the fundamental conflict with our national founding covenant, most of America is distracted with debates over policy differences without understanding the true conflict with our founding principles. Many have disengaged entirely because of all the political acrimony.
- The church that was so instrumental during the founding era

in educating colonial America on liberty and freedom is mostly disengaged from the civil arena. Additionally, many pastors are parroting back the progressive, negative narrative about America and the founding generation. Many have simply declared any political discussion off limits and discouraged their congregants from bringing it up. Some have even removed the American flag from the sanctuary, claiming it is divisive.

Lincoln summarized the test America was facing during his presidency in the Gettysburg Address as seeing "if a nation conceived in liberty can long endure." We are facing this same test today, only the question can be stated more specifically: Will Christians rise to the challenge as so many previous generations have, to protect and defend the Declaration, our national founding covenant that the Constitution is based on? And will church leaders reclaim their role as the moral conscience of society and actively teach biblical principles of governing to their congregations?

If Christians and the Church do not reengage en masse, America will become like many other nations where sovereignty rests not in "We the People" under God but in those who seize power and decide how everyone else should think and live. This is the great decision before us today: Will Christians engage in or retreat from the political fray and let progressives impose their godless agenda on America?

To prevent this, Christians must rediscover the theology behind the American founding, and through citizenship duties, defend our national founding covenant. This citizenship responsibility applies to all Christians in the communities and nations in which they live. This is not just the responsibility of American Christians; it is the responsibility of all Christians around the world, wherever they live.

As believers rediscover these principles, they will not only understand their responsibility but also see a whole new strategy to take evangelism to the next level. This strategy will become more relevant as the American culture continues to decline. At some point, there will be a growing population asking "Where did we go wrong? How do we restore liberty and justice for all in America?" The Bible provides the answers to these questions, and our true American history shows that our founders followed the biblical template.

And, in explaining how biblical principles were applied at the time of the founding, one cannot help but explain the gospel.* Contrary to the position the modern Church takes with regard to politics, I believe we are on the cusp of the greatest evangelistic opportunity in my lifetime, because Americans will be looking for reasonable answers to understand the political way forward for America during this present crisis.

THE FOCUS OF THIS BOOK

Christians need to be ready to lead the way by explaining what the Christian faith teaches about achieving a just civil authority that secures liberty and justice for everyone, regardless of where they are on their faith journey. They need not only to be able to explain the history behind the *American founding* but also to be able to explain the biblical principles behind the *American founding covenant*—the Declaration of Independence. Equipping Christians to do that is the focus of this book.

In the chapters to come, we will address the following questions Christians should be able to answer:

- What does the Bible teach about civil government, and whom does God expect to provide for a just civil authority?
- What principles about governing do we learn from Israel?
- What is the connection between securing justice and evangelism?
- How did these biblical principles for governing influence the American founding?
- What is the unique formula to achieve freedom in America?
- What did the founders mean by the phrase "pursuit of happiness"?
- How does the progressive worldview compare to America's founding principles?
- What are the responsibilities Christians have regarding citizenship?

---

* This will be more fully explained later in the book.

- What roles should churches be playing in local communities?
- What are the critical steps to restoring America to be a God-honoring nation?

As you continue to read, you will discover that Christian citizenship is not only the way to restore law and order but it also creates a natural opportunity to share the gospel. It is not only the responsibility of every believer; it is a mark of the mature believer, one who is not only concerned about injustice but willing to act and take on responsibility in civil government to ensure liberty and justice for all. No matter how difficult, Christians must not give up this responsibility, especially given all those who fought to preserve American freedom over the past 250 years.

RENEWING OUR COVENANT

While the state of the union is cause for great concern, we understand this is a common problem for nations, and it has a clear remedy. Israel experienced cycles of disobedience and judgment from God we can learn from.* One of the few good kings to come after Solomon was King Josiah, who came to power around 623 BC. In 2 Kings 22, we read the account of Josiah wanting to repair the temple, and during the process, the high priest found the missing "Book of the Law." This Book of the Law referred to the writings of Moses that include the Mosaic covenant. This was when God presented the moral law, and the Israelites agreed to follow it to secure God's blessing. In other words, this was Israel's *national covenant*—and they had forgotten it!

Once discovered, the Book was read before the king. In verse 11, we are told he tore his robes and gave instructions to Hilkiah the priest:

> Go and inquire of the LORD for me and for the people and for
> all Judah about what is written in this book that has been found.

---

* We can learn many things from studying Israel in the Old Testament. Understanding the cycle of blessing and judgment as a result of their adherence to biblical guidance on governing a nation is one of the more important things, yet this source of insight is mostly ignored by the modern Church.

Great is the LORD's anger that burns against us because those who have gone before us have not obeyed the words of this book; they have not acted in accordance with all that is written there concerning us. (2 Kings 22:13)

Later, in 2 Kings 23, Josiah renews the covenant with all the people pledging themselves to the covenant:

Then the king called together all the elders of Judah and Jerusalem. He went up to the temple of the LORD with the people of Judah, the inhabitants of Jerusalem, the priests and the prophets—all the people from the least to the greatest. He read in their hearing all the words of the Book of the Covenant, which had been found in the temple of the LORD. The king stood by the pillar and renewed the covenant in the presence of the LORD—to follow the LORD and keep his commands, statutes and decrees with all his heart and all his soul, thus confirming the words of the covenant written in this book. Then all the people pledged themselves to the covenant. (2 Kings 23:1–3)

This is consistent with what the Lord spoke to Solomon during his reign:

If my people, who are called by my name, will humble themselves and pray and seek my face and turn from their wicked ways, then I will hear from heaven, and I will forgive their sin and will heal their land. (2 Chron. 7:14)

The American covenant is different from the covenant God made through Moses to the Israelites, but they are both based on the moral law. And as we will see in later chapters, there are many principles for civil government we learn from Israel that create a governing blueprint for other nations to follow. What we see in 2 Kings 23 and 2 Chronicles 7 is the remedy for nations that do turn away from God.

Just like Israel, nations can be restored if their leaders come together, confess their national sin, and renew their governing covenant with God. This is what must happen in America, which I will further explain in the last chapter.

SUMMARY

America is in the midst of an ideological civil war where the battleground is between two different worldviews informing the purpose and mission of civil government. If we depart from our founding covenant, we will lose the liberty and civil justice that America has long enjoyed. If this is lost, the entire world will suffer the consequences. Some Christians suggest this decline is inevitable, perhaps leading to the "end times," but remember, most generations believed they were living in the end times. Regardless of where we are in God's eternal plan, the fact remains that we are to live our lives every day as the Bible teaches. Not just in our *relationship* with God but also meeting the *responsibilities* we have to take care of ourselves, our families, and the communities where we live. This includes establishing and maintaining a just civil authority.

All that is required is for people to understand America's founding covenant and engage at the local, state, and national level to defend our republic. The goal is not so much to "save America" as it is to do our best to live out biblical principles of governing in our communities as part of living the Christian life. This is what Christians are called to do, regardless of what nation or era they live in. Christians meeting this responsibility is the only way the American experiment, conceived in liberty, can continue to endure. To embrace this responsibility and have the conviction the founders had to see it through, we must first look to the Bible to understand the origin and purpose of civil government. We will look at this in the next chapter.

SUMMARY POINTS

The state of the union is precarious—but we have been here before.

- The key governing principles and vision behind the American founding are captured in the Declaration of Independence—our national founding covenant.
- For the first 200 years, America's leaders referenced the Christian faith as central to the American form of government.
- In the mid-nineteenth century, secular progressivism emerged as an alternative governing philosophy—one that is at odds with America's founding covenant.
- Many Christians are asking questions about civil government and public policy, but pastors avoid these topics, even suppress them—claiming political discussion hinders evangelism.
- All Christians have a duty to engage in the business of governing in the communities in which they live.
- God has provided a blueprint for governing, which our founders codified for us in America's founding documents. He has also provided a mechanism for us to humbly repent as individuals and as a nation and restore his favor.

CHAPTER 2

THE SOURCE OF CIVIL GOVERNMENT

Why a Covenant?

Now the earth was corrupt in God's sight and was full of violence.
God saw how corrupt the earth had become, for all the people on
earth had corrupted their ways.
—Genesis 6:11–12

The Americans combine the notions of Christianity and of liberty
so intimately in their minds, that it is impossible to make them
conceive the one without the other…. They brought with them
into the New World a form of Christianity which I cannot better
describe than by styling it a democratic and republican religion.
—Alexis de Tocqueville

CHAPTER 2

THE SOURCE OF CIVIL GOVERNMENT

Why a Covenant?

Now the earth was corrupt in God's sight and was full of violence.
God saw how corrupt the earth had become, for all the people on
earth had corrupted their ways.
—Genesis 6:11–12

The Americans combine the notions of Christianity and of liberty
so intimately in their minds, that it is impossible to make them
conceive the one without the other.... They brought with them
into the New World a form of Christianity which I cannot better
describe than by styling it a democratic and republican religion.[24]
—Alexis de Tocqueville

The modern church views civil government as an institution
to which Christians have several obligations. These include
submission to the civil authority, because God establishes
them as described in Romans 13, and prayer for our civil
leaders, given the instruction in 1 Timothy 2. These principles are correct but do not capture the entire context regarding civil government
provided throughout the Bible. The Old Testament provides the context and much more information on the purpose and mission of civil
government through thousands of passages. A correct biblical position on the role of civil government must incorporate Old and New
Testament guidance to form a complete and accurate interpretation.

In this chapter we will start by looking at the earliest mention of civil government in the Old Testament and the context for why it was established. Then we will look at God's view of justice and his plan for the nations. Lastly, we will address typical questions around the scope of civil government and accountability for establishing a just civil authority.

IN THE BEGINNING

The opening chapters of Genesis provide an account of God in creation: God created the heavens and the earth; he formed man in his image and placed them in the garden; he would regularly fellowship with them (Gen. 1–2). By bringing together Adam and Eve, God ordained the first and most important institution on earth: marriage between a man and a woman. From this institution comes the family unit, a subset of every community and the model for propagation of the human race. At this point, no need for civil government existed, but this paradise was short lived. Adam and Eve disobeyed God when they ate from the tree of knowledge of good and evil. As a result, God expelled them from the garden and from his presence. Beyond the boundaries of paradise, they began having children who would form future families, communities, and nations.

These future generations inherited the knowledge of good and evil, along with the God-given blessing of a conscience to distinguish right from wrong. Armed with this internal sense, they could govern their personal conduct and dealings with others. Many of their struggles were due to losing direct fellowship with God. In addition to being alienated from him, they also found themselves at odds with each other. As they grew in numbers, they began to face more challenges because of this interpersonal conflict.

Genesis 5 provides a genealogy that spans the next 1,500 years. Various models estimate that by the time God instructed Noah to build the ark, the world's population could have been anywhere between one million and three billion people.[25] Regardless of the actual number, the questions are, "How well did their consciences guide this large population to do the right thing when interpersonal conflict arose among them? To what extent was there peace, harmony, and justice in these early communities?"

While we can only approximate how many people were alive at that time, we do not need to guess about the quality of community life. God tells us that violence was pervasive across all communities on the earth:

> The LORD saw how great the wickedness of the human race had become on the earth, and that every inclination of the thoughts of the human heart was only evil all the time. (Gen. 6:5)

> Now the earth was corrupt in God's sight and was full of violence. God saw how corrupt the earth had become, for all the people on earth had corrupted their ways. So God said to Noah, "I am going to put an end to all people, for the earth is filled with violence because of them. I am surely going to destroy both them and the earth." (Gen. 6:11–13)

It is hard to imagine what a violent society in antiquity would have been like, but we get a glimpse through modern equivalents where dictators force subjection and use poverty and fear to govern (e.g., Cuba, Libya, North Korea, Pakistan, Syria, and others).[26]

God did not intend for mankind to live in communities where people disrespect the lives or the property of others. His concern for humanity and the widespread violence prompted him to destroy all mankind and start over. God chose Noah—the one righteous man on earth in those days—from whom to repopulate the earth. God told Noah to build an ark to house his family and two of each animal. Then God sent a global flood that destroyed the rest of mankind. Only Noah, his family, and the animals aboard the ark survived. The flood waters receded, and God instructed Noah to repopulate the earth: "Then God blessed Noah and his sons, saying to them, 'Be fruitful and increase in number and fill the earth'" (Gen. 9:1).

God promised Noah that he would not repeat such extreme

measures, like the flood, to stop mankind's wickedness—but one big question remained: What would prevent an escalation of violence such as occurred prior to the flood?

GOD ORDAINS CIVIL GOVERNMENT

The first mention of civil government occurs in Genesis 9 when God is relaying instructions to Noah after leaving the ark. It is in these several verses, very seldom discussed from the pulpit, where we see God's remedy to civil unrest. God commanded Noah that individuals should be held accountable for the taking of innocent life. This is what is needed to prevent a repeat of the violent society that existed prior to the flood.

> And for your lifeblood I will surely demand an accounting. I will demand an accounting from every animal. And from each human being, too, I will demand an accounting for the life of another human being. Whoever sheds human blood, by humans shall their blood be shed; for in the image of God has God made mankind. (Gen. 9:5–6)

There are several important points in these verses. First, this passage is communicating God's ordination of a new institution that he deemed critical to address the civil unrest that existed prior to the flood. This institution is a civil governing authority charged with establishing and maintaining justice in the local community.* God's solution to the widespread violence problem is to have a group of people establish and maintain civil order to provide equal justice to everyone.†

Next, notice that God uses the word *demand* three times with respect to holding those accountable who take an innocent life. The clear meaning is that God expects mankind to deal with evil behavior in the local community. God names murder, the worst crime a person can commit, as an example.

---

* This should first be applied locally, then at the state or national level. See chapter 3 for details.

† This interpretation of these verses is widely accepted across all denominations. I have never had a pastor or theologian assert this passage meant something other than God ordaining the institution of civil government.

God's directive for this new institution also shows his concern for the lives of mankind. It reveals that human life is sacred—having been made in God's image—and that every individual has a "right to life." Notice also this directive comes early in the biblical narrative, after about 1,500 years proving that violence dominates human existence. Without a civil authority to keep evil in check, people would have had to keep living in fear, but God intended men and women to live without fearing for their lives. A life without fear affords humans the opportunity to ponder the mysteries of God and to live out their God-given lives in society, as God created them to do.

This is God's initial call to active citizenship to every person, community, and nation coming after Noah. It is clearly articulated and leaves no doubt as to what God expects. It is also prescribed before the calling of Abraham and the Jewish nation, meaning this applies to all mankind that follows Noah. From this passage we see the responsibility, or duty, every nation has to help establish and maintain justice.

GOD'S FIRST PRIORITY FOR CIVIL GOVERNMENT: JUSTICE

The first and primary task of the institution of civil government is to keep the citizenry safe by ensuring justice is provided equally to all. God's ongoing priority to provide justice through members of the community is reiterated throughout the Old and New Testaments.

OLD TESTAMENT

Appoint judges and officials for each of your tribes in every town the LORD your God is giving you, and they shall judge the people fairly. Do not pervert justice or show partiality. Do not accept a bribe, for a bribe blinds the eyes of the wise and twists the words of the innocent. Follow justice and justice alone, so that you may live and possess the land the LORD your God is giving you. (Deut. 16:18–20)

God presides in the great assembly; he renders judgment among the "gods": How long will you defend the unjust and show partiality to the wicked? Defend the cause of the weak and fatherless; maintain the rights of the poor and oppressed. Rescue the weak and needy; deliver them from the hand of the wicked. (Ps. 82:1–4)

Speak up for those who cannot speak for themselves, for the rights of all who are destitute. Speak up and judge fairly; defend the rights of the poor and needy. (Prov. 31:8–9)

Woe to those who make unjust laws, to those who issue oppressive decrees, to deprive the poor of their rights and withhold justice from the oppressed of my people, making widows their prey and robbing the fatherless. (Isa. 10:1–2)

Do not deprive the foreigner or the fatherless of justice, or take the cloak of the widow as a pledge. Remember that you were slaves in Egypt and the LORD your God redeemed you from there. That is why I command you to do this. (Deut. 24:17–18)

"Does it make you a king to have more and more cedar? Did not your father have food and drink? He did what was right and just, so all went well with him. He defended the cause of the poor and needy, and so all went well. Is that not what it means to know me?" declares the LORD. (Jer. 22:15–16)

He has shown you, O mortal, what is good. And what does the LORD require of you? To act justly and to love mercy and to walk humbly with your God.* (Mic. 6:8)

NEW TESTAMENT

God's call to keep his commands and his concern for leaders to ensure

---

* Many other verses in the Bible speak to God's call for justice: Exod. 12:49; Lev. 19:15, 33–34; Deut. 24:17–18; 1 Kings 10:9; 2 Chron. 9:8; Ps. 82:3–4; Prov. 21:15; Isa. 1:23, 56:1; Lam. 3:31–36; Matt. 5:19; John 14:21; 1 Tim. 5:17–21; Titus 1:5–9; Heb. 11:32–33.

justice does not change but rather is affirmed in the New Testament by Jesus and through various epistles.

> Woe to you, teachers of the law and Pharisees, you hypocrites! You give a tenth of your spices—mint, dill and cumin. But you have neglected the more important matters of the law—justice, mercy and faithfulness. You should have practiced the latter, without neglecting the former. You blind guides! You strain out a gnat but swallow a camel. (Matt. 23:23–24)

> Let everyone be subject to the governing authorities, for there is no authority except that which God has established. The authorities that exist have been established by God. Consequently, whoever rebels against the authority is rebelling against what God has instituted, and those who do so will bring judgment on themselves. For rulers hold no terror for those who do right, but for those who do wrong. Do you want to be free from fear of the one in authority? Then do what is right and you will be commended. For the one in authority is God's servant for your good. But if you do wrong, be afraid, for rulers do not bear the sword for no reason. They are God's servants, agents of wrath to bring punishment on the wrongdoer. Therefore, it is necessary to submit to the authorities, not only because of possible punishment but also as a matter of conscience. (Rom. 13:1–5)

> Submit yourselves for the Lord's sake to every human authority: whether to the emperor, as the supreme authority, or to governors, who are sent by him to punish those who do wrong and to commend those who do right. (1 Pet. 2:13–14)

> Yet now I am happy, not because you were made sorry, but because your sorrow led you to repentance. For you became sorrowful as God intended and so were not harmed in any way by us. Godly sorrow brings repentance that leads to salvation and leaves no regret,

but worldly sorrow brings death. See what this godly sorrow has produced in you: what earnestness, what eagerness to clear yourselves, what indignation, what alarm, what longing, what concern, what readiness to see justice done. At every point you have proved yourselves to be innocent in this matter. (2 Cor. 7:9–11)

Anyone who does wrong will be repaid for their wrongs, and there is no favoritism. (Col. 3:25)

I list many additional passages in the footnote to make the point that God really does care about justice, evidenced by the hundreds of passages given to the subject throughout the Bible. This is not a minor topic or a narrow field for "experts only." While many areas of today's legal system require specialized training (contract law, patents, international law, etc.), the basics of "how to live in community with our neighbors" are surprisingly simple. It starts with protecting life. God's call to establish and maintain justice is a consistent and common theme throughout the Bible, and God cares deeply about equal justice for everyone, regardless of race, social class, or nationality.* All mankind is to be concerned about securing justice, but no one should be more involved in ensuring justice nor care more when injustice occurs than Christians.

GOD'S SECOND PRIORITY FOR CIVIL GOVERNMENT: PROPERTY

The second priority for civil government is to protect the property of citizens, making sure all people can accumulate and manage property as they see fit. We also see this in verses throughout the Bible:

You shall not steal. (Exod. 20:15)

Whoever steals an ox or a sheep and slaughters it or sells it must

---

* *Justice* means *civil justice*, not *social justice*, which carries a different definition in contrast to biblical civil justice. We will examine this further in chapter 8.

47

pay back five head of cattle for the ox and four sheep for the sheep. (Exod. 22:1)

Do not defraud or rob your neighbor. Do not hold back the wages of a hired worker overnight. (Lev. 19:13)

Honor the LORD with your wealth, with the first fruits of all your crops; then your barns will be filled to overflowing and your vats will brim over with new wine. (Prov. 3:9–10)

Jesus replied, "You shall not murder, you shall not commit adultery, you shall not steal, you shall not give false testimony." (Matt. 19:18)

Anyone who has been stealing must steal no longer, but must work, doing something useful with their own hands, that they may have something to share with those in need. (Eph. 4:28)

On the first day of every week, each one of you should set aside a sum of money in keeping with your income, saving it up, so that when I come no collections will have to be made. (1 Cor. 16:2)

These verses clearly reveal from the Bible that people have a right to accumulate and manage their property as they see fit.

In the century leading up to the American founding, civil leaders (mostly Christian) regarded it as obvious ("self-evident") that all individuals possess the rights of life, liberty, and property. We will talk about liberty in a later chapter; the point here is to see clearly how the Bible speaks to the right of all individuals to have full possession of their life and property. This is first presented in Genesis 9 and reinforced through thousands of passages in the Old and New Testaments.

GOD'S PLAN FOR THE NATIONS

After God tells Noah about the institution of civil government, we are given more information about God's expectation for the nations that would follow:

> Then God blessed Noah and his sons, saying to them, "Be fruitful and increase in number and fill the earth." (Gen 9:1)

> These are the clans of Noah's sons, according to their lines of descent, within their nations. From these the nations spread out over the earth after the flood. (Gen. 10:32)

What is clearly implied is that these nations would all adopt God's institution of a just civil government that he demanded in Genesis 9. In this way, these new nations would provide justice by keeping evil in check, thereby governing in a way that honors God. The Old Testament reinforces this charge to nations, especially throughout the book of Psalms, where it is a recurring theme:

> Therefore, you kings, be wise; be warned, you rulers of the earth. Serve the Lord with fear and celebrate his rule with trembling. (Ps. 2:10–11)

> He rules forever by his power, his eyes watch the nations—let not the rebellious rise up against him. Praise our God, all peoples [nations], let the sound of his praise be heard; he has preserved our lives and kept our feet from slipping. (Ps. 66:7–9)

> All the nations you have made will come and worship before you, Lord; they will bring glory to your name. (Ps. 86:9)

> I will praise you, Lord, among the nations; I will sing of you among the peoples (nations). (Ps. 108:3)

> May all the kings of the earth praise you, Lord, when they hear what you have decreed. May they sing of the ways of the Lord, for the glory of the Lord is great. (Ps. 138:4–5)

The Old Testament clearly and consistently reveals that God wants all the nations of the world that would come after Noah to govern themselves justly. The New Testament again confirms God's desire that there be nations around the world whose justice would enable individuals to seek out God. As Paul preached to the people of Athens:

> The God who made the world and everything in it is the Lord of heaven and earth and does not live in temples built by human hands. And he is not served by human hands, as if he needed anything. Rather, he himself gives everyone life and breath and everything else. From one man he made all the nations, that they should inhabit the whole earth; and he marked out their appointed times in history and the boundaries of their lands. God did this so that they would seek him and perhaps reach out for him and find him. (Acts 17:24–27)

When civil authorities ensure justice, they make it possible for more people to reach out for God and find him. The Great Commission is consistent with this principle, first delivered in the Old Testament. It affirms that Christians are to enter other nation-states to share the gospel so the people in those nations can turn to God:*

> Then Jesus came to them and said, "All authority in heaven and on earth has been given to me. Therefore go and make disciples of all nations, baptizing them in the name of the Father and of the Son and of the Holy Spirit, and teaching them to obey everything I have commanded you. And surely I am with you always, to the very end of the age." (Matt. 28:18–20)

From all these verses spanning the whole Bible, we see God wants individuals to turn to him and all nations to honor him. Nations do this by governing in a way that secures equal justice for all, enabling every individual to go on his or her own faith journey—even if it means rejecting God.

---

* We will unpack the Great Commission much more in chapter 4.

CITIZENSHIP RESPONSIBILITY: WHOSE IS IT?

Understanding God's call for law and order in the nations leads us to several questions. The first is, to whom is God directing this demand to establish and maintain justice in the nations that follow Noah?

The directive in Gen 9:5–6 is prior to the calling of Israel, which means it is directed to all nations going forward and is completely independent from whatever we learn about the nation of Israel later. This does not automatically mean all nations will govern in a way that honors God, only that this is what God expects—in fact, *demands*—from all nations. The question is, whom does God expect to perform this function? To whom is he talking?

There are four possible groups to whom God is directing this demand for justice:

1. Those who do not know God
2. Those who reject God
3. Those who acknowledge there is a God but do not know the Bible
4. Those who know God and generally read the Bible

Let us consider the first group. Is it at all reasonable to assume that people who do not know God, or have not read the Bible, are able to govern following biblical principles? It is possible that a group of people informed by their God-given conscience might identify biblical principles to govern themselves justly, but history shows that is not likely. It is not reasonable to assume this is the group God expects to be leaders in civil government.

The second group flat out rejects God, which means they may not only be ignorant of biblical principles for governing but they are also most likely hostile to how God expects mankind to govern. Genesis 6 tells us of a time when "every inclination of the thoughts of the human heart was only evil all the time," and "the earth was corrupt in God's sight and was full of violence." In Romans 1, we see a similar description of how those who reject God behave:

They have become filled with every kind of wickedness, evil, greed and depravity. They are full of envy, murder, strife, deceit and malice. They are gossips, slanderers, God-haters, insolent, arrogant and boastful; they invent ways of doing evil; they disobey their parents; they have no understanding, no fidelity, no love, no mercy. (Rom. 1:29–31)

This description from Paul explains how nations run by leaders who reject God can be so corrupt and oppressive. How could this group, that tends to "become filled with every kind of wickedness," be expected to establish and maintain justice in a way that honors God? It seems clear that people who reject God would not even consider what he has to say about securing justice. Given this, it is not reasonable to conclude that this second group is the one God expects to step in and provide justice in the civil arena.

The third group acknowledges God and desires a just civil authority, which is a big advantage over the first two groups. This third group may include those who embrace the gospel message (like Christians in the modern age) and people who agree with the general principles of civil government from the Bible but have not made a personal commitment to accept the gospel. An unbeliever in this third group has a better chance to govern justly than a person who rejects God. For example, many unbelievers acknowledge the Ten Commandments as a good moral standard to live by and could govern according to those principles. But this group does not routinely read the Bible, where more information on how to govern justly is given. Would it be reasonable to assume God is relying on this third group to ensure a just civil authority when they do not understand biblical principles for securing justice?

This brings us to the fourth group: believers who acknowledge God and generally read their Bible. This group should know better than anyone what the Bible has to say on key topics, including principles of justice found in the Old Testament that are critical to providing a just civil government today. Even Christians who think civic duty stops at submitting to civil government and praying for their leaders understand those leaders are to be God's servants "for your good" (Rom. 13:4). The people most eligible to use positions of civil authority "for your good" are people who embrace "goodness" according to the Bible, especially the principles of justice and mercy.

There is only one reasonable conclusion in looking at the available groups to assume the responsibility of establishing and maintaining a just civil authority in keeping with God's demand in Genesis 9:5–6. It can only be the fourth group, those who claim to follow God, acknowledge the Bible as God's life-giving word, and seek to apply it to daily living, including the civil arena. Who else could it be? How is it logical that God would communicate his expectation that mankind secure justice through a civil authority, provide all the details necessary on how to accomplish this in his word that only his followers revere, and then expect his followers to sit on the sidelines and hand this task over to those who do not read his word or who reject him altogether?

It seems inconceivable that God would expect Christians to rely on unbelievers to ensure civil justice and exclude any teaching on civil government in church, yet this is the position the modern Church reflects by its inaction and suppression of political discussion. Churches make this theological mistake by focusing only on New Testament passages: Romans 13 and 1 Timothy 2, instead of rooting their position on this topic in the whole counsel of God, starting in the Old Testament. The New Testament verses commonly cited do not present all we need to know about civil government, nor are they new teaching on the topic. These passages are simply *an affirmation of Genesis 9:5–6 and other truths in the Old Testament* (which we will cover in later chapters).

Because of this incorrect approach to the topic, most modern-day Christians act as though they have a responsibility only to pray for and submit to their civil government. Without noting Genesis 9, where God demands justice, and all the Old Testament information about the need and call for civil government, they see themselves only as having a responsibility *to* civil government: submit and pray. This is not biblically correct. Christians do not have a responsibility *to* civil government; they have a responsibility *for* civil government, to ensure that a just civil authority exists in their communities. Christians are the ones who are supposed to care about justice the most and should be most upset when it is denied to anyone.

We will say much more about this in the next few chapters, but the question of whom God expects to ensure a just civil government should be crystal clear: it has always been people who actively follow God and study his word, because only this group of people heeds the principles of justice God provides in the Bible. Christians living today are responsible for this activity—*period*.

HAS THIS RESPONSIBILITY CHANGED SINCE THE TIME OF THE OLD TESTAMENT?

The second question to ask is, has anything changed in the New Testament that would alter whom God would expect to ensure a just civil authority? Is there anything that would alter what God clearly explains back in Genesis 9 and expands on through the example of Israel? The answer is "No"; nothing has changed to alter God's expectation on this question. The New Testament is about the coming of Christ to declare "the year of the LORD's favor" (Isa. 61:2), where Jesus urges repentance and then dies for the sins of the world. But none of this negates the need for a just civil authority across the nations of the world, nor God's demand for justice back in Genesis 9.

Many New Testament passages affirm that Christians are responsible *for* civil government. First, during his ministry, Jesus declared everything in the Old Testament true and unchanged:

> For truly I tell you, until heaven and earth disappear, *not the smallest letter, not the least stroke of a pen, will by any means disappear from the Law until everything is accomplished.* Therefore anyone who sets aside one of the least of these commands and teaches others accordingly will be called least in the kingdom of heaven, but whoever practices and teaches these commands will be called great in the kingdom of heaven. (Matt. 5:18–19, emphasis added)

Second, the New Testament affirms God's desire that people of faith be a part of administering justice in the nations and that they would be blessed as a result of fulfilling this citizenship duty:

> And what more shall I say? I do not have time to tell about Gideon, Barak, Samson and Jephthah, about David and Samuel and the prophets, *who through faith conquered kingdoms, administered justice, and gained what was promised.* (Heb. 11:32–33, emphasis added)

Third, we get reinforcement that seeking justice is part of the Christian walk:

> Godly sorrow brings repentance that leads to salvation and leaves no regret, but worldly sorrow brings death. See what this godly sorrow [conviction] has produced in you: what earnestness, what eagerness to clear yourselves what indignation, what alarm, what longing, what concern, what *readiness to see justice done.* (2 Cor. 7:10–11, emphasis added)

Last, we learn Christians are uniquely enabled to lead in pursuit of justice because of the equipping of the Holy Spirit, who helps us discern what is right and true in a godly way:

> But the fruit of the Spirit is love, joy, peace, forbearance, kindness, goodness, faithfulness, gentleness and self-control. *Against such things there is no law.* (Gal. 5:22–23, emphasis added)

The New Testament not only affirms the role of civil government; it confirms the citizenship duty that Christians have to secure equal and impartial justice for all. While it is certainly possible for non-Christians to serve well in positions in government, Christians seeking to honor God with their lives and promote justice as defined by the Bible are much better equipped to secure justice, provided they have the gifts and calling.

America's founders understood this truth and affirmed the importance of having Christians serve in civil government:

> Providence has given our people the choice of their rulers, and it is
> the Duty, as well as privilege and interest, of a Christian nation to
> select and prefer Christians for their rulers.
> — John Jay, October 12, 1816[27]

> Our Constitution was made only for a moral and religious people.
> It is wholly inadequate to the government of any other.
> — John Adams, October 11, 1798[28]

> Public business must always be done by somebody—if wise men
> decline it, others will not; if honest men refuse it, others will not.
> — Abigail Adams[29]

The founders' sense of duty aligns with God's initial call in Genesis
9 to active citizenship with the purpose of restraining evil so everyone
can go on his or her own personal faith journey. This is a call to every
individual who came after Noah, although many throughout history
have failed to recognize this obligation since the days of Noah. Today,
this citizenship duty falls to Christians, who are responsible not just *to*
civil government but also *for* ensuring there is a just civil authority in
their communities.

In 1831, a French political philosopher named Alexis de Tocqueville
spent nine months touring America. In 1835, nearly sixty years after
the American founding, he published *Democracy in America* with his
observations from that visit. They included the following:

> The Americans combine the notions of Christianity and of liberty
> so intimately in their minds, that it is impossible to make them
> conceive the one without the other.... They brought with them
> into the New World a form of Christianity which I cannot better
> describe than by styling it a democratic and republican religion.[30]

These observations reflect the acknowledgment that Christians living during the founding era believed they were responsible for establishing a just civil authority. Fifty years later, during de Tocqueville's visit, the philosophy of active Christian citizenship was still firmly embedded and active in maintaining the American experiment. The Church was instrumental in stressing this responsibility up to and through the founding era and is still responsible today for ensuring a just civil authority.

WHAT RESPONSIBILITY LOOKS LIKE

Many Christians are immediately repelled by the notion they should get involved in politics, but involvement can take many forms. Some are called to vocations in civil service, including law enforcement or being a lawyer or a judge. Others are called to run for office or volunteer in their local communities or state legislature.

It is important to remember that God equips the local church with all the skills needed for a complete ministry, which includes supporting the maintenance of the local civil authority. God has given all Christians spiritual gifts—talents or abilities God intends us to apply as part of our personal ministry. These are clearly spelled out in the following passages:

And God has placed in the church first of all apostles, second prophets, third teachers, then miracles, then gifts of healing, of helping, of guidance, and of different kinds of tongues. Are all apostles? Are all prophets? Are all teachers? Do all work miracles? Do all have gifts of healing? Do all speak in tongues? Do all interpret? Now eagerly desire the greater gifts. (1 Cor. 12:28–31)

We have different gifts, according to the grace given to each of us. If your gift is prophesying, then prophesy in accordance with your faith; if it is serving, then serve; if it is teaching, then teach; if it is to encourage, then give encouragement; if it is giving, then give generously; if it is to lead, do it diligently; if it is to show mercy, do it cheerfully. (Rom. 12:6–8)

So Christ himself gave the apostles, the prophets, the evangelists, the pastors and teachers, to equip his people for works of service, so that the body of Christ may be built up until we all reach unity in the faith and in the knowledge of the Son of God and become mature, attaining to the whole measure of the fullness of Christ. (Eph. 4:11–13)

Those with the gifts of leadership, administration, and knowledge are the ones who should consider engaging in public service, which could look like being on the school board or city council. For those not called to civil service, they still have a critical role—to vote for godly leaders who have demonstrated their belief in biblical principles for civil government. This means being able to articulate biblical principles for governing and understand the key issues related to their application. We will describe this more in chapter 9, but the point here is to recognize that God expects Christians to step up to ensure everyone receives equal and impartial justice, because we are the ones to whom God has entrusted the principles on how this is accomplished.

SCOPE OF GOVERNMENT – IMPOSE RIGHTEOUSNESS OR EXTEND LIBERTY?-

A common point of debate among Christians during the Church Age has been the scope of responsibility for the civil authority.* Specifically, should the government impose certain Christian doctrines on the citizenry beyond the moral law, even though citizens do not embrace the Christian faith?† Both religious and civil leaders claiming to represent God have been guilty of imposing certain doctrinal positions and of persecuting dissenters during the Church Age, even to the extent of torture and killings. These different positions were driven in large part by different views on the manner and time when Jesus would return and how he would establish his kingdom, which many Bible verses describe. A detailed explanation of these different views and how they evolved

---

* The Church Age – the time since the resurrection of Christ to today, about 2,000 years.

† The basics of the moral law that apply to all are protection of life and property. We will talk more about the moral law in the next chapter.

during the Church Age is beyond the scope of this book. However, we can at least define the different governing positions and compare them to the point of view that will be explained in the remainder of this book.

Finding a simple explanation of the different positions on the proper role of civil government and the church turned out to be very difficult. Serendipitously, years ago a friend gave me *Christian Theology of Public Policy*, by John M. Cobin. In his book Cobin provides a table explaining the various positions, which I include and expand upon in Table 2.1. While there are a lot of variations within these different positions, I will explain the basic differences that traditionally distinguish these views from one another and the resulting actions of the civil authority. I fully recognize many variations within these views exist that this simple explanation will not address; however, I believe this is a good model to understand how people have generally viewed the role of civil government throughout the Church Age.

Cobin calls out two general interpretive approaches to this question. In the first, the church or state ruler imposes Christianity on the citizenry to varying degrees, claiming a biblical or divine right to do so. In this view Jesus reigns on earth through the church or through the state ruler as "established by God" (a way to interpret Rom. 13). Some holding this view believe that not only the civil code should be imposed but also the penalties God prescribed for the Israelites, including the death penalty (by stoning) for adultery, incest, and homosexuality.[31] During the Church Age, civil leaders have often claimed a divine right to impose laws on their citizens as they see fit—often viewing themselves as above the law. The drafting of the Magna Carta by barons living in Runnymede in 1215 and the signing of it by King John is the classic example of citizens challenging the king's supposedly limitless power. The American founders were essentially claiming the same problem with King George when they listed twenty-seven ways in the Declaration of Independence of how the king had exceeded his God-given authority and governed improperly. The common thread in these positions is an imposition of what the civil leader or state-sponsored church believes is best. This often leads to the infringement of rights at best and persecution and martyrdom at worst.

The second view is very different in that it recognizes there are two kingdoms: God's Kingdom in heaven where he is ruling now and earthly kingdoms where God allows mankind to govern using principles laid out in the Old Testament. This two-kingdom view believes that Jesus reigning on earth is a future event.* It has two sub-views: one where the church is responsible *to* civil government and is more passively involved (SEPARATE & SUBMISSIVE), and the other where the church is responsible *for* civil government (SEPARATE & RESPONSIBLE). Importantly, this SEPARATE & RESPONSIBLE view, also seeking to apply biblical principles of civil justice, differs from the first two views in that it embraces liberty as the foundational principle. This difference is what prohibits the persecution by state or church leaders of dissenters (religious or not) that has been prevalent during much of the Church Age.

This SEPARATE & RESPONSIBLE view is what motivated the American founders. They recognized that violating a person's liberty led to persecution, and they believed God wants everyone to make his or her own choice regarding faith. Thomas Jefferson articulated this well in his "Virginia Statute for Religious Freedom" (1786):

> Whereas, Almighty God hath created the mind free; That all attempts to influence it by temporal punishments or burthens, or by civil incapacitations tend only to beget habits of hypocrisy and meanness, and therefore are a departure from the plan of the holy author of our religion, who being Lord, both of body and mind yet chose not to propagate it by coercions on either, as was in his Almighty power to do, That the impious presumption of legislators and rulers, civil as well as ecclesiastical, who, being themselves but fallible and uninspired men have assumed dominion over the faith of others, setting up their own opinions and modes of thinking as the only true and infallible, and as such endeavoring to impose them on others, hath established and maintained false religions

---

* Theologians debate the details of when and how Jesus will reign in the future, but these differences do not materially change the resulting view that God appoints civil governments as part of this "two-kingdom" view.

over the greatest part of the world and through all time...."[32]

Table 2.1 – The Different Views on The Role and Scope of Civil Government[33]

Two Basic Approaches	Integrated Authority of State & God's Law Imposing Biblical Laws & Penalties		'Two-Kingdom' View with God's Kingdom Preeminent & the Moral Law as the Legal Standard	
Different Positions	State Authority: Divine Right of Kings	Religious Authority: Post Millennialism Theonomy, Reconstruction, Christian Nationalism	Separate & Submissive: Support and Pray for Civil Leaders	Separate & Responsible To Establish Civil Gov: Protect Liberty and Justice for All
Different Viewpoints Regarding Church and Government	Impose God's will as discerned by the King	Church imposes doctrinal positions through a state-sponsored Church. Church imposes Old Testament law through the king.	Limited church involvement in civil government Focus on building God's heavenly Kingdom through evangelism	View government as an institution given by God to enable nations to honor God by securing justice The Church should be active in training civil leaders and be the moral conscience for society, including government officials.

---

* Modern historians often cite passages like this to promote the idea that Jefferson was anti-church, but this is not the case. When looking at all of what he wrote over his life, what is clear is that he did not approve of state-sanctioned churches that subsidized their clergy. He found it especially bad when this clergy forced or imposed their beliefs on others yet were not living out moral principles clearly taught by Jesus himself. He fought to disestablish the state church in Virginia for this reason, instead promoting the idea that churches should directly pay for their pastors based on a voluntary congregation. This is the model most churches in America follow today—paying for their clergy directly.

Two Basic Approaches	Integrated Authority of State & God's Law Imposing Biblical Laws & Penalties		'Two-Kingdom' View with God's Kingdom Preeminent & the Moral Law as the Legal Standard	
Kingdom Perspective	King/Ruler not subject to earthly laws given they are ordained by God[34] The King or Queen may impose what he or she feels is best.	Government to be used to usher in God's kingdom by imposing Christianity on the citizenry[35]	See earthly kingdoms as hopelessly corrupt and a distraction to the Great Commission See themselves as "citizens of another kingdom," with that heavenly kingdom being the primary focus of Christians	Dual citizenship, but ultimate allegiance to God's Kingdom, which is yet to fully come[36] Recognize the challenge of corrupt government but see government as a blessing from God and believe he expects us to do our best to apply biblical principles of liberty, rights, and justice in civil government

CHAPTER 2 : THE SOURCE OF CIVIL GOVERNMENT

| Typical Beliefs | Rulers have supreme authority because they are all appointed by God. They should legislate as they feel best to conform the citizenry to God's moral law. | The Church has been given a mandate to Christianize the world through active legislative or executive action. Some hold that the Old Testament law should be fully enforced, including penalties. | Submit to and pray for civil leaders. Limited Church support and involvement in civil government Believe focus should be on the Great Commission versus engaging in political arena because of potential division and threat to evangelism See the government as inherently evil and run by Satan, justifying no involvement **Several subgroups:** Sincere Christians across denominations Separatists or pacifists | Believe God has given principles of civil government to mankind after the flood and expects nations to govern justly Believe the Church is responsible to be the moral conscience for societies where they exist View Christians as having a patriotic duty to establish and maintain "liberty and justice for all" and support the leaders and nation they live in In any nation, the Church should be active in training those called to serve in the civil arena, so they can be the "ministers of God" referred to in Romans 13 to "do good." View involvement of Christians in the public arena to impact the culture for Christ along with evangelizing and discipling the lost |

PURPOSE AND MISSION OF CIVIL GOVERNMENT

We will take a detailed look at the responsibilities of civil government in a later chapter as we work our way through the Bible, but it is helpful to summarize the purpose and mission of civil government based on what we know at this point. From Genesis 9 we can see the purpose of a civil authority is to restrain evil to prevent a violent society. In Genesis 8:20–21 we see that Noah worshipped God by offering sacrifices, and this pleased God. This passage affirms God's desire that we pursue and worship him, which the civil authority is intended to protect. From this, we can say the purpose of civil government is *to restrain evil so every individual can go on his or her own personal faith journey, worshipping God (or not), without fear of persecution from any person or institution.*

We can also begin to build a mission statement for civil government based on what we know so far. Civil government should:

1. Provide justice for all by ensuring individual rights are protected, especially the right to one's life and property.
2. Provide personal protection either from a fellow citizen or an outside force.

These are the primary obligations the Bible describes as the mission of civil government based on what we have covered so far.

KEY POINTS ON CIVIL GOVERNMENT

4000 BC	2400 BC
The Garden Ideal community environment & relationship with God. No need for government.	**Global Violence** God destroys the earth with a flood.
The Fall Man isolated from God with a conscience to enable mankind to live in harmony.	**Post Flood** General command for justice through civil government. **Repopulate** and form nations that honor God.

IMPLICATIONS FOR THE MODERN CHURCH

What does this initial survey of God's plan for civil government mean to the modern Church? The Church has a much bigger role to play regarding civil government than many understand or acknowledge. The colonial clergy were active in reinforcing biblical principles, and they trained their congregations in God's vital—yet limited—purpose of government. This church-centric governance training lasted until the middle of the twentieth century, when the Church pivoted to focus more on evangelism and having a personal relationship with God. The concept of citizenship duty—responsibilities Christians have with respect to the maintenance "of liberty and justice for all"—began to wane.

Over the last half century, the Church has retreated from recognizing the civic duty all Christians have to engage politically. Consequently, culture no longer looks to the Church as the moral conscience of the nation, and the Church has become much less relevant. This is because the Church has abandoned God's demand for justice and appears to have no solutions to the injustice that is front and center in America today. The modern Church needs to return to the biblical role God commissioned people of faith to hold in Genesis 9. We will pick up this topic in chapter 10.

SUMMARY

Without just civil governments, societies will slip into chaos in which the leadership eventually oppresses the citizenry. This was the condition prior to the flood, which is why a governing covenant is needed when people come into community to live together. In Genesis 9 God ordained the institution of civil government so that life would be different than it was before the flood. This is his provision to restrain evil and allow each of us to go on our own personal faith journey and follow our liberty of conscience as we pursue God—*or not.*

The Church has a stewardship responsibility to train Christians to understand and follow the basic design of civil government. At minimum, all Christians should be involved in the voting process to appoint leaders who will follow biblical principles of justice and governing (discussed more in chapter 9). Some Christians are called to serve and should be encouraged and supported. This is not a job for those who reject or do not know God; it is for those who understand God's purpose and mission of civil government and embrace Judeo-Christian principles of justice. These individuals are uniquely capable of governing in a way that honors God and provides justice for the masses.

In this chapter we examined where the idea of a civil authority came from. In Genesis 9 we learn that God ordained civil government, but how to do this arguably requires more information. We get this additional insight by examining instructions God gave to the nation of Israel. Understanding these instructions and seeing how they can be put into practice is the topic of the next chapter.

SUMMARY POINTS

- When Adam and Eve were created and living in the Garden of Eden, there was no need for a civil authority.
- After eating from the tree of knowledge of good and evil, they were expelled from the garden and began having children who populated the earth.
- There was no civil authority during this time, but they had their conscience to guide their personal behavior.
- After 1,500 years, God surveyed the earth and found only widespread violence.
- God spared Noah and his family on the ark but destroyed the rest of mankind to eliminate the violence.
- Civil government was ordained by God after the flood to restrain evil, so the world would not fall into a state of widespread violence as existed prior to the flood.
- Through the institution of civil government, God demands that justice be served, especially with respect to the taking of an innocent life.
- This is God's initial call to active citizenship for all people going forward throughout all ages.
- God's call for justice through civil government is universal to all mankind. Its pre-Israel origin makes the topic of governing independent of any particular prophetic scenario regarding Israel.
- With just civil government to keep evil in check, a nation could be stable and productive, allowing individuals to go on their own personal faith journey—hopefully to choose to follow God.

CHAPTER 3

LEARNING FROM ISRAEL

Governing through a Covenant

Then Moses went up to God, and the LORD called to him from the mountain and said, "This is what you are to say to the descendants of Jacob and what you are to tell the people of Israel: 'You yourselves have seen what I did to Egypt, and how I carried you on eagles' wings and brought you to myself. Now if you obey me fully and keep my covenant, then out of all nations you will be my treasured possession. Although the whole earth is mine, you will be for me a kingdom of priests and a holy nation.' These are the words you are to speak to the Israelites." So Moses went back and summoned the elders of the people and set before them all the words the LORD had commanded him to speak. The people all responded together, "We will do everything the LORD has said." So Moses brought their answer back to the LORD.
—Exodus 19:3–8

"I will insist that the Hebrews have done more to civilize men than any other nation. If I were an atheist, and believed in blind eternal fate, I should still believe that fate had ordained the Jews to be the most essential instrument for civilizing the nations."
—John Adams, December 27, 1816

CHAPTER 3

LEARNING FROM ISRAEL

Governing through a Covenant

Then Moses went up to God, and the LORD called to him from the mountain and said, "This is what you are to say to the descendants of Jacob and what you are to tell the people of Israel: 'You yourselves have seen what I did to Egypt, and how I carried you on eagles' wings and brought you to myself. Now if you obey me fully and keep my covenant, then out of all nations you will be my treasured possession. Although the whole earth is mine, you will be for me a kingdom of priests and a holy nation.' These are the words you are to speak to the Israelites." So Moses went back and summoned the elders of the people and set before them all the words the LORD had commanded him to speak. The people all responded together, "We will do everything the LORD has said." So Moses brought their answer back to the LORD.
—Exodus 19:3–8

I will insist that the Hebrews have done more to civilize men than any other nation. If I were an atheist, and believed in blind eternal fate, I should still believe that fate had ordained the Jews to be the most essential instrument for civilizing the nations. If I were an atheist of the other sect, who believe or pretend to believe that all is ordered by chance, I should believe that chance had ordered the Jews to preserve and propagate to all mankind the doctrine of a supreme, intelligent, wise, almighty, sovereign of the universe, which I believe to be a great essential principle of all morality, and consequently of all civilization.
—John Adams, December 27, 1816[37]

I n Genesis 9, God instructed Noah to establish civil authority to secure justice and deter violence. His instructions were more of a sketch, not a blueprint; clearly more information was needed. Generations later, God gave Moses the plan: free the Jews from Egyptian slavery, travel toward the Promised Land, and officially incorporate the nation of Israel. What happened through the leadership of Moses was the revealing of a complete governing blueprint from God. This blueprint showed the Israelites how to establish civil authority to administer justice in a way that honors God. It also provided a template for all other nations to follow.* Through Scripture, future nations have access to God's blueprint; through ancient Israel, they have a living example of what a just civil government looks like—and of what happens when people abandon God's design for just civil authority. Equally important, from Israel we learn what to do to turn a nation back to God when things go wrong.

In this chapter, we will extract the Bible's blueprint for establishing a God-honoring nation by looking at the instructions God gave Israel through Moses. I will focus on key principles pertaining to the creation of a just civil government and show how these same principles were adopted to initiate the American founding. Lastly, I will look at typical questions people have when reflecting on Israel as a blueprint for civil government that other nations can learn from.

THE CALLING OF ISRAEL

To learn about how God was using Israel to provide a blueprint for governing, one must understand the Abrahamic covenant. With this covenant, God made an unconditional promise to give Abraham a great land, to establish a great nation, and to bless the world through him. This covenant unfolds over many centuries, and Christians around the world are still experiencing the greatest blessing—the full payment of our sins by Jesus. Understanding this covenant is critical to understanding the Bible, because much of the word of God relates

---

* We will not address the ceremonial law, which is unique to Israel and part of a different aspect of Jewish life. With the resurrection of Jesus, the rules for worship given to Israel changed. The guidelines given to other nations for civil government and establishment of justice did *not* change.

to how God was keeping his end of the bargain. This covenant is presented in Genesis 12 and is codified in Genesis 15:

> The LORD had said to Abram, "Go from your country, your people and your father's household to the land I will show you. I will make you into a great nation, and I will bless you; I will make your name great, and you will be a blessing. I will bless those who bless you, and whoever curses you I will curse; and all peoples on earth will be blessed through you." (Gen. 12:1–3)

> When the sun had set and darkness had fallen, a smoking firepot with a blazing torch appeared and passed between the pieces. On that day the LORD made a covenant with Abram. (Gen. 15:17–18)

In these passages we see the scope of God's promise and the binding nature of the agreement. When the smoking firepot with a blazing torch (an ancient irrevocable symbol), passed between the pieces, an unbreakable covenant was confirmed.* God would honor his covenant with Abraham even if Israel was disobedient. God intentionally chose Abraham and created a nation through him. God not only provided a blueprint for creating a great nation; in Israel, he built a model house for future generations to examine—an example for how a nation can govern itself in a God-honoring way.

In the previous chapter we established God's desire for nations to administer justice in order to live in a way that would honor him (Gen 9:5–6). To do this, it would be helpful, arguably necessary, to provide principles and more detailed instruction on how this was to be accomplished. God chose to communicate these governing principles through the nation of Israel by explaining to them exactly how to establish and maintain a just civil government. This process started when God called the people of Israel to publicly declare they would follow him.

---

* The word *covenant* literally means "to cut." Scholars believe that the practice described in Genesis 15 was common in the Old Testament. By splitting an animal in half with the parties walking between the bloody pieces, they were pledging, "May God do the same thing to me if I break my covenant." The modern expression "to cut a deal" may date back to this Old Testament symbol.

PRINCIPLE #1 – START A NATION BY DECLARING A COVENANT

The first thing we learn about governing a nation through Israel is that you need to declare it through a public covenant. Covenants in general are used to codify legal agreements between parties toward a mutual purpose. A number of specific covenants are given by God throughout the Bible: covenants with Adam, Noah, David, etc., each with a specific purpose.

While the Abrahamic covenant was first communicated in Genesis 12 and cemented in Genesis 15, it did not mark the start of the nation of Israel. Israel was officially incorporated when God delivered his moral law to Abraham's descendant, Moses. This Mosaic covenant communicated God's foundational governing building block to the Israelites: the moral law.

The moral law was the basis of the covenant with God, adding an important conditional clause. The Israelites agreed to follow the moral law in exchange for God's blessing:

> " 'Now if you obey me fully and keep my covenant, then out of all nations you will be my treasured possession. Although the whole earth is mine, you will be for me a kingdom of priests and a holy nation.' These are the words you are to speak to the Israelites."
> So Moses went back and summoned the elders of the people and set before them all the words the LORD had commanded him to speak. The people all responded together, "We will do everything the LORD has said." So Moses brought their answer back to the LORD. (Exod. 19:5–8)

The conditional nature of the Mosaic covenant clearly differs from the unconditional nature of the Abrahamic covenant. This raises an important question: Why would God ask the Jews to agree to this? Was it to amend his earlier unconditional covenant? No. The reason is that God wanted the Jews to choose to make a public declaration of their intentions to govern according to God's standard, the moral law.

They heard God's terms and publicly stated their intentions to adhere to it. With this declaration, the nation of Israel obligated themselves to a contract with God and officially began as a nation.

Not only did the Mosaic covenant establish the template for starting a community or nation, it provided the framework for contract law still used in most societies. Whenever parties come together to exchange significant property or form a legal entity, they follow this pattern of declaring mutual obligations in front of witnesses. In our times, this is written up as a contract with notarized signatures, not symbolized by two parts of a sacrificed cow. The church rarely talks about the legal implications of the Mosaic covenant, even though the pattern plays out whether we are forming a business, a civic organization, a marriage, or even a church.* In each case, a document states the intent of the covenant and outlines the terms and conditions.

It is important to clarify some nuances of the Mosaic covenant, as there is sometimes some confusion on how it applies to other nations. First, the Mosaic covenant is a direct agreement between God and the nation of Israel. God personally sponsored Israel and intervened supernaturally to preserve her. Second, the process God used to establish Israel serves as the incorporation template for other nations to follow.

Bible-believing Christians today are familiar with God's blessing when we follow his principles for living. We understand the need for God's guidance on how to manage our families to receive his ongoing blessing. When we read "Be sure you know the condition of your flocks, give careful attention to your herds; for riches do not endure forever, and a crown is not secure for all generations" (Prov. 27:23–24), we understand that our "flocks" refers to our families and that future blessing is not guaranteed. We also recognize a general principle that people who acknowledge God and seek to live in a way that honors him are generally blessed. The same is true for nations. conversely,

---

* My wife and I were involved in starting several churches; in the second one I was the administrative elder. Pulling from various sources, we drafted a document describing our purpose for forming the church and summarizing our beliefs. The founding families talked through the document, making several changes. With the document in hand, we incorporated, filing for our 501(c)(3) certification. While I did not appreciate it at the time, we were following the Old Testament template as we started that church.

nations that ignore God and his governing principles can expect *not* to be blessed, or even to be judged.

Many verses in Psalms and Proverbs describe God's desire for nations to govern his way and what happens when they fail to secure justice for their citizenry:

> Therefore, you kings, be wise; be warned, you rulers of the earth. Serve the LORD with fear and celebrate his rule with trembling. (Ps. 2:10–11)

> When the righteous thrive, the people rejoice; when the wicked rule, the people groan. (Prov. 29:2)

> By justice a king gives a country stability, but those who are greedy for bribes tear it down. (Prov. 29:4)

> Let all the earth fear the LORD ; let all the people of the world revere him…. Blessed is the nation whose God is the LORD, the people he chose for his inheritance…. But the eyes of the LORD are on those who fear him, on those whose hope is in his unfailing love…. We wait in hope for the LORD; he is our help and shield. In him our hearts rejoice, for we trust in his holy name. May your unfailing love rest upon us, O LORD, even as we put our hope in you. (Ps. 33:8–22)

> He rules forever by his power, his eyes watch the nations—let not the rebellious rise up against him. Praise our God, all peoples [nations], let the sound of his praise be heard; he has preserved our lives and kept our feet from slipping. (Ps. 66:7–9)

> All the nations you have made will come and worship before you, Lord; they will bring glory to your name. (Ps. 86:9)

Praise the LORD, all you nations; extol him, all you peoples. For great is his love toward us, and the faithfulness of the LORD endures forever. (Ps. 117)

May all the kings of the earth praise you, LORD, when they hear what you have decreed. May they sing of the ways of the LORD, for the glory of the LORD is great. (Ps. 138:4–5)

Praise the LORD from the earth, you great sea creatures and all ocean depths, lightning and hail, snow and clouds, stormy winds that do his bidding, you mountains and all hills, fruit trees and all cedars, wild animals and all cattle, small creatures and flying birds, kings of the earth and all nations, you princes and all rulers on earth. (Ps. 148:7–11)

What we learn by reading further in the Old Testament is how Israel went through cycles of rebellion against God. Their biggest offense was idolatry, but ignoring God's demand for justice was also called out frequently by the prophets:

Wash and make yourselves clean. Take your evil deeds out of my sight; stop doing wrong. Learn to do right; seek justice. Defend the oppressed. Take up the cause of the fatherless; plead the case of the widow. (Isa. 1:16–17)

Among my people are the wicked who lie in wait like men who snare birds and like those who set traps to catch people. Like cages full of birds, their houses are full of deceit; they have become rich and powerful and have grown fat and sleek. Their evil deeds have no limit; they do not seek justice. They do not promote the case of the fatherless; they do not defend the just cause of the poor. Should I not punish them for this? (Jer. 5:26–29)

He answered me, "The sin of the people of Israel and Judah is exceedingly great; the land is full of bloodshed and the city is full of injustice. They say, 'The Lord has forsaken the land; the Lord does not see.' So I will not look on them with pity or spare them, but I will bring down on their own heads what they have done." (Ezek. 9:9–10)

There are those who turn justice into bitterness and cast righteousness to the ground. (Amos 5:7)

This first step in starting a nation, acknowledging God's moral law as the legal standard, was exactly the model applied in the American founding. America's covenant is the Declaration of Independence, which was unanimously adopted by the original thirteen colonies. To be clear, America is not "the new Israel." She is simply one in a long list of nations that came after Israel. But America's use of a covenant patterned after Israel is part of what makes her unique—in fact, exceptional.* The founders believed they would also receive God's blessing if they followed his plan as they formed a new nation. We see this in a number of writings from the founding era:-

With a firm reliance on the protection of divine Providence, we mutually pledge to each other our Lives, our Fortunes and our sacred Honor.
—The last line in the Declaration, calling out the signers' reliance on God's protection to see the separation through.

God who gave us life gave us liberty. And can the liberties of a nation be thought secure when we have removed their only firm basis, a conviction in the minds of the people that these liberties are of the Gift of God? That they are not to be violated but with His wrath? Indeed, I tremble for my country when I reflect that God is just; that His justice cannot sleep forever.[38]

---

* How all this informed the American founding will be explained further in chapter 5.

—Thomas Jefferson making the connection to suffering God's judgment if we were to abandon God. From Jefferson's *Notes on the State of Virginia*, 1781, also inscribed on the Jefferson Memorial.

How has it happened, Sir, that we have not hitherto once thought of humbly applying to the Father of lights to illuminate our understanding? In the beginning of the Contest with G. Britain, when we were sensible of danger, we had daily prayer in this room for Divine protection.—Our prayers, Sir, were heard, & they were graciously answered. All of us who were engaged in the struggle must have observed frequent instances of a superintending Providence in our favor. To that kind Providence we owe this happy opportunity of consulting in peace on the means of establishing our future national felicity. And have we now forgotten that powerful Friend? or do we imagine we no longer need His assistance? I have lived, Sir, a long time, and the longer I live, the more convincing proofs I see of this truth—that God Governs in the affairs of men. And if a sparrow cannot fall to the ground without His notice, is it probable that an empire can rise without His aid? We have been assured, Sir, in the Sacred Writings, that "except the Lord build the House, they labor in vain that build it." I firmly believe this; and I also believe that without his concurring aid we shall succeed in this political building no better than the Builders of Babel.... I therefore beg leave to move—that henceforth prayers imploring the assistance of Heaven, and its blessing on our deliberations, be held in this Assembly every morning before we proceed to business, and that one or more of the clergy of this city be requested to officiate in that service.[39]

—Ben Franklin at the Constitutional Convention, June 28th, 1787, in an address to the delegates when progress toward a new Constitution stalled. His recommendation was to pray for guidance so they might discern God's will for how to create a more robust governing structure.

Such being the impressions under which I have, in obedience to the public summons, repaired to the present station; it would be peculiarly improper to omit in this first official Act, my fervent supplications to that Almighty Being who rules over the Universe, who presides in the Councils of Nations, and whose providential aids can supply every human defect.... The propitious smiles of Heaven, can never be expected on a nation that disregards the eternal rules of order and right, which Heaven itself has ordained.[40]
—George Washington, excerpts from his first inaugural address, April 30, 1789. He was stating that the government must remain in God's will as it began governing under the new constitution and never ignore his moral law (eternal rules of order and right).

The moral or natural law was given by the Sovereign of the universe to all mankind.... It is true that the law was given by Moses, not however in his individual or private capacity, but as the agent or instrument, and by the authority of the Almighty.[41]
—John Jay, April 15, 1818.

The Declaration was not the first use of a covenant in the New World. The Pilgrims followed the same template in 1620 when 102 settlers, attempting to join the Jamestown colony, instead landed in Plymouth, Massachusetts. Realizing they needed to establish a new community, they drafted the Mayflower Compact, declaring their mutual commitment. This compact made by the Pilgrims rendered them the first group in the New World to voluntarily establish a civil government.

As the colonies in New England began to spread, other important documents detailed their beliefs about governance. In 1638, Thomas Hooker drafted the Fundamental Orders of Connecticut, which were adopted in 1639. Hooker spoke for the contemporary understanding that governments were ordained by God and existed to honor him:

For as much as it hath pleased Almighty God by the wise disposition of his divine providence so to order and dispose of things that we the Inhabitants and Residents of Windsor, Hartford and Wethersfield are now cohabiting and dwelling in and upon the River of Connectecotte and the lands thereunto adjoining; and well knowing where a people are gathered together the word of God requires that to maintain the peace and union of such a people there should be an orderly and decent Government established according to God, to order and dispose of the affairs of the people at all seasons as occasion shall require.[42]

Many historians view Hooker's Fundamental Orders as the first written constitution in the American colonies.[43*] Throughout the colonies it was colonial pastors who were adopting biblical principles for governance that created the blueprint to follow as the colonies grew.

So, the first governing principle we learn from Israel is the need for those starting a community or nation to declare their intentions through a formal covenant. If a nation does this and remains faithful to God, that nation can generally expect to be blessed by him. Colonial documents throughout the American founding confirm that our forefathers believed in this template for starting communities or a nation. This is exactly the process followed with the drafting and signing of the Declaration of Independence, which is America's national founding covenant.

PRINCIPLE #2 – EMBRACE GOD'S MORAL LAW AS THE STANDARD FOR INDIVIDUAL BEHAVIOR AND LAWMAKING

The second principle for establishing a community or nation is to embrace God's moral law as the legal standard. The moral law is summarized in the Ten Commandments, which serves as the universal legal standard. The Ten Commandments were first presented in Exodus 20:

And God spoke all these words: "I am the Lord your God, who brought you out of Egypt, out of the land of slavery. You shall have

---

* This is why Connecticut's state nickname is "The Constitution State."

no other gods before me. You shall not make for yourself an image in the form of anything in heaven above or on the earth beneath or in the waters below. You shall not bow down to them or worship them; for I, the Lord your God, am a jealous God, punishing the children for the sin of the parents to the third and fourth generation of those who hate me, but showing love to a thousand generations of those who love me and keep my commandments. You shall not misuse the name of the Lord your God, for the Lord will not hold anyone guiltless who misuses his name. Remember the Sabbath day by keeping it holy. Six days you shall labor and do all your work, but the seventh day is a sabbath to the Lord your God. On it you shall not do any work, neither you, nor your son or daughter, nor your male or female servant, nor your animals, nor any foreigner residing in your towns. For in six days the Lord made the heavens and the earth, the sea, and all that is in them, but he rested on the seventh day. Therefore, the Lord blessed the Sabbath day and made it holy. Honor your father and your mother, so that you may live long in the land the Lord your God is giving you. You shall not murder. You shall not commit adultery. You shall not steal. You shall not give false testimony against your neighbor. You shall not covet your neighbor's house. You shall not covet your neighbor's wife, or his male or female servant, his ox or donkey, or anything that belongs to your neighbor." (Exod. 20:1–17)

Hundreds of years after its origin, Jesus validated the importance of the moral law in the following declaration:

Do not think that I have come to abolish the Law or the Prophets; I have not come to abolish them but to fulfill them. For truly I tell you, until heaven and earth disappear, not the smallest letter, not the least stroke of a pen, will by any means disappear from the Law until everything is accomplished. Therefore anyone who sets aside one of the least of these commands and teaches others accordingly will be called least in the kingdom of heaven, but whoever practices and teaches these commands will be called great in the kingdom of heaven. (Matt. 5:17–19)

In this passage Jesus acknowledges that the moral law is still in force and worth teaching. He also states that all that the prophets foretold will come true, which includes his substitutionary death on the cross that paid for the sins of the world. Mankind constantly falls short, sinning against God and is consequently hopelessly separated from him. But Jesus's death and resurrection restores this relationship, because he was able to live according to the moral law. One of the purposes of the moral law is to show us we are sinners in need of a Savior, and that Savior must be Jesus Christ.

The Ten Commandments are also meant to govern the actions of individual citizens. This means civil laws must advance the same standard community-wide. Said differently, any law that contradicts the moral law would create a double standard, violating the boundaries of God's governing blueprint. This would be an unjust law, which is condemned in Scripture:

> Woe to those who make unjust laws, to those who issue oppressive decrees, to deprive the poor of their rights and withhold justice from the oppressed of my people, making widows their prey and robbing the fatherless. (Isa. 10:1–2)

This idea about the absolute supremacy of the moral law directly influenced the American founding. In the years leading up to the founding, several individuals were critical in establishing the clear connection between the moral law and civil law. John Locke advanced this belief in his 1689 "Two Treaties on Civil Government":

> It is plain, in fact, that human reason unassisted failed men in its great and proper business of morality. It never from unquestionable principles, by clear deductions, made out an entire body of the "law of nature." And he that shall collect all the moral rules of the

philosophers, and compare them with those contained in the New Testament, will find them to come short of the morality delivered by our Saviour, and taught by his apostles.[44]

Sir William Blackstone, an English jurist and judge in the mid-1700s, affirmed Locke's belief in the supremacy of the moral law. He was famous for *Commentaries on the Laws of England* (1765–1770), which helped establish the validity of the Common Law based on the Judeo-Christian concept of natural rights given by God.

The founders knew Blackstone and his *Commentaries*. As one collector has stated,

Bell's edition [of *Commentaries*] has a 22-page subscribers list (listing names, cities, and professions), which includes John Adams, John Dickinson, James Wilson, John Jay (later the first Chief Justice of the Supreme Court), and Thomas Marshall, who bought it for his teenaged son John Marshall (John read it four times by the age of twenty-seven and became the fourth Chief Justice). Sixteen subscribers became signers of the Declaration of Independence and six became members of the Constitutional Convention....

Adams's annotated copies of the 1771 Bell edition and a 1768 Oxford edition are at the Boston Public Library....

James Madison mentioned in a 1773 letter that he was reading the work and commented: "I am most pleased with & find but little of that disagreeable dryness I was taught to expect." Madison included Blackstone in his 1783 list of "books proper for the use of Congress."[45]

In *Commentaries*, Blackstone, like Locke, challenged the notion that laws passed in conflict with God's moral law were valid:

Man, considered as a creature, must necessarily be subject to the laws of his creator, for he is entirely a dependent being…. It is necessary that he should in all points conform to his maker's will. This will of his maker is called the law of nature…. It is binding over all the globe, in all countries, and at all times: no human laws are of any validity, if contrary to this…. The doctrines thus delivered we call the revealed or divine law, and they are to be found only in the holy scriptures…. Upon these two foundations, the law of nature and the law of revelation, depend all human laws; that is to say, no human laws should be suffered to contradict these.[46]

What Locke and Blackstone were affirming is that the moral law transcends all eras and cultures. Furthermore, it provides a framework for personal behavior and community harmony that is critical for citizens to embrace in order to achieve equal and impartial justice.

The founders revered God's moral law and embraced Locke's and Blackstone's ideas that the moral law is in effect at all times and is non-negotiable.* And they clearly attributed the source of the moral law to God, as evidenced by his people, the Israelites:

I will insist that the Hebrews have done more to civilize men than any other nation. If I were an atheist, and believed in blind eternal fate, I should still believe that fate had ordained the Jews to be the most essential instrument for civilizing the nations. If I were an atheist of the other sect, who believe or pretend to believe that all is ordered by chance, I should believe that chance had ordered the Jews to preserve and propagate to all mankind the doctrine of

---

* The idea of a divine law that governs the universe led some to also seek to understand the natural world. Concepts and formulas in physics, chemistry, and astronomy are examples of laws that are fixed, timeless, and part of God's divine law. The pursuit of understanding these laws by people like Newton, Boyle, and Kepler was a direct result of the Reformation and the concept that God is the architect of the universe, who sustains it through a series of laws that are discoverable by mankind and can be used to improve the human condition. Many scientists during this era were Christians, viewing the discovery of these laws as learning about God himself. Some of them even wrote commentaries on various biblical topics like apologetics and prophecy. Far from being at odds with science, Christianity creates the *foundation* for science, where the constant objective is to search for the truth about our physical world, recognizing that God created it and sustains it through a series of laws that are discoverable by mankind.

a supreme, intelligent, wise, almighty, sovereign of the universe, which I believe to be a great essential principle of all morality, and consequently of all civilization.
—John Adams, December 27, 1816. [47]

Moreover, they believed civil leaders needed to hold the moral law in high regard. It was the king's repeated violation of the moral law over a long period of time that drove them to declare their independence. So, the second governing principle we learn from Israel is the need to embrace the Ten Commandments as the moral and legal standard for personal behavior, community living, and lawmaking.

PRINCIPLE #3 – APPOINT GOD-FEARING REPRESENTATIVES TO CIVIL GOVERNMENT

An all-important consideration when forming a civil government is determining who is in charge. Originally, Moses was the sole leader and arbiter of civil disputes, but the number of cases brought to him soon became overwhelming. God used Jethro, Moses's father-in-law, to suggest training other honorable men who would serve as regional judges to help bear the judicial load Moses was carrying:

The next day Moses took his seat to serve as judge for the people, and they stood around him from morning till evening. When his father-in-law saw all that Moses was doing for the people, he said, "What is this you are doing for the people? Why do you alone sit as judge, while all these people stand around you from morning till evening?" Moses answered him, "Because the people come to me to seek God's will. Whenever they have a dispute, it is brought to me, and I decide between the parties and inform them of God's decrees and instructions." Moses' father-in-law replied, "What you are doing is not good. You and these people who come to you will only wear yourselves out. The work is too heavy for you; you cannot handle it alone. Listen now to me and I will give you some advice, and may God be with you. You must be the people's representative before

God and bring their disputes to him. Teach them his decrees and instructions, and show them the way they are to live and how they are to behave. But select capable men from all the people—men who fear God, trustworthy men who hate dishonest gain—and appoint them as officials over thousands, hundreds, fifties and tens. Have them serve as judges for the people at all times. (Exod. 18:13–22)

God's solution for the Israelites was to appoint elders in every community who would handle civil leadership responsibilities, including settling disputes. This model of representative government allowed for scalability of government as the Jewish nation grew. Both the Old and New Testaments leveraged God's design in establishing communities that would honor him. This is reinforced in Deuteronomy 16 and 18:

Appoint judges and officials for each of your tribes in every town the LORD your God is giving you, and they shall judge the people fairly. Do not pervert justice or show partiality. Do not accept a bribe, for a bribe blinds the eyes of the wise and twists the words of the innocent. Follow justice and justice alone, so that you may live and possess the land the LORD your God is giving you. (Deut. 16:18–20)

But select capable men from all the people—men who fear God, trustworthy men who hate dishonest gain—and appoint them as officials over thousands, hundreds, fifties and tens. (Exod. 18:21)

The apostle Paul applied these same principles to New Testament church leadership. While this is a different sphere of leadership, the basic qualifications are the same:*

---

* One qualification that is not the same is the gender limitation on serving in civil government. Most evangelical churches follow Paul's teaching that the role of elder in the church is reserved for men, but women are very involved in all other aspects of ministry, including teaching. As for civil service, the Bible never suggests women cannot fill those roles. In fact, the Bible has examples of women in civil leadership positions: Deborah and the Queen of Sheba. Today, many very capable women are in leadership positions in public service and private business.

The reason I left you in Crete was that you might put in order what was left unfinished and appoint elders in every town, as I directed you. An elder must be blameless, faithful to his wife, a man whose children believe and are not open to the charge of being wild and disobedient. Since an overseer manages God's household, he must be blameless—not overbearing, not quick-tempered, not given to drunkenness, not violent, not pursuing dishonest gain. Rather, he must be hospitable, one who loves what is good, who is self-controlled, upright, holy and disciplined. He must hold firmly to the trustworthy message as it has been taught, so that he can encourage others by sound doctrine and refute those who oppose it. (Titus 1:5–9)

The elders who direct the affairs of the church well are worthy of double honor, especially those whose work is preaching and teaching. For Scripture says, "Do not muzzle an ox while it is treading out the grain," and "The worker deserves his wages." Do not entertain an accusation against an elder unless it is brought by two or three witnesses. But those elders who are sinning you are to reprove before everyone, so that the others may take warning. I charge you, in the sight of God and Christ Jesus and the elect angels, to keep these instructions without partiality, and to do nothing out of favoritism. (1 Tim. 5:17–21)

Clearly, elders are to govern in a God-honoring way, protecting the rights of all according to the moral law within the sphere of their influence. Affirming this same role of civil government, the apostle Paul describes civil authorities as God's servants, charged with doing what is right and just for the public good:

Let everyone be subject to the governing authorities, for there is no authority except that which God has established. The authorities that exist have been established by God. Consequently, whoever rebels against the authority is rebelling against what God has instituted, and those who do so will bring judgment on themselves. For rulers hold no terror for those who do right, but for those who do wrong. Do you want to be free from fear of the one in authority? Then do what is right and you will be commended. For the one in authority is God's servant for your good. But if you do wrong, be afraid, for rulers do not bear the sword for no reason. They are God's servants, agents of wrath to bring punishment on the wrongdoer. (Rom. 13:1–4)

A critical detail of God's design for civil leadership rests in a term tarnished in the modern era: *public servant*. Too many times, elected officials elevate themselves, but God calls for civil leaders to *serve* the people whom God has entrusted to them. Peter appeals to fellow elders, urging them to fulfill this leadership principle in the church:

Be shepherds of God's flock that is under your care, watching over them—not because you must, but because you are willing, as God wants you to be; not pursuing dishonest gain, but eager to serve; not lording it over those entrusted to you, but being examples to the flock. (1 Pet. 5:2–3)

History demonstrates that, all too often, when one person or an elite group rises to power, they subdue their citizens through manipulation or force. Not all kings or queens are tyrants, but history bears the truth articulated by Lord Acton (1887): "Power tends to corrupt and absolute power corrupts absolutely."[48] God's preferred design is to appoint a group of respected leaders who will adhere to the governing covenant and moral law as the legal standard. This approach provides a vital check on civil leaders from usurping the rights of those they serve.

So, the third governing principle we learn from Israel is the need to appoint, or elect, leaders to represent their citizens and govern as God's servants. Importantly, these appointed leaders must govern in a moral and ethical way, keeping with the moral law. This leads to the next principle about lawmaking.-

PRINCIPLE #4 – HARMONIZE LEGITIMATE RIGHTS AND LAWS WITH THE MORAL LAW AND INSTITUTIONS GOD ORDAINED FOR MANKIND

Once representative government is in place, God calls on it to protect legitimate individual rights. The most basic right, the right to life, came early in God's design and applies universally. While an oppressive governance model grants rights only to the elite, God calls for just governance for *all* citizens, with no prerequisites:

> God presides in the great assembly; he renders judgment among the "gods": "How long will you defend the unjust and show partiality to the wicked? Defend the weak and fatherless: uphold the cause of the poor and oppressed. Rescue the weak and the needy; deliver them from the hand of the wicked." (Ps. 82:1–4)

> Speak up for those who cannot speak for themselves, for the rights of all who are destitute. Speak up and judge fairly; defend the rights of the poor and needy. (Prov. 31:8–9)

> For no one is cast off by the Lord forever. Though he brings grief, he will show compassion, so great is his unfailing love. For he does not willingly bring affliction or grief to anyone. To crush underfoot all prisoners in the land, to people their rights before the Most High, to deprive them of justice—would not the Lord see such things? (Lam. 3:31–36).

God's design calls for legitimate individual rights to be applied to all citizens, but how do we determine which are legitimate and which are not? The answer lies in always looking to the moral law. Legitimate human rights must be in harmony with the moral law. Conversely, any claim that goes against the moral law fails to pass the legitimacy test. Consider the following examples.

MURDER

The moral law forbids willfully taking someone's life other than as an act of self-defense. The moral law protects the right to life for young or old, slave or free, male or female.

A modern example challenging this biblical right to life is a women's right to choose to have an abortion. Many today claim that a woman has "reproductive rights," including the right to terminate an unwanted pregnancy. In recent years, this right has extended to a full-term pregnancy. Those with a Christian worldview see the conflict with the moral law's right to life and instead embrace a pro-life position. It is not that Christians want to deny women's rights; it is that we see the clear conflict with God's moral law when a pregnancy is willfully terminated. This is the taking of an innocent life, which is exactly what God is concerned with in Genesis 9 and in the sixth commandment, "You shall not murder."

STEALING

Taking an individual's property by mandate or force and giving it to someone else violates the eighth commandment, "You shall not steal." Such an action would result in prosecution if an individual burglarized a house and walked off with a big-screen television. For some, the picture becomes muddier when the burglar is an inequitable tax code that takes the wealth of some and distributes it to others. In both instances, a possession is being taken by mandate or force, without the consent of the governed, and thus, it violates the moral law.

MARRIAGE

The moral law established boundaries that govern who may marry and who may not, whom one may have sexual relations with and who is outside the boundaries. Leviticus 18:1–23 contains a list of those one should not have sex with: a close relative, one's father's wife, grandchildren, a sister, a daughter-in-law, someone of the same gender, an aunt, etc.—even animals. Modern thinking attempts to rewrite the standard and make legitimate what the moral law forbids. In President

Obama's speech in 2015 lauding the SCOTUS ruling legitimizing gay marriage, he said, "All Americans are entitled to the equal protection of the law. That all people should be treated equally, regardless of who they are or who they love."[49] If he is right, then "regardless of who they are or who they love" would extend to close relatives, daughters-in-law, and adult-child sexual relationships if they were consensual. All of these acts are forbidden by the moral law and, therefore, are not legitimate rights. Since these rights are illegitimate, any laws passed to protect them are unjust and illegitimate. As shown earlier, God is very clear about the need for laws to be just.

This is why Christians object to same-sex marriage. They are not trying to deny someone his or her rights; they are holding to God's definition of marriage. It is his institution, and Christians do not believe they are in a position to modify it as if it were a man-made institution.[*]

SANCTUARY CITIES

One practical scenario the Bible speaks to is when a person accidentally kills someone. To maintain balance with the moral law, the Bible provides a scenario and a remedy for a community to follow to provide justice. The example provided still resonates today despite all modern advances:

> This is the rule concerning anyone who kills a person and flees there for safety—anyone who kills a neighbor unintentionally, without malice aforethought. For instance, a man may go into the forest with his neighbor to cut wood, and as he swings his ax to fell a tree, the head may fly off and hit his neighbor and kill him. That man may flee to one of these cities and save his life. Otherwise, the avenger of blood might pursue him in a rage, overtake him if the distance is too great, and kill him even though he is not deserving of death, since he did it to his neighbor without malice

---

[*] See Lev. 18:22, 20:13; 1 Kings 14:24, 15:12; 2 Kings 23:7; Mark 10:6–9; Rom. 1:24–28; 1 Cor. 6:9–11; 1 Tim 1:8–11; Heb. 13:4; Jude 7.

aforethought. This is why I command you to set aside for yourselves three cities. (Deut. 19:4–7)

In this passage God outlines the legal principle for involuntary manslaughter. God also gave provision to establish a sanctuary city—a place where an accused person can go to get a fair trial when he accidentally kills someone.

Today, the concept of a sanctuary city has been turned upside down. Rather than establish a place where a person accused of a crime can go to be protected while the crime is being investigated, a person can go to a city where the crime will be ignored. Those supporting this modern definition would argue immigration laws are unjust or immoral. This position rejects the notion that sovereign nations have a right to manage their borders to protect their citizens, whether it be from theft, the flow of addictive drugs, or criminals trafficking women in the sex trade or murdering people. Those making this argument not only ignore the most fundamental aspects of the moral law but they also assert a right that prevents securing justice based on the moral law.

GOD-ORDAINED INSTITUTIONS

Legitimate rights and laws must also be consistent with the boundaries of the two key institutions God ordained: the family unit and civil government. This book is largely about the institution of civil government and God's principles for the proper role of government in a community, but all communities are made up of families. God ordained families in Genesis 2 with the marriage of Adam and Eve. When civil leaders deviate from God's design for either of these two institutions, they violate this vital principle and should be confronted. This is essentially what happened in colonial America, which we will explore further in chapter 5.

So, the fourth principle we see in examining God's governing blueprint through Israel is that to live safe and productive lives, legitimate individual rights and the laws supporting them must be in harmony with the moral law and the key institutions God gave mankind.

PRINCIPLE #5 – PROVIDE EQUAL JUSTICE FOR ALL WITH THE PENALTY MATCHING THE CRIME

While the moral law provides clarity to establish just laws, justice must be applied to everyone in a way that is equitable and impartial. This means everyone deserves the same level of justice, regardless of race, gender, class, or nationality. Securing justice to meet this standard is an incredibly challenging task, but the Bible provides all the guidance we need through legal principles about judges found in hundreds of passages in the Old Testament.

IMPARTIAL

Judges should apply justice to everyone, regardless of race, gender, class, or nationality.* To the best of their ability, judges must apply God's moral law equitably and fairly.

He has made you king to maintain justice and righteousness. (1 Kings 10:9)

Do not deprive the foreigner or the fatherless of justice, or take the cloak of the widow as a pledge. Remember that you were slaves in Egypt and the LORD your God redeemed you from there. (Deut. 24:17–18)

Appoint judges and officials for each of your tribes in every town the LORD your God is giving you, and they shall judge the people fairly. Do not pervert justice or show partiality. Do not accept a bribe, for a bribe blinds the eyes of the wise and twists the words of the innocent. Follow justice and justice alone, so that you may live and possess the land the LORD your God is giving you. (Deut. 16:18–20)

---

* This does not mean a nation cannot establish laws regarding the flow of people in and out of the country. Nations have the right to manage their borders, especially to ensure the protection of their citizens and their governing institutions. What it *does* mean is that a foreigner legally visiting a country has the same rights as citizens of that nation in relation to the moral law. The practical implication is that foreigners have a right to their life, liberty, and property.

Do not pervert justice; do not show partiality to the poor or favoritism to the great, but judge your neighbor fairly. (Lev. 19:15)

EQUALLY JUST

Judges must dispense justice universally, especially to the poor, the disadvantaged, and the foreigner.

Woe to those who make unjust laws, to those who issue oppressive
decrees, to deprive the poor of their rights and withhold justice
from the oppressed of my people, making widows their prey and
robbing the fatherless. (Isa. 10:1–2)

Cursed is anyone who withholds justice from the foreigner, the
fatherless or the widow. (Deut. 27:19)

Defend the weak and the fatherless; uphold the cause of the poor
and the oppressed. Rescue the weak and the needy; deliver them
from the hand of the wicked. (Ps. 82:3–4)

ACCIDENTAL OFFENSES

Judges must allow for due process when a person injures or kills his
neighbor accidentally, to ensure a fair trial.

Then Moses set aside three cities east of the Jordan, to which anyone who had killed a person could flee if they had unintentionally
killed a neighbor without malice aforethought. They could flee
into one of these cities and save their life. (Deut. 4:41–42)

Determine the distances involved and divide into three parts the
land the LORD your God is giving you as an inheritance, so that
a person who kills someone may flee for refuge to one of these
cities. This is the rule concerning anyone who kills a person and
flees there for safety—anyone who kills a neighbor unintentionally,
without malice aforethought. (Deut. 19:3–4)

JUSTICE-DISPENSING
Judges must punish and bring guilty people to justice.

How long will you defend the unjust and show partiality to the wicked? (Ps. 82:2)

Acquitting the guilty and condemning the innocent—the LORD detests them both. (Prov. 17:15)

REASONABLE
Judges should dispense punishment in keeping with the severity of the crime.

If men who are fighting hit a pregnant woman and she gives birth prematurely but there is no serious injury, the offender must be fined whatever the woman's husband demands and the court allows. But if there is serious injury, you are to take life for life, eye for eye, tooth for tooth, hand for hand, foot for foot, burn for burn, wound for wound, bruise for bruise. (Exod. 21:22–25)

Anyone who takes the life of a human being is to be put to death. Anyone who takes the life of someone's animal must make restitution—life for life. Anyone who injures their neighbor is to be injured in the same manner: fracture for fracture, eye for eye, tooth for tooth. The one who has inflicted the injury must suffer the same injury. Whoever kills an animal must make restitution, but whoever kills a human being is to be put to death. You are to have the same law for the foreigner and the native-born. I am the LORD your God. (Lev. 24:17–22)

GOD-HONORING
Judges should honor God by correctly dispensing justice.

To do what is right and just is more acceptable to the LORD than sacrifice. (Prov. 21:3)

To accomplish this, judges should be fair and impartial as they apply the law. Ideally they are God-fearing and recognize they will be held accountable in the next life for their rulings. This is why the taking of an oath is so important: it recognizes that the person will be held accountable to God in the next life.

Fear the LORD your God, serve him only and take your oaths in his name. (Deut. 6:13)

George Washington stressed the importance of oaths when he took the oath of office as the first president, adding "So help me God." He stressed this point again in his farewell address:

Let it simply be asked where is the security for property, for reputation, for life, if the sense of religious obligation desert the oaths, which are the instruments of investigation in Courts of Justice? And let us with caution indulge the supposition, that morality can be maintained without religion. Whatever may be conceded to the influence of refined education on minds of peculiar structure—reason & experience both forbid us to expect that National morality can prevail in exclusion of religious principle.[50]

THE CITIZEN'S RESPONSE TO INJUSTICE

When judges fail to execute justice, the citizens are to leave retaliation to God. This has to do with the individual who is wronged.

It is mine to avenge; I will repay. In due time their foot will slip; their day of disaster is near and their doom rushes upon them. (Deut. 32:35)

Do not take revenge, my friends, but leave room for God's wrath, for it is written: "It is mine to avenge; I will repay," says the

Lord.... Do not be overcome by evil, but overcome evil with good. (Rom. 12:19, 21)

This does not mean Christians should not seek redress when an injustice is done. This was the process the founders followed in the decade leading up to the struggle for independence. And what swayed the colonies to collectively declare separation was the widespread tyranny the king was imposing, with no end in sight. To them, it was a defensive response to the king's aggression on all the colonies. When an individual does not receive justice, however, that individual is not to take matters into his or her own hands.

The verses above show how God has provided clear guidance in all areas needed to provide justice in a community, including principles to administer fair punishment. So, the fifth principle we see in examining God's governing blueprint through Israel is that civil leaders must provide equal and impartial justice for all, with the penalty matching the level of the crime.

PRINCIPLE #6 – EXTEND LIBERTY TO ALL

The sixth principle we glean from Israel and throughout the Bible is the idea that while people living in community should respect lives and property, they should not be coerced into believing in God. Instead, they should be allowed to follow their conscience, ideally through the free exchange of ideas while the civil authority maintains civil order. This is what liberty is—the ability to have and express opinions. We see this principle by examining a number of verses that show a pattern where God gives boundaries but always allows mankind to make a volitional choice.

The LORD God took the man and put him in the Garden of Eden to work it and take care of it. And the LORD God commanded the man, "You are free to eat from any tree in the garden; but you must not eat from the tree of the knowledge of good and evil, for when you eat from it you will certainly die." (Gen. 2:15–17)

"Now if you obey me fully and keep my covenant, then out of all nations you will be my treasured possession. Although the whole earth is mine, you will be for me a kingdom of priests and a holy nation." These are the words you are to speak to the Israelites. So Moses went back and summoned the elders of the people and set before them all the words the LORD had commanded him to speak. The people all responded together, "We will do everything the LORD has said." So Moses brought their answer back to the LORD. (Exod. 19:5–8)

"Come now, let us settle the matter," says the LORD. "Though your sins are like scarlet, they shall be as white as snow; though they are red as crimson, they shall be like wool." (Isa. 1:18)

But my people would not listen to me; Israel would not submit to me. (Ps. 81:11)

This is good, and pleases God our Savior, who wants all men to be saved and to come to a knowledge of the truth. (1 Tim. 2:3–4) He is patient with you, not wanting anyone to perish, but everyone to come to repentance. (2 Pet. 3:9)

We will explore this concept more fully in chapter 6, but we mention it here because liberty was extended to all in that they were not forced to believe something—only to live according to the moral law based on the Mosaic covenant. This was the critical missing piece of the governing puzzle that so many earnest Christians overlooked during the Church Age. Not extending liberty is what led to the persecution and murder of many people during the medieval and early colonial period. Whether they were Christians or not does not matter. What we clearly see through the Bible is that God does not demand that we impose doctrinal beliefs on people, only that we establish and retain civil order as first described in Genesis 9. With civil order in place, we can live our lives in a way that honors God, including by sharing the gospel.

Additionally, the first five basic principles do not require adherence or complete agreement to a long list of doctrinal positions that characterize all the different Christian denominations. All that is required is an acknowledgment of the moral law as the legal standard to provide equal and impartial justice. Liberty is what allows all the Christian sects to live together along with those who are ambivalent or reject Christianity. This is why liberty is so critical and must be extended to all.

So, the sixth principle we learn from examining the nation of Israel is the need to extend liberty to all.

PRINCIPLE #7 – TEACH THE NEXT GENERATION IMPORTANT INSTITUTIONS AND TRADITIONS

If establishing a just nation that honors God were not difficult enough, maintaining one through many generations proves even more precarious. Keeping a nation thriving and securing justice over time requires the next generation to live productive, God-honoring lives, recognizing the key institutions God ordained for mankind: the family unit and a just civil authority. In America the church has traditionally communicated this information to the next generation along with other institutions, like public schools, universities, and the Girl Scouts and the Boy Scouts.*

Furthermore, it is important to pass on defining national traditions to the next generation. In the case of Israel, God laid out seven annual holidays with unique meanings for Israel to remind future generations about their founding covenant and reliance on God. (See Table 3.1.)

---

* Unfortunately, many public schools, universities, and civic-minded clubs like the Girl Scouts and Boy Scouts have become politicized and no longer represent traditional American values that reflect our national founding covenant. In nearly all cases, however, these institutions were founded by Christians to develop Christian character and to improve life in America.

Table 3.1[51]

Feast	Text	Date	Significance
Passover	Lev. 23; Num. 28; Deut. 16	Nisan 14 Spring	Passover speaks of redemption. The Messiah, our Passover lamb, would be sacrificed for us.
Unleavened Bread	Lev. 23; Num. 28; Deut. 16	Nisan 15–21 Spring	Unleavened bread speaks of sanctification. The Messiah's body would not decay in the grave.
Firstfruits	Lev. 23	Nisan 16 Spring	Firstfruits speaks of resurrection. The Messiah would rise triumphantly from the grave on the third day.
Weeks (Pentecost)	Lev. 23; Num. 28; Deut. 16	50 days after Firstfruits Spring	Weeks/Shavuot speaks of origination. The Messiah would send the Holy Spirit to initiate a New Covenant and the Church Age.
Trumpets	Lev. 23; Num. 29	Tishri 1 Fall	Trumpets/Rosh Hashanah points to the future day when the Messiah returns to rescue the righteous (Rapture) and judge the wicked.
Yom Kippur (Day of Atonement)	Lev. 23; Num. 29	Tishri 10 Fall	Yom Kippur/Day of Atonement points to the future day when Israel repents of her sins and turns to the Messiah for salvation.
Tabernacles (Booths)	Lev. 23; Num. 29; Deut. 16	Tishri 15–21 Fall	Tabernacles/Sukkot points to the future day when the Messiah sets up his messianic Kingdom and tabernacles among us.

Scattered throughout the year and each with a unique meaning, these annual reminders urged Israel to remain steadfast and gave them a mechanism to pass God's design to their children and grandchildren. Failing to pass on the foundational governance principles leaves posterity without the critical knowledge to continue living in a way that will result in God's blessing. God knew man's forgetfulness would be detrimental, so he commanded Israel to communicate his plan to their children:

> Only be careful, and watch yourselves closely so that you do not forget the things your eyes have seen or let them fade from your heart as long as you live. Teach them to your children and to their children after them. Remember the day you stood before the LORD your God at Horeb, when he said to me, "Assemble the people

before me to hear my words so that they may learn to revere me as long as they live in the land and may teach them to their children." (Deut. 4:9–10)

These verses are describing God's direction to teach all of what Moses wrote in the first five books of the Bible. There is additional admonishment in Old Testament passages to pass on this knowledge to the next generation:

He decreed statutes for Jacob and established the law in Israel, which he commanded our ancestors to teach their children, so the next generation would know them, even the children yet to be born, and they in turn would tell their children. (Ps. 78:5–6)
Start children off on the way they should go, and even when they are old they will not turn from it. (Prov. 22:6)

This appeal to teach the Judeo-Christian worldview to the next generation is repeated in the New Testament. For example:

Fathers, do not exasperate your children; instead, bring them up in the training and instruction of the Lord. (Eph. 6:4)
The American founders were aware of the need for traditions, and they designated the anniversary of our founding as a key day of remembrance. John Adams articulated it this way:

The second day of July, 1776, will be the most memorable epoch in the history of America. I am apt to believe that it will be celebrated by succeeding generations as the great anniversary Festival. It ought to be commemorated, as the Day of Deliverance, by solemn acts of devotion to God Almighty. It ought to be solemnized with pomp and parade, with shows, games, sports, guns, bells, bonfires and illuminations, from one end of this continent to the other, from this time forward forever.[52]*

---

* The Declaration of Independence was approved on July 2 but signed by most of the delegates on

In time, additional holidays were added to pass on the values of our history. Thanksgiving dates to a 1621 celebration of gratitude to God for his provision, to which the settlers of Plymouth Plantation celebrated with local Native Americans. Remembering this a century and a half later, the first official Thanksgiving of the United States of America was inaugurated in 1777 by the Continental Congress, following the victory of the Battle of Saratoga:

> That with one heart and one voice the good people may express the grateful feeling of their hearts, and consecrate themselves to the service of their Divine Benefactor; and that together with their sincere acknowledgements and offerings, they may join the penitent confession of their manifold sins whereby they had forfeited every favour, and their humble and earnest supplication that it may please God, through the merits of Jesus Christ, mercifully to forgive and blot them out of remembrance; that it may please Him graciously to … inspire our commanders both by land and sea, and all under them, with that wisdom and fortitude which may render them fit instruments, under the providence of Almighty God, to secure for these United States, the greatest of all human blessings, independence and peace.[53]

On October 3, 1863, during the Civil War, the current tradition of our annual, national Thanksgiving was established. President Abraham Lincoln issued a formal proclamation, passed by an Act of Congress, stating the following:

> No human counsel hath devised nor hath any mortal hand worked out these great things. They are the gracious gifts of the Most High God, who, while dealing with us in anger for our sins, hath nevertheless remembered mercy. It has seemed to me fit and proper that they should be solemnly, reverently, and gratefully acknowledged, as

---

July 4. Interestingly, both John Adams and Thomas Jefferson died on July 4, 1826, fifty years after the signing of the Declaration. Dying within hours of each other, many viewed this as a providential sign of God's approval of America.

with one heart and one voice, by the whole American people. I do therefore invite my fellow-citizens in every part of the United States, and also those who are at sea and those who are sojourning in foreign lands, to set apart and observe the last Thursday of November next as a day of thanksgiving and praise to our beneficent Father who dwelleth in the heavens.[54]

Over the years, other national holidays have been added to commemorate various aspects of American faith and experience.

The key institutions in America that have traditionally been responsible to teach the story of America are the public schools, universities, civil authorities, churches, and families. During the twentieth century, nearly all these institutions largely abandoned this responsibility, teaching instead history through a progressive worldview. This has contributed to America's identity crisis and opened the door to "cancel culture"—a deliberate attempt to erase all aspects of our Christian national heritage, both good and bad.

The Israelites fell into a similar cycle of forgetting the covenant and feasts meant to remind them how they were to live and govern themselves. What we also see, however, is that God will restore a nation that repents, which Israel did under several of its leaders:

> If my people, who are called by my name, will humble themselves and pray and seek my face and turn from their wicked ways, then I will hear from heaven, and I will forgive their sin and will heal their land. (2 Chron. 7:14)

This is the opportunity and challenge for American patriots today: To call attention to how America has forsaken our founding principles and encourage repentance and a turning back to the governing principles that were put into place during our founding.

So, the seventh principle we see in examining God's governing blueprint through Israel is the need to teach the next generation these principles and how they have been applied in America.

GOVERNING PRINCIPLES ALSO APPLY TO THE FAMILY

The purpose and mission for civil government, along with the seven principles for governing, also apply to the family unit. This is not by accident; they must apply since communities are made up of families. Families are where children are supposed to learn their Christian citizenship responsibilities, among other things. In fact, the material in this book could be repackaged as "how to govern your household in a way that honors God." Table 3.2 illustrates how each of the seven principles plays out in the family dynamic and can help parents assess how well they are managing their homes to provide liberty and justice for all.

Table 3.2

Community	Family
1. Governments are established and declared through a mutual covenant.	1. Marriage is started through a mutual covenant declared in front of witnesses, with a marriage license.
2. Governments are to embrace God's moral law as the standard to guide personal behavior and lawmaking.	2. Couples agree to love and care for each other, forsaking all others and embracing God's moral law.
3. Representatives to civil government should be God-fearing.	3. Mom and Dad are the authorities in the home and promise to raise and govern their household according to God's ways.
4. The moral law provides context to the rights of individuals.	4. The moral law provides the standard for how parents treat their children.
5. Laws passed must be enforced through equal justice where punishment matches the level of the crime.	5. Mom and Dad make rules within the home that must conform to the moral law. They discipline their children as best they can, through equal justice where the punishment matches the level of the crime.*

---

* As a father of four children with very different personalities, I particularly understand the challenge in making and enforcing rules in a house where children have different compliance profiles. There were many times when my wife and I "retired to our chambers" to try to figure out how to dispense justice to one of our children in a particularly difficult case.

6. Liberty is to be extended to all, regardless of religious belief.	6. Parent tell their kids "You can ask us anything," extending liberty instead of being legalistic task masters. As the kids get older, their parents give them more responsibility as equal family members. This prepares them to be good citizens.
7. The community needs to be educated on these principles.	7. Mom and Dad are responsible to educate their kids on these principles.

These principles we learn from Israel further refine our understanding of how God expects the nations of the world to govern themselves. Nations that follow these principles will generally be blessed, and nations that violate these principles will generally be judged.

KEY POINTS ON CIVIL GOVERNMENT

4000 BC	2400 BC	2000 BC	1500 BC
The Garden Ideal community environment & relationship with God. No need for government.	**Global Violence** God destroys the earth with a flood.	**Abrahamic Covenant** Promise to make a great nation. Gen: 12, 15	**National Covenant** God established Israel through the Mosaic covenant.
The Fall Man isolated from God with a conscience to enable mankind to live in harmony.	**Post Flood** General command for justice through civil government. **Repopulate** and form nations that honor God.		**Moral Law** As the legal standard for justice. **Guidelines** for community and home governing. **Teaching** principles of governing to the next generation.

QUESTIONS

Several common questions arise when learning from Israel to govern through a covenant. Two of these are captured in this list and discussed in detail in the Appendix.

- Didn't Jesus teach that we should forgive instead of hold to "an eye for an eye"?
- What about the harsh penalties in the Old Testament?

SUMMARY

In this chapter, we reviewed the basic governing principles God provided to Israel—principles to govern through a covenant. These are principles all the other nations of the world can apply to establish a God-honoring nation. Those who choose to do so can generally expect to be blessed, and those who turn their backs on God can generally expect to be judged. We saw dozens of Old Testament verses that speak to this matter with New Testament affirmation. This is further evidence refuting the notion that government is an optional topic for the modern-day Christian. Instead, from cover to cover, the Bible shows us how important establishing a just civil authority is to God.

Tragically, many Christians do not appreciate how foundational the Bible's principles of government are to enable evangelism. It should be self-evident that the best possible environment in which to share the gospel is a civil community that respects and protects free expression. A civil authority is God's provision to create this kind of environment, where people are free to hear and receive the gospel. Furthermore, many Christians believe the mere mention of civil government, or politics in general, hampers evangelism. The Bible teaches the exact opposite, which we will show in the next chapter.

SUMMARY POINTS

- The Bible provides basic principles for how to govern in a God-honoring way, demonstrated through the nation of Israel.
- Nations that follow these principles can generally expect to be blessed, and those who reject them can generally expect not to be blessed and may face judgment.
- Communities and nations are established through a mutual declaration of the people agreeing to join them.
- The moral law is the legal standard for personal behavior and lawmaking.
- The primary governing body should be made up of representatives appointed by the citizenry who fear God and promise to govern according to these principles.
- Legitimate individual rights and just laws must be in harmony with the moral law. If they violate the moral law, they are not true rights, nor are they just laws.
- Civil leaders are to provide equal and impartial justice for all, where the penalties match the level of the crime.
- The citizenry is to teach the next generation about these governing principles, key institutions, and traditions in order to maintain a unified national identity and provide liberty and justice for all.

CHAPTER 4

EVANGELISM THROUGH JUSTICE
How God Uses National Covenants

See, I have taught you decrees and laws as the Lord my God commanded me, so that you may follow them in the land you are entering to take possession of it. Observe them carefully, for this will show your wisdom and understanding to the nations.
—Deut. 4:5–8

For we must Consider that we shall be as a City upon a Hill, the eyes of all people are upon us; so that if we shall deal falsely with our God in this work we have undertaken and so cause him to withdraw his present help from us, we shall be made a story and a by-word through the world.
—John Winthrop
March 21, 1630

CHAPTER 4

EVANGELISM THROUGH JUSTICE

How God Uses National Covenants

See, I have taught you decrees and laws as the LORD my God commanded me, so that you may follow them in the land you are entering to take possession of it. Observe them carefully, for this will show your wisdom and understanding to the nations, who will hear about all these decrees and say, "Surely this great nation is a wise and understanding people." What other nation is so great as to have their gods near them the way the LORD our God is near us whenever we pray to him? And what other nation is so great as to have such righteous decrees and laws as this body of laws I am setting before you today?
—Deut. 4:5–8

We shall find that the God of Israel is among us, when ten of us shall be able to resist a thousand of our enemies; when He shall make us a praise and glory, that men of succeeding plantations shall say, "The Lord make it like that of New England." For we must Consider that we shall be as a City upon a Hill, the eyes of all people are upon us; so that if we shall deal falsely with our God in this work we have undertaken and so cause him to withdraw his present help from us, we shall be made a story and a by-word through the world.
—John Winthrop
March 21, 1630[55]

W hen I talk with pastors and church leaders about Christian citizenship, the number one reason they give for why it should not be discussed in the church is because it is divisive and threatens evangelism. Because of the clear emphasis on evangelism in the New Testament, this argument is like kryptonite when used against the believer trying to motivate fellow Christians to engage in the political process. It thoroughly neutralizes any attempt to have a discussion on what the Bible might have to say about the topic. But is the pursuit of justice following biblical principles truly at odds with the evangelistic process?

In this chapter, I will challenge this premise. I will show how God's Old Testament evangelistic strategy was based on Israel's success in creating a nation according to God's blueprint of providing equal and impartial justice to all. Second, I will explain why this strategy changed in the New Testament with the Great Commission in Matthew 28. Finally, we will examine how God's original evangelistic strategy is timeless and has played out with the American experiment given the desire of the destitute around the globe to come to America in search of freedom.

EVANGELISM IN THE OLD TESTAMENT

When we hear the word *evangelism*, we tend to think of it as a New Testament activity—but God was just as interested in evangelism in the Old Testament. In reading through the Old Testament, it is easy to miss God's desire and strategy for drawing people to himself, but in Deuteronomy 4:5–8, Moses describes what the strategy is:

> See, I have taught you decrees and laws as the LORD my God commanded me, so that you may follow them in the land you are entering to take possession of it. Observe them carefully, for this will show your wisdom and understanding to the nations, who will hear about all these decrees and say, "Surely this great nation is a wise and understanding people." What other nation is so great as to have their gods near them the way the LORD our God is near

us whenever we pray to him? And what other nation is so great as to have such righteous decrees and laws as this body of laws I am setting before you today?

God's plan for evangelizing the nations of the world in the Old Testament is very clear, especially when considering God placed this tiny nation at the crossroads of civilization at that time.* When observing Israel, the nations of the world were to see God's blueprint for governing in a way that honors him. They were to see an equitable legal system administering liberty and justice for all in a way that enabled the citizens and nation to flourish. When governing this way, Israel was blessed by God and was a magnetic draw for other nations to come and see what made Israel different.

During Solomon's reign, we learn about a *seeker*—a queen from the south. This queen was searching for God, and at the time, Israel was at its zenith and was renowned as a nation that followed the one true God. This queen had to come check out this nation. What follows is an expanded narrative based on 1 Kings 10 about this seeking queen. I have added some details to frame the account, but it is consistent with the biblical narrative.

A VISIT FROM A QUEEN SEARCHING FOR TRUTH

The year was 970 BC, and Solomon had been ruling the nation of Israel in Jerusalem for twenty-three years, having succeeded his father, King David.† Under David's leadership, Israel had become a world power, strategically located on the only natural land bridge between the major continents of the known world. Anyone traveling by land would have passed through Israel and learned about the wise rule of King Solomon.

Solomon had successfully established law and order, having

---

* Israel is located on the only land bridge between the major continents of that era. Anyone traveling between nations would pass through the land of Israel and encounter this tiny but special nation.

† The year quoted is an estimate of the year based on chronology in the Old Testament.

followed the Mosaic covenant captured in the Pentateuch.* He also built the temple with exacting precision to God's design, and he established the ceremonial practices God gave Moses 400 years earlier—a key element of the blueprint for the Jewish nation. Because of Solomon's obedience as Israel's civil leader, God poured out the blessing he had promised. Israel had become a great nation in keeping with the promise God made to Abraham, but also great in riches (1 Kings 3:5–15). Many of those closest to Solomon argued that he was one of the wisest men to ever live.

Because of his wisdom, Solomon understood God's blueprint for governing, especially in administering justice. First, he understood that God demanded justice for all (Gen. 9:5–6). Second, he understood that God's moral law served as a universal standard for civil laws, and any law contrary to the moral law was unjust and illegitimate. Third, he understood he needed leaders and judges capable of administering justice in the communities beyond Jerusalem. Fourth, he understood God's ceremonial law and the need to observe the sacrifices and feasts as regular reminders of Israel's sins and God's subsequent forgiveness. Solomon understood that teaching God's design to the next generation was critical for Israel to continue in God's blessing after his reign. Lastly, he understood that God made a conditional covenant through Moses to bless Israel if they lived by his design and to judge them if they did not. Solomon understood God's promise to make Abraham "into a great nation" (Gen. 12:2)—and God fulfilled that promise during his reign.

Because of the success Israel enjoyed, many nations took notice, making inquiries to Solomon as to the source of this prosperity. One such inquiry came from the Queen of Sheba, who wanted to see firsthand if Israel was as prosperous—and if the king was as wise—as she had heard. Having traveled for many weeks, she approached Jerusalem.†

---

* The Pentateuch is the first five books of the Bible, also called the *Torah*.

† We cannot be sure of the exact location where the Queen of Sheba lived, but most historians believe it was either southern Arabia or Ethiopia, about 1,500 and 1,200 miles from Israel, respectively. Either location would have taken many weeks to travel from, especially with a large caravan described in the biblical narrative. (Joshua J. Mark, "Queen of Sheba," World History Encyclopedia,

As she arrived and settled just outside the eastern gate, the queen was amazed by the walls that surrounded this city, which seemed nearly impregnable. The ramp winding its way up the steep incline to the eastern gate gave a sense of scale to the city and the height of its walls. From the valley they were encamping in, it was an imposing sight.

As her entourage set up camp, Solomon's emissaries escorted the queen and her advisors to the Mount of Olives to provide more details for her pending audience with Solomon. From this view, she gained a sense of the grandeur of the city's architecture, including the king's palace and the temple.

As she surveyed the entire city, the aides told her about the king and how Israel's God had granted him unparalleled wisdom. She learned that Israel had enjoyed a time of relative peace, and that King David—Solomon's father—was a warrior-king. They told of how God had called Solomon to serve a different purpose: to build a magnificent temple that would be the center of Jerusalem. This explanation helped the queen to see that Solomon was not a warrior-king, bent on making war with other nations. To the queen, this was odd, because most kings secured their kingdoms through force and often oppressed their people to prevent a hostile overthrow from within. Solomon's greatness was different: his apparent wisdom and power were given by his God, and

March 26, 2018, https://www.worldhistory.org/Queen_of_Sheba/.)

CHAPTER 4 : EVANGELISM THROUGH JUSTICE

she pondered this as an alternative to ruling by force. In this, the queen saw Israel as a unique nation and was eager to have an audience with King Solomon.

Solomon's emissaries also explained how he had used Israel's strategic location as the only natural land bridge between the continents, employing a kind of toll on the commerce in the region. This had afforded Israel to become wealthy and to finance the building of the temple. From her vantage point, the temple was awe-inspiring. Then the emissaries pointed out Solomon's palace, which was also impressive. The queen stared at the city for a few minutes, trying to take in all she was seeing.

The emissaries then described how their God clearly explained how he expected them to live, summarized in what they called the Ten Commandments, and handed down by a great prophet named Moses. Through Moses, God had also provided guidelines for how to set up regional leadership structures, make laws, and provide justice for everyone, regardless of social standing. All of this was captured in sacred Jewish writings given through Moses. They explained how Jewish priests were responsible to teach these principles to their local gatherings to ensure all citizens would understand their God and his design for how they should live. Unlike other nations, Israel viewed education for its citizens as critical for their success. This notion of widespread education among the citizenry on how they were to live was novel to the queen, and she wondered how Solomon kept all these educated people from forming factions to challenge his power.

The queen asked for an example of how the justice system worked, so Solomon's emissaries explained one of Solomon's more difficult rulings. Two prostitutes had appeared before him with a child, each claiming she was the mother. Both women had recently given birth, but one of the newborns had died, and both women claimed the remaining baby belonged to her. Their case was deemed inconclusive in a lower court and was brought before Solomon. Having heard the testimony of each woman, Solomon shocked the court with an order to cut the child in two, giving each mother half. As the guard drew his sword, one of the women protested, offering to spare the infant's life and to allow the other woman to take the living child. Solomon knew she was the real mother; only a mother's love would explain her willingness to spare the child's life, even if it meant giving up her baby. What was a seemingly unsolvable case was resolved in a matter of minutes with no doubt behind the verdict.* Stories like this about Solomon's wisdom drew the queen's respect. Clearly, the relationship Solomon enjoyed with his Hebrew God appeared to be the power behind his success. She wanted to hear more.

Solomon's emissaries explained further how the Ten Commandments were the foundation of civil justice and the focal point of Jewish life. They shared how these commands from God created an unachievably high standard—one that no one can uphold perfectly. They called the falling short "sin," and God's law required sacrifice as a temporary covering for the sin of the nation and of its individual citizens. As part of the queen's stay in Jerusalem, she would visit Solomon's temple, where this process would be explained further by Solomon and the high priest.

The queen would also be shown the court where King Solomon heard and settled only the most difficult civil cases, those that the lower courts could not decide. Ultimately, the Queen of Sheba would tour Solomon's royal palace and enjoy a meal and an interview with the man of enviable wisdom and power. Having shared remaining details of the queen's introduction to the king the next day, Solomon's emissaries departed.

The queen's mind teemed with questions. After her long journey, she was poised to meet the king of the greatest nation in the known world. She was hours away from seeing for herself what made this nation unique.

The next day started early. Anticipation filled the air as the details of the historic meeting came to fruition. A highly decorated caravan assembled to transport the queen and her retinue: horses and camels were groomed and outfitted with regal garments and banners representing her homeland. The king's emissaries arrived to escort the queen through the eastern city gate.

---

* This is an actual account from 1 Kings 3:16–28.

As the queen passed through the gate, she was led through the narrow streets winding toward Solomon's palace. Cheering crowds lined the roads, bowing in respect. Their genuine demeanor welcomed their royal guest, and the significance of her visit was beginning to sink in.

Upon entry to the royal hall, trumpeters greeted her with majestic fanfare. She hesitated a moment, ensuring her retinue was ready to make a ceremonial entrance. The backdrop for her royal appointment was a room with a large, vaulted ceiling supported by dozens of pillars with ornate capitals atop each gilded pillar. Not fifty paces from her, Solomon raised his scepter and smiled to indicate his approval for her approach.

She surveyed the royal officials—adorned in beautifully designed robes and arranged on either side of the main aisle. Beautiful music was playing, and the whole scene was unlike anything she had ever seen. She stopped at the foot of the steps leading to the throne and slowly bowed. Solomon descended the steps to greet her, an unusual act of respect and humility for a great king. After each of them made customary remarks and they exchanged gifts, Solomon led her out of the royal hall and into his palace for the remainder of the day.

Along the way, Solomon inquired about her trip and if she needed anything at her encampment. As they entered the palace, he pointed out unique features of the architecture and explained how the city had expanded under his leadership. As they entered a large dining room, Solomon escorted the queen to the head of the table and seated her next to him. Through the window, the queen caught sight of the temple. It was impressive from a distance, but even more so just a few hundred yards away. After a prayer by the high priest, the feast began.

During the meal, the queen inquired about the history of Israel and how it functioned. Solomon explained how God called Abraham and promised him a great nation, a great land, and a future great blessing—a reference to the coming Messiah who would ultimately deliver the Jewish people from their sin. He summarized generations of their history: time spent in Egypt, 400 years of slavery, and God's deliverance through Moses, who led them to the land where Jerusalem was built. He explained that their God is holy and just and how the

Ten Commandments are an expression of his divine attributes. In this short expression of God's holiness, Israel sees how they fall short and are under God's judgment, he said. He explained God's instructions to Moses to build a temple where God's wrath would be appeased through a sacrificial system.* Solomon explained how the offering of these sacrifices, along with seven annual feasts, served as the focus of life in Israel.

After the meal, Solomon escorted the queen to a side chamber with a full view of the temple. He explained the history of the various temples and how his father, King David, had prepared for this temple's construction but was instructed by God not to build it. This responsibility fell to Solomon, so David told Solomon about his preparations so he could build it.

The queen asked a few questions, but she had so many more: How did Solomon rule his kingdom so effectively? How did he acquire officials who were capable and loyal? How did the citizenry come to be so orderly without a strong military force to impose order? Why did other kingdoms arrest, torture, or even execute their political enemies, but Israel did not? Israel was unique, and the queen wanted to know how it became so.

In gracious manner, Solomon explained how the Ten Commandments were not only a summary of God's holiness but also the standard for providing justice to all Israelites, regardless of social status. God ensured certain rights for everyone, even foreigners traveling through Israel. As monarch, Solomon had a solemn responsibility to ensure that these rights were protected. For instance, Israel's God had declared human life sacred, having created it himself. Therefore, murder was prohibited in the Ten Commandments—a crime punishable by death; other provisions dealt with death resulting from accidents or self-defense. God's prohibition of murder meant the king could not

---

* And how much more would the Queen of Sheba have been astonished had she known that the sacrifices were just a picture of the final sacrifice of God's Son to fully atone for the sins of mankind? Exactly what Solomon understood of this we cannot know, but he did have access to Genesis 3:15, which alludes to injury of the seed of the woman ("bruise his heel"). He also had access to Psalm 22, in which David describes the future crucifixion.

arrest his enemies without cause or have them executed unless they committed a capital crime—as defined in God's law, not by the king's whims. All life was declared sacred, and God had given Solomon the responsibility to see that Israel honored his standard.

Another key protection was individual private property. Israel's God said that to take away someone's property without that person's permission was a sin. The king was under divine orders to provide equal justice regarding property—even for the widow, orphan, or visiting alien, like the queen. To ensure equal justice, Solomon's God had given clear instructions for the selection of elders: they were responsible to enforce laws that were in harmony with God's moral law. These same elders presided over civil cases, rendering judgments when an infraction of laws occurred. God had even included a provision for sanctuary cities if someone felt he or she needed an unbiased official to preside over a particular case. These principles for justice and governing were new to the queen, but she was seeing the clear benefits of a society that followed them.

The queen asked Solomon how it was that the people of Israel understood these principles, so he described the role of the local priests to provide ongoing education. In each town, a priest taught from the sacred writings left by Moses, ensuring students understood God's principles and his promise to bless those who obey him. This ongoing education led to a generally peaceful society—one where citizens had a greater measure of freedom to pursue interests unlike in the dictatorships typical of the era.

The beauty of God's blueprint was making sense to the Queen of Sheba. She realized she was touring the model nation, built according to God's design. The queen turned her questions to a broad range of topics. Solomon answered all with ease as wisdom guided his logic and prescribed his words. After several hours of discussion, the queen paused to reflect on all she had seen and heard. When she "saw all the wisdom of Solomon and the palace he had built, the food on his table, the seating of his officials, the attending servants in their robes, his cupbearers, and the burnt offerings he made at the temple of the LORD, she was overwhelmed."*

She said to the king, "The report I heard in my own country about your achievements and your wisdom is true. But I did not believe these things until I came and saw with my own eyes. Indeed, not even half was told me; in wisdom and wealth you have far exceeded the report I heard. How happy your people must be! How happy your officials, who continually stand before you and hear your wisdom! Praise be to the LORD your God, who has delighted in you and placed you on the throne of Israel. Because of the LORD's eternal love for Israel, he has made you king to maintain justice and righteousness."†

Solomon smiled. He understood that the queen had seen in Israel a unique nation set apart by God—a great nation that had a unique approach to governing that respected every individual and guaranteed justice to everyone. In living out God's promises faithfully, Israel was providing a glimpse into the holiness and justice of God to the surrounding nations. Solomon understood that nations that decided to apply what they had seen in Israel would be blessed and that nations

---

* Sourced from 1 Kings 10:4–5.

† From 1 Kings 10:1–9, 2 Chron. 9:1–8. The Queen stated exactly what Moses had predicted in Deuteronomy 4:6–8.

that did not would most likely have problems. His job was to set the example, and today Solomon had fulfilled his responsibility. The queen was rightly overwhelmed, as the holiness and justice of God should be overwhelming and convicting to all who take the time to consider him.

After spending the afternoon together, the two monarchs bid their farewells. Many nations had come to visit Israel before the Queen of Sheba, and many more would follow. Some would leave eager to apply what they had heard and seen in Israel; others would not. Solomon understood his dual role: to govern according to God's design and to explain that design to inquisitive visitors. An obedient Israel stood as a shining city on a hill for surrounding nations to see and inquire about. For the first part of his reign, Solomon accomplished this, and the nations of the world flocked to Jerusalem. God's plan for evangelism was working exactly as intended.

THE EVANGELISM STRATEGY WORKED

From the Old Testament narrative, it is not entirely clear whether the Queen of Sheba accepted and chose to follow the God of Israel. Certainly, she was impressed, but did she have saving faith because of the encounter? The answer came centuries later as Jesus was talking to the Pharisees.

During Jesus's ministry on earth, he restored sight to the blind, healed the lepers, fed multitudes, walked on water, calmed storms, made the paralyzed walk, etc.—all to give evidence that he was the Messiah foretold in the Old Testament. While myriads saw these miracles and believed, the religious leaders were reluctant to recognize Jesus as the promised Messiah. Despite seeing the miracles with their own eyes, they demanded a sign to prove Jesus was sent by God. Jesus rebuked them for demanding this, and in the process answered the question about the queen's conversion:

> A wicked and adulterous generation asks for a sign! But none will
> be given it except the sign of the prophet Jonah. For as Jonah was
> three days and three nights in the belly of a huge fish, so the Son of

Man will be three days and three nights in the heart of the earth. The men of Nineveh will stand up at the judgment with this generation and condemn it; for they repented at the preaching of Jonah, and now something greater than Jonah is here. The Queen of the South will rise at the judgment with this generation and condemn it; for she came from the ends of the earth to listen to Solomon's wisdom, and now something greater than Solomon is here. (Matt. 12:39–42)

Jesus confronts the Pharisees' lack of faith by pointing to people who repented because of what they had seen and heard:

- Men of Nineveh: The reluctant prophet, Jonah, traveled to their city and preached a "turn or burn" sermon. One sermon was all it took for them to repent and believe in God.
- Queen of the South: The Queen of Sheba was searching like our modern day "seekers." She was so intent on finding the truth she took the initiative to travel a long distance to find an answer. Seeing the nation of Israel and God's plan for establishing a just nation was all it took for her to believe in God.

The Pharisees heard the truth. They had even seen God perform many miracles. But they still did not believe in Jesus or repent. As a result, Jesus called them out as a wicked generation.

Through this encounter in the Gospels, we know that the Queen of Sheba was converted. Part of what caused her conversion was seeing how blessed Israel was because of Solomon governing as a "king to maintain justice and righteousness." This is exactly what Moses indicated would happen if Israel was faithful in governing justly:

See, I have taught you decrees and laws as the LORD my God commanded me, so that you may follow them in the land you are entering to take possession of it. Observe them carefully, for this will show your wisdom and understanding to the nations, who will hear about all these decrees and say, "Surely this great nation is a wise and understanding people." What other nation is so great as to have their gods near them the way the Lᴏʀᴅ our God is near us whenever we pray to him? And what other nation is so great as to have such righteous decrees and laws as this body of laws I am setting before you today? (Deut. 4:5–8)

The Queen of Sheba was not the only one to notice that Israel must have been blessed by God. We know that "the whole world sought audience with Solomon to hear the wisdom God had put in his heart" (1 Kings 10:24–25). God's evangelistic plan for Israel had the desired effect on the nations of the world.

When Solomon and all of Israel's leaders administered equal justice to all, they were governing in a way that honored God. Many people saw this just government in Israel and visited the nation to understand why. Still today, governing justly is a draw to people, especially those who may be oppressed or searching for freedom.

NEW TESTAMENT AFFIRMATION OF GOD'S EVANGELISTIC PLAN

There is further guidance in the New Testament on the role of nations and Christians in God's evangelistic plan. During his ministry to the Gentile nations, Paul affirmed God's evangelistic role of nations from Genesis 9 and 10:

The God who made the world and everything in it is the Lord of heaven and earth and ... does not live in temples built by human hands. And he is not served by human hands, as if he needed any-thing. Rather, he himself gives everyone life and breath and every-thing else. From one man he made all the nations, that they should inhabit the whole earth; and he marked out their appointed times in history and the boundaries of their lands. God did this so that they would seek him and perhaps reach out for him and find him. (Acts 17:24–27)

In this passage Paul looks back to God's demand for justice and plan for the nations that was clarified after the flood. God's desire was for nations to form, spread over the world, and govern justly so citizens could "seek him and perhaps ... find him."

Affirming the desired relationship between Christians and civil government, Paul instructed his protégé, Timothy, with these words:

> I urge, then, first of all, that petitions, prayers, intercession and thanksgiving be made for all people—for kings and all those in authority, that we may live peaceful and quiet lives in all godliness and holiness. This is good, and pleases God our Savior, who wants all people to be saved and to come to a knowledge of the truth. (1 Tim. 2:1–4)

In other words, a just civil government is a key prerequisite to living peaceful, godly lives in a society conducive to fellowshipping with God and spreading the gospel. This is completely consistent with teaching about civil government in the Old Testament.

In reinforcing the importance of faith in action, the writer of Hebrews notes "administering justice" as the catalyst for many Old Testament individuals gaining what was promised to them:

> And what more shall I say? I do not have time to tell about Gideon, Barak, Samson and Jephthah, about David and Samuel and the prophets, who through faith conquered kingdoms, administered justice, and gained what was promised. (Heb. 11:32–33)

In 2 Corinthians, Paul identifies virtues that should come with Christian growth, including the desire to secure justice:

> Godly sorrow brings repentance that leads to salvation and leaves no regret, but worldly sorrow brings death. See what this godly sorrow has produced in you: what earnestness, what eagerness to clear yourselves... what indignation, what alarm, what longing, what concern, what readiness to see justice done. (2 Cor. 7:10–11)

Lastly, Paul highlights the role of the Holy Spirit in producing the virtues Christians need to live at peace with God and their neighbors. This makes the Christian even more capable of achieving a just society:

> But the fruit of the Spirit is love, joy, peace, forbearance, kindness, goodness, faithfulness, gentleness and self-control; against such things there is no law. (Gal. 5:22–23)

Equipped with the Holy Spirit and empowered by a growing understanding of Scripture, believers can become God's agents of administering justice in the communities and nations in which they live. We have ready access to God's design to live out our Christian faith with increasing success. Supported by the Holy Spirit, our godly demeanor "teaches us to say 'No' to ungodliness and worldly passions, and to live self-controlled, upright and godly lives in this present age" (Titus 2:12).

Christians who live by God's design in their personal lives become like Solomon's Israel, attracting others in their orbit like the Queen of Sheba. In this way, God's Old Testament evangelism strategy becomes ours as well. As individuals, we each become a city on the hill, a light-house for the gospel.

AMERICA'S EVANGELISTIC IMPACT

A free and just nation like America will always attract people. God designed humans to want to be treated with respect, to have their property protected, and to be dealt with fairly. Liberty and justice for all is more of a DNA issue than just a line from our Pledge of Allegiance. Free nations have long served as beacons of hope. The light of American freedom has shone throughout America's history just as it did in ancient Israel. People from all corners made, and still make, the difficult decision to pull up stakes, leaving family and the familiar to come to America for the promise of this freedom. And when they come and desire to join the American family, there is an opportunity to see the Christian faith on display and share the gospel. This has been the idea in New England since the start.

"A Model of Christian Charity" is a sermon John Winthrop preached at Holyrood Church in Southampton, England, on March 21, 1630, to a group of Puritans ready to embark across the Atlantic and stake their claim for a free society. His words included the now iconic expression of what the new world offered: "a city on a hill."* He prophesied that the eyes of the world would be upon them to see if the American experiment offered true freedom:

> We shall find that the God of Israel is among us, when ten of us shall be able to resist a thousand of our enemies; when He shall make us a praise and glory, that men of succeeding plantations shall say, "The Lord make it like that of New England." For we must Consider that we shall be as a City upon a Hill, the eyes of all people are upon us; so that if we shall deal falsely with our God in this work we have undertaken and so cause him to withdraw his present help from us, we shall be made a story and a by-word through the world.
> — John Winthrop, March 21, 1630[56]

His words echoed what Jesus said in the Sermon on the Mount:

> You are the light of the world. A town built on a hill cannot be hidden. Neither do people light a lamp and put it under a bowl. Instead they put it on its stand, and it gives light to everyone in the house. In the same way, let your light shine before others, that they may see your good deeds and glorify your Father in heaven. (Matt. 5:14–16)

A constant stream of immigrants to America since our founding validated Winthrop's prediction.

The nations of the world also acknowledged America's distinctive

---

* In his 1988 State of the Union address, Reagan called America "this shining city on a hill." (Ronald Reagan, Address Before a Joint Session of Congress on the State of the Union, January 25, 1988, online by Gerhard Peters and John T. Woolley, The American Presidency Project, https://www.presidency.ucsb.edu/node/255154).

of protecting individual liberty.* In 1885, France gifted America with the Statue of Liberty, motivated in part by the abolition of slavery. With a torch held high, Lady Liberty stands as a metaphor for John Winthrop's "shining city on a hill." While France paid for the statue, America agreed to pay for the pedestal. Some of the fundraising came from an auction of art and literary works, one of which was a sonnet by Emma Lazarus entitled "The New Colossus." First read in 1883, the poem captured the concept of the unique haven America had become for the oppressed who sought a better life:

> Not like the brazen giant of Greek fame,
> With conquering limbs astride from land to land;
> Here at our sea-washed, sunset gates shall stand
> A mighty woman with a torch, whose flame
> Is the imprisoned lightning, and her name
> Mother of Exiles. From her beacon-hand
> Glows world-wide welcome; her mild eyes command
> The air-bridged harbor that twin cities frame.
> "Keep, ancient lands, your storied pomp!" cries she
> With silent lips. "Give me your tired, your poor,
> Your huddled masses yearning to breathe free,
> The wretched refuse of your teeming shore.
> Send these, the homeless, tempest-tost to me,
> I lift my lamp beside the golden door!"[57]

America began as a place where the tired, poor, and oppressed masses could come and experience religious and civil liberty. It was a nation where they could pursue their passions, knowing their lives, liberty, and property would be protected. Despite continuing challenges in modern America, many still yearn to come, willing to leave family and all that is familiar to carve out a path to American citizenship.

As in the days of Solomon, explaining a unique national vision for a just civil government presents an opportunity to share the gospel.

---

* The First Amendment in the US Bill of Rights protects our individual religious and civil liberties.

When Christians understand the biblical principles that led our founders to make America free, they can point the oppressed masses to the God who drafted the moral law. Whether the masses convert to Christianity or not, believers who are faithful will have planted seeds of the gospel in the pursuit of liberty and justice.

Sadly, the modern-day church is missing out on this evangelistic opportunity. Rather than explain the biblical meaning behind a "shining city on a hill" and link to the American founding, the church intentionally avoids talking about political matters. Evangelism is often the singular focus and has become the lens through which every other Christian responsibility is viewed. Ironically, this view of the faith has become a stumbling block to the very objective of gaining more converts and influencing the culture for Christ. This narrow view comes in part from a fundamental misunderstanding of the Great Commission.

THE GREAT COMMISSION – A CHANGE IN STRATEGY

For sincere Christians living today, the most important passage that seems to guide our daily priorities is in Matthew 28, where Jesus tells the disciples to spread the gospel to the nations of the world:

> Then Jesus came to them and said, "All authority in heaven and on earth has been given to me. Therefore go and make disciples of all nations, baptizing them in the name of the Father and of the Son and of the Holy Spirit, and teaching them to obey everything I have commanded you. And surely I am with you always, to the very end of the age." (Matt. 28:18–20)

Considering all we have learned up to this point about civil government in the Old Testament, what else might this passage be telling us?

If we read this verse only from a New Testament standpoint, it might seem that Jesus is giving new marching orders, but this is not the case. First, notice the focus on nations, which is not new; it's only another reinforcement from the Old Testament:

I will praise you, LORD, among the nations; I will sing of you among the peoples. (Ps. 108:3)

Praise the LORD, all you nations; extol him, all you peoples. For great is his love toward us, and the faithfulness of the LORD endures forever. (Ps. 117)

Second, Jesus commands the disciples to teach new believers *everything he has commanded* them. This includes the Old Testament and principles for establishing a just civil authority. There is nothing Jesus taught that would suggest instructions in the Old Testament about civil government are no longer important. Additionally, other New Testament writers affirm the intent of civil government in passages like Romans 13 and 1 Timothy 2. So, what is Jesus conveying in Matthew 28 with the Great Commission?

God's plan to draw nations to himself has not changed, *but his evangelistic strategy has*. Critical to God's evangelistic plan for Israel was for Israel to *stay* in the land he gave them. God knew the power of location; he gave Israel the only natural land bridge between the major continents. Anyone traveling in the ancient world would travel through Israel, taking note of the unique governance design and divine blessings this nation enjoyed.

God's strategy changed when Jesus came into the world and paid the penalty for the world's sin. Jesus's crucifixion and resurrection reconciled to God those who believe in him. Old Testament sacrifices—which were only a temporary covering of sin—were no longer necessary, and anyone could have access to God through his Son in any location. With the risen Christ, God's plan for evangelism entered a new stage. No longer were the disciples (who were Jews) to *stay* in the land God gave them and govern justly as the primary vehicle for making God known to the world. Now, given the gospel based on the risen Christ, Jesus's disciples were to *go*, taking the gospel to all the nations of the world.

In our effort to fulfill the Great Commission, the modern evangelical church has made a strategic error, avoiding topics like politics out of fear they will hamper evangelism. Church leaders ramp up the intensity around missions and evangelism, hoping to engage their congregants to "impact the culture for Christ." We hire senior pastors and fill church boards with people God has gifted as evangelists. In their zeal, they say things like, "If you are not fishing for men, you are not following the Jesus of the Bible." With this approach, they pressure people into believing they ought to be evangelists themselves if they are to take their faith seriously. Few would dispute the importance of evangelism, but there is more God calls his followers to do, including leading in the civil arena.

There are many Christians who are engaging in the civil arena but not because they are encouraged by their church leaders. I find these folks are usually gifted and feel called to use their God-given leadership in the civil arena as their personal ministry. Unfortunately, they are often criticized or censured in the local church for wanting to talk about political issues that they wish the church would address. Church leaders often say, "You should be more interested in God's heavenly kingdom instead of man's earthly kingdom and focus on reaching the lost for Christ." This attitude marginalizes or silences congregants whom God has gifted in the civil arena. Disillusioned, their Christian faith becomes compartmentalized from their civil service, and they often do not see it as a legitimate and critical ministry.

Meanwhile, the church that avoids the topic of biblical citizenship becomes less relevant to one of the most critical problems facing the church today—government encroachment on religious liberty, including the freedom to evangelize. Most churches are unwittingly working against the evangelistic objective they claim to pursue at home and abroad.

God's directive to his people in Genesis 9 shows that establishing and maintaining justice is one of his top priorities. Without Christian involvement in civil affairs to protect liberty and justice for all, culture will collapse, and with it, evangelism will become increasingly difficult if not nearly impossible. It's not that God cannot still move to reach individuals with the gospel, but a post-Christian secular culture will restrict liberty. We are seeing this already as traditional Christian positions on things like marriage are increasingly characterized as hate speech. This environment does not provide the best ground for citizens to openly discuss Christianity or the gospel. The people will instead bear the weight of the unjust, godless government. This was an overarching theme of the twentieth century: the communist takeover of Russia, China, and North Korea, as well as the rise of Nazi Germany. All are examples of godless regimes inflicting oppression, persecution, and misery on the masses. The catalyst in all these cases was the direct and intentional abandonment of God and his governing principles for nations.

For much of American history, our nation adhered to the biblical blueprint—and blessing followed. More recently, the blueprint has been questioned, abandoned, or redrawn altogether—and we have suffered signs of collapse. Sadly, the modern church bears much of the blame. The narrow interpretation of the Great Commission pushed by the modern church ignores God's blueprint for establishing just civil governments that allow individuals to go on their own personal faith journey. As a result, American culture is in serious decline, and the church seems to have no answer.

Furthermore, much of the church has accepted the cultural decline as inevitable and does not believe the church bears any responsibility. I often hear messages from the pulpit where speakers provide updates on the moral decline as if they were reporting the weather, as though moral decline is something they are not responsible for or have any control over. At some point, Christians must step back and ask, "Are we missing something that is leading to the cultural decline and narrowing the window of evangelism as a result?" "If God has given us his word so we can live peaceful and quiet lives (as 1 Timothy 2 describes), why isn't it working?"

Unlike the modern church's separation of evangelism and politics, one of America's most prolific evangelists had a different view on the role of the church in political affairs. Charles Finney is widely recognized as one of the catalysts of the Second Great Awakening in America in the mid 1800s. His approach to revival meetings—the tent meeting—became the pattern for the modern evangelical crusade with leaders like Billy Graham. In an article entitled "The Decay of Conscience" dated December 4, 1873, Finney stated the following about the role of the church, specifically the senior pastor:*

> If immorality prevails in the land, the fault is ours in a great degree. If there is a decay of conscience, the *pulpit* is responsible for it. If the public press lacks moral discrimination, the *pulpit* is responsible for it. If the church is degenerate and worldly, the *pulpit* is responsible for it. If Satan rules in our halls of legislation, the *pulpit* is responsible for it. If our politics become so corrupt that the very foundations of our government are ready to fall away, the *pulpit* is responsible for it.[58]

It is up to church leaders, especially senior pastors, to embrace our responsibility to establish and maintain just civil governments. This is not only clearly what the Bible teaches, it also provides a pathway to evangelism the church has totally ignored in recent years. Pastors must rebalance efforts between evangelism and providing leadership in the public square. The Bible provides the blueprint for just civil government, and we must encourage those gifted in this area to learn these principles and serve where called. This will be hard, but who said establishing liberty and justice for all would be easy? Jesus was very clear that his message would be controversial and would even split families. Taking a stand on moral issues in the public square will certainly increase friction but cannot be ignored. Leaders in the modern church should not believe things will be different today as we seek to establish and maintain justice in the communities in which we live.

---

* The orthodoxy of some of Finney's theological beliefs have been questioned—perhaps justifiably—but his push for civil engagement was very much in line with biblical principles for civil government. Finney's call for Christians to engage in politics in order to seek justice arguably prepared America for its biggest trial after achieving independence: the Civil War.

QUESTIONS

A number of questions arise when discussing biblical governing as a way to evangelize. A few of these are captured in this list and discussed in detail in the Appendix.

- Don't politically active Christians come across as unloving and end up inhibiting evangelism?
- What if the candidates are immoral and my conscience prevents me from voting for any of them?
- Shouldn't all Christians in government roles use their jobs as a platform for evangelism?
- Shouldn't all Christians just seek to know God?

The common solution to all these questions is education. The colonial church understood its citizenship duty because pastors in the founding era consistently preached sermons to educate their congregations. The modern church needs to return to God's blueprint, teaching congregants to develop and support civic leaders who will faithfully execute their public offices as ministers of God's plan. God has gifted capable leaders in the church with the talent and calling to do this important work. They need both encouragement and education to embrace these roles in society as a legitimate ministry important to God and society at large.

SUMMARY

The modern church has accepted the narrative that politics and evangelism do not mix, but in this chapter, we saw how God actually used Israel's national covenant—with a focus on justice—as his evangelistic strategy. When God's blueprint was faithfully followed in Israel, it had the desired effect—and it has had a similar effect in America, drawing millions to realize the freedom our national founding covenant offers. Governing justly and evangelism are interrelated, and both activities are part of the Christian walk ordained by God to enable every individual the freedom to go on his or her personal faith journey. The church needs to alter her evangelistic strategy, prioritizing teaching on biblical citizenship and the principles of civil government as a key part of living out the Christian faith, along with evangelism.

Thus far, we have shown how God ordained civil government after the flood to all the nations that would follow. We saw how God provided additional guidance on how to govern through the nation of Israel, not only for law and order but also to support his evangelistic strategy for the nations. The next question is, "How might a group living under unjust rule form a new nation that follows these biblical insights?" This is the focus of the next chapter.

SUMMARY POINTS

- Churches do not talk about politics, because they fear it hinders evangelism; but this view is inconsistent with Old Testament and New Testament teaching about God's call for a just civil authority.
- The pursuit of justice goes hand in hand with evangelism, as both are based on the moral law.
- God's strategy for evangelism in the Old Testament was for Israel to live justly and be blessed by him.
- We see Israel achieving this objective during the reign of Solomon, who, for a season, administered justice as God instructed him to do.
- The nations of the world saw the greatness of Israel during Solomon's reign and came to see for themselves the product of his success.
- The Queen of Sheba was one such visiting dignitary; she asked Solomon many questions and was overwhelmed by Israel's uniqueness.
- Jesus confirmed the Queen of Sheba's conversion, and Scripture reveals that the nations of the world came to see the blessing on Israel.
- Just governance is crucial because it prevents societies from devolving into chaos.
- This is not in conflict with the Great Commission, as this was just a change in strategy, not a change in vision.
- The church's almost singular focus on evangelism and marginalization of biblical citizenship has sidelined many believers who may be called to serve in civil leadership.
- The faithful administration of justice is something many desire today, so it still serves as an evangelistic hook.
- America's history demonstrates the same magnetism, attracting millions of immigrants yearning to be free. The church should be using this opportunity to explain the biblical principles behind our nation's founding as another way to evangelize.

CHAPTER 5

STARTING A NATION

Establishing a Covenant

Blessed is the nation whose God is the LORD, the people he chose for his inheritance. From heaven the LORD looks down and sees all mankind; from his dwelling place he watches all who live on earth—he who forms the hearts of all, who considers everything they do.
—Psalm 33:12–15

There are instances of, I would say, an almost astonishing Providence in our favor; our success has staggered our enemies, and almost given faith to infidels; so we may truly say it is not our own arm which has saved us. The hand of Heaven appears to have led us on to be, perhaps, humble instruments and means in the great providential dispensation, which is completing.
—Samuel Adams, August 1, 1776

CHAPTER 5

STARTING A NATION

Establishing a Covenant

Blessed is the nation whose God is the LORD, the people he chose for his inheritance. From heaven the LORD looks down and sees all mankind; from his dwelling place he watches all who live on earth—he who forms the hearts of all, who considers everything they do.
—Psalm 33:12–15

There are instances of, I would say, an almost astonishing Providence in our favor; our success has staggered our enemies, and almost given faith to infidels; so we may truly say it is not our own arm which has saved us. The hand of Heaven appears to have led us on to be, perhaps, humble instruments and means in the great providential dispensation, which is completing.
—Samuel Adams, August 1, 1776[59]

After the enormous cost it took to defend the American colonies in the French and Indian War, England needed to refill her national treasury. To accomplish this, the king imposed a number of different acts from 1764 through 1775 to raise revenue from the colonies. However, colonial leaders had grown accustomed to governing themselves and objected not only to the excessive taxation but also to being imposed upon without their consent. By the spring of 1776, after many attempts to seek redress for their grievances, the colonies concluded the king would never acknowledge their right to govern themselves as English citizens. The

colonists realized their only path forward was to live under the tyranny of the king or to separate from the mother country. Once they
chose independence, the question before them was how to form a new
nation.

The colonists' Christian faith informed not only their rationale for
separation but also the process they followed. Their faith was informed
by a series of events and experiences in the preceding 250 years, which
were triggered by the Reformation. In this chapter I will explain how
these events shaped the theology and faith of the founding generation. I will also show how the governing principles covered in previous
chapters informed the process they followed to separate from England
and the rationale they captured in the Declaration of Independence.

THE REFORMATION

Long before America's founders declared independence, a revolution of
theological freedom had paved the way. Prior to the fifteenth century
and the invention of the printing press, Bibles were hand-copied and
written in Latin, making Scripture accessible to educated church leaders but not to the common citizen. This gave the church and its clergy
tremendous power over the citizenry as they alone could explain what
the Bible taught. This problem began to change, however, with the
invention of the moveable type printing press by Johannes Gutenberg
around 1440.

The first book printed using this new "printing press" was the
Latin Bible. The first English Bible became available in 1535, thanks
to the translating work of William Tyndale.* The first Bible that resem-
bles our modern-day Bible was the Geneva Bible, produced in 1560.[60]
This Bible was the first to divide the text into numbered chapters and
verses. Each book had a summary introduction and included marginal
notes to help explain the meaning of verses. It also included visual aids

---

* Because of his work translating the Bible for common people, Tyndale was arrested in 1535 and
convicted of heresy in 1536. He was strangled to death then burned at the stake. His dying prayer
was that the King of England's eyes would be opened and that he would permit the dissemination
of Bibles. It seemed God answered his prayer when a year later, King Henry VIII authorized work
on the Matthew Bible.

and a topical and name index. By the late 1500s the Geneva Bible had replaced earlier translations. With the printing press reducing the cost to produce books, it became possible for more people to have access to the word of God and to draw their own conclusions about its meaning.[61] Within one generation, biblical literacy had spread from pulpit to pew, and a spiritual revolution was underway.

Historians generally agree the catalyst for the Reformation was in 1517 when Martin Luther challenged Catholic doctrine. Although a monk himself, Luther posted his "95 Theses" opposing many long-held church doctrines, such as the selling of indulgences.* He argued that many of these doctrines and practices were out of line with Scripture. He also raised other issues, such as how people achieved salvation, how Christians should live out their faith, and how they should be governed. Luther sought to tie these doctrinal questions to the Bible, and many Reformers continued his mission. Eventually this movement led to the formation of Baptist, Lutheran, Methodist, Congregationalist, and Presbyterian denominations.

English believers who joined these new denominations often found themselves at odds with their civil leaders. Among them was a group of Separatists who boarded the Mayflower in the fall of 1620 and began their journey to the New World in search of religious liberty. Prior to the Pilgrims' arrival, a colony had been founded in Jamestown, Virginia. The differences in these two colonies are important as we seek to understand how early colonial American faith and practice informed key events surrounding the American founding.

GOVERNING IN COLONIAL AMERICA

Jamestown, founded in 1607, was the first permanent colony in America.[62] It was established by the Virginia Company of London and governed by men appointed by the company. Rather than seeking religious liberty, the primary goal of Jamestown was to turn a profit by searching for gold and silver deposits. But the colony struggled with

---

* The idea of indulgences at that time was that people who sinned could pay the church to earn forgiveness. The "95 Theses" listed reasons Luther believed this practice and other manipulations and misapplications of Scripture were unbiblical.

the local Indians and had trouble sustaining itself.

One notable event occurred in 1614, when John Rolfe married Pocahontas, who was the daughter of Chief Powhatan. She became a Christian, adopting the name Rebecca, and her conversion is captured in one of the large paintings in the Capitol rotunda. Their marriage improved relations between the settlers and the Native people. But during a trip to England in 1617, Pocahontas became sick and died, and shortly thereafter, her father died as well. After the death of Chief Powhatan, relations between the settlers and Natives deteriorated.[63]

In 1619, several important developments occurred. Jamestown established a representative assembly, which convened in the Jamestown Church. This assembly was the first of its kind in the English colonies. Also in that year, the first African slaves arrived, around fifty men, women, and children. They began working as indentured servants, which meant that after working for a period of time, they would gain their freedom.[64] Early records do show an increasing number of free blacks, confirming that Jamestown was following typical principles of indentured servitude, but this did not last.[65]

A few years later, in 1622, "the Powhatan Indians staged an uprising, which wiped out a quarter of the European population of Virginia."[66] In 1624, after years of instability with the local Indians and growing debt, King James I intervened and made Virginia a royal colony. In 1627 the king granted royal approval of the Virginia Assembly and governor, which remained the governing structure in force until 1776.[67*]

By the 1680s, the system of indentured servitude the first Africans experienced devolved into the race-based slavery system that existed at the time of the founding. As early as 1640, the first African was ordered[†] by the court "to serve his said master or his assigns for the time of his natural life here or elsewhere."[68] By the time of the founding, indentured servitude had fully transitioned to racial slavery.[69]

The Jamestown colony clearly struggled to self-govern. The most

---

* Consequently, the Anglican church became the official church for the Virginia colony.

† The sentence may have been because he was a not a Christian rather than because he was black.

troubling part of its legacy was the institution of slavery that led to the Civil War. Even 150+ years after the "War between the States," America is still dealing with the negative effects of this terrible practice.

The Pilgrims sailing on the *Mayflower* in 1620 and the northern colonies that followed had a very different story.* The Pilgrims intended on joining the colony in Jamestown, but the prevailing winds prevented them from sailing south after arriving at Plymouth. Believing God was calling them to settle there instead of at Jamestown, they did so. But they had an unforeseen problem: How would they govern themselves? Following their faith, they drafted a unique document aboard the *Mayflower* that became their founding covenant. They were still obligated to the Virginia Company, which financed their journey, but the covenant they signed had a much different tone to it. In this document they declared their intent to advance the Christian faith and form a political body "for their better ordering" because they would not be joining the colony in Jamestown. The "Mayflower Compact," as it is known today, followed the biblical template for starting a community, which was demonstrated by Moses. It is a unique document that was clearly motivated by the Pilgrims' desire to form a new community God's way:

> In the name of God, Amen. We, whose names are underwritten, the loyal subjects of our dread Sovereign Lord King James, by the Grace of God, of Great Britain, France, and Ireland, King, defender of the Faith, etc.
>
> Having undertaken, for the Glory of God, and advancements of the Christian faith and honor of our King and Country, a voyage to plant the first colony in the Northern parts of Virginia, do by these presents, solemnly and mutually, in the presence of God, and one another, covenant and combine ourselves together into a civil body politic; for our better ordering, and preservation and furtherance of the ends aforesaid; and by virtue hereof to enact,

---

* The Pilgrims brought with them the 1599 Geneva Bible. This is captured in one of the large portraits in the Capitol rotunda.

constitute, and frame, such just and equal laws, ordinances, acts, constitutions, and offices, from time to time, as shall be thought most meet and convenient for the general good of the colony; unto which we promise all due submission and obedience.

In witness whereof we have hereunto subscribed our names at Cape Cod the 11th of November, in the year of the reign of our Sovereign Lord King James, of England, France, and Ireland, the eighteenth, and of Scotland the fifty-fourth, 1620.*

As in Jamestown, the Plymouth colonists were ill-equipped to settle in the New World, and half of the first 102 settlers died the first winter. But unlike in Jamestown, the Plymouth colonists put God first, and God blessed the colony in unique ways. They respected the local Indians and received help from one named Squanto, who previously had lived in that area, a member of the Patuxet tribe. He had been captured years earlier and sold into slavery in Europe. Monks helped him escape, and he eventually made his way back to Plymouth, only to find out his tribe had been wiped out several years earlier by a plague. He decided to help the new settlers, "teaching them to hunt, fish, and raise crops."[70] As a result of this collaboration, they celebrated the first harvest that fall with a three-day party. This celebration included the local Indians, with whom the colonists had a good relationship.[71]

The chief of the neighboring Wampanoag tribe was Massasoit, who negotiated a treaty with the colonists in March 1621. Massasoit was concerned about negative political dynamics with neighboring tribes, so his aim for this treaty was to form a political alliance with the new settlers who might provide additional protection. This relationship was tested in 1623 when Massasoit became gravely ill, but colonist Edward Winslow successfully nursed him back to health. As the Plymouth colony grew, the colonists were careful to negotiate the acquisition of additional land

---

* John Robinson was the pastor for the Pilgrims prior to sailing to the New World. He was the one who taught them the basic principles of self-government they applied when they settled in Plymouth. The impact of this single pastor on the American founding is incalculable. He planned on coming to the New World after the *Mayflower* sailed, but he died before he could make the journey.

directly with the chief.[72] This consistent pattern of the colonists governing justly led to peaceful relations for the next forty years.[73]

Interestingly, the Plymouth colony experimented in its early days
with socialism, where the work to plant crops and sustain the new
colony was to be shared by all. Noting the lack of production with
this arrangement, William Bradford decided to implement a different
system. He gave each family a plot and declared they would enjoy the
fruits of their labor. Immediately, production increased, and the new
system became permanent.[74]

As the "New England" colonies grew, new communities emerged,
each needing to establish governing principles. To meet these new
challenges, Rev. Thomas Hooker delivered a sermon in Hartford,
Connecticut, on May 31, 1638, entitled "The Foundation of
Authority is Laid In the Free Consent of the People."[75] He also drafted
the "Fundamental Orders of Connecticut,"[76] which were adopted on
January 14, 1639. The "Fundamental Orders of Connecticut" included
many biblical ideas about politics. This document had a major impact
on the founding generation. Historian John Fiske writes that the government of the United States is "in lineal descent more nearly related
to that of Connecticut than to any other of the thirteen colonies."[77]
Two years after this document was adopted, Nathaniel Ward drafted
"The Massachusetts Body of Liberties," which listed nearly one hundred specific liberties for men, women, children, animals, and the
church. This was also the first document of its kind in America and
became a forerunner of the Bill of Rights. Both Hooker and Ward were
clergymen, and they both directly contributed to the establishment of
biblical principles as the foundation of civil government in America.

The contrast between the Jamestown and Plymouth colonies is
clear. Jamestown was focused on profit; the colonists struggled to live
in harmony with the local Native Americans, poorly governed themselves, and accepted a culture where slavery could take root. Plymouth
followed biblical principles for starting a new colony and governing
God's way. These principles also guided their interactions with the
Native Americans, which led to decades of peace. When a slave ship

landed in Plymouth in 1646, the colonists freed the slaves and then imprisoned the slave traders.[78] Slavery would not get a foothold in the northern colonies. Furthermore, as more people arrived and the challenges of self-government increased, the colonists continued to identify key governing principles from the Bible to clarify rights for all individuals. These efforts were led by pastors whose writings provided the theology behind the American founding that followed.

DEFENSE AS A CHRISTIAN VIRTUE

The people who were settling the New World were seeking religious liberty and law and order. They were generally not eager to engage in armed conflict. As the colonies grew, however, settlers began moving west and were confronted with the realities of living near hostile Indians. As we have seen with northern colonies, there are examples where the early colonists engaged with the Indians in a positive way.[*] Despite this, there were times of conflict, one of which I explain below, leaning heavily on Dr. Thomas West's essay "The Transformation of Protestant Theology as a Condition of the American Revolution."[79]

During King Philip's War in 1675,[†] the Indians "staged a massive attack" that led to many slaughtered families and destroyed towns. West points out that this war "caused a crisis in Puritan theology," and "two rival interpretations of the war agreed New Englanders had sinned and that the work was a divine punishment. But what was the sin?"[80]

According to West, Puritan pastor Increase Mather believed the sin was that the settlers had become ungrateful and were conforming too much to the sinful world. His solution was to appoint a day of humiliation that included fasting and prayer. The government then

---

* The Pilgrim colony in Plymouth and William Penn (who founded the city of Philadelphia) are good examples of colonists respecting the Indians and their right to the land they lived on. In both cases, careful negotiations were made for the purchase of land for these growing colonies. They were following the Judeo-Christian blueprint for governing and respecting the property rights of others.

† King Philip's name was Metacom, and he was Chief Massasoit's grandson and leader of the tribe. Originally, there were no hostilities. But the Indians became increasingly concerned they were losing their way of life, especially as more and more of them converted to Christianity. This was the main catalyst for the war, which lasted fifteen months (David Barton and Tim Barton, *The American Story* [Aledo, Texas: WallBuilder Press, 2020], 61–63).

passed laws to suppress any "proud excesses ... excessive drinking, swearing, etc."[81]

Samuel Nowell proposed a different sin the settlers had committed. He believed that the settlers' sin was a lack of battle preparedness. In his sermon "Abraham in Arms," he spoke to the need for Christians to learn to fight in order to defend against random attacks. West explains that Nowell founded his argument on Genesis 14, stating, "Abraham organized and trained an informal militia ... to rescue Lot and defeat his enemies. For this exploit, Abraham received a blessing from Melchizedek, a priest of God."[82] Nowell also noted Luke 22:36, in which Jesus says, "And if you don't have a sword, sell your cloak and buy one." Nowell concluded it is a commendable practice to train men in military discipline so they may be ready for war. In fact, he said it is a duty that God expects from his followers wherever they may live. In Nowell's view, war was something God's people need to be prepared for.

Nowell's interpretation of events won the day. The narrative that emerged was that Christians must "learn to defend ourselves, or resolve to be vassals."[83] Being prepared to fight was soon seen as part of Christian civic duty. West sums up how Nowell's sermon paved the way for the American Revolution:

Nowell taught that God requires men to train and to kill in defense of their lives and liberties. His was a fighting Christianity that was quick to repel evil and stood firm in defense of civil liberty.[84]

As West notes, the emphasis that the colonists learn the art of war to defend their freedom was a pivotal change in theology—one we can learn from today. As Ecclesiastes 3:8 tells us, there is a season for all things, including war. In Psalm 144:1 King David says, "Praise be to the LORD my Rock, who trains my hands for war, my fingers for battle." Viewing the willingness to fight for one's freedom as a Christian virtue is what inspired the colonists to fight for their God-given rights when the time came.

REDISCOVERING LIBERTY

Back in England, John Locke was advancing the development of the philosophy of civil government. He published his "Two Treaties on Civil Government"* in 1689, which codified many of the emerging ideas from the Reformation, such as religious tolerance, liberty of conscience, and the social contract, which described the relationship between citizens and their civil leader. He argued against the concept of the divine right of either a king or pope to have absolute authority over the citizenry he governs, which had long been supported by a misapplication of Romans 13.† Locke also discussed the idea of a social contract, where laws must be passed by the consent of the citizenry.-

> In the state of nature, liberty consists of being free from any superior power on Earth. People are not under the will or lawmaking authority of others but have only the law of nature for their rule. In political society, liberty consists of being under no other lawmaking power except that established by consent in the commonwealth. People are free from the dominion of any will or legal restraint apart from that enacted by their own constituted lawmaking power according to the trust put in it.[85]

Locke's theory deeply influenced the thinking of America's founders, who understood that the Bible limits the government's rightful scope to administer justice, deter violence, and maintain a peaceful society. By the early 1700s, Locke's theory of the liberty of conscience was influencing colonial thinking. In 1717, John Wise published *Vindication of the Government of New England Churches*, stating that violating an individual's liberty is tantamount to violating the law of nature, which was written on the hearts of men and made known through their consciences. Wise makes the biblical case for individual liberty yet warns against unrestrained liberty:

---

* In this work, he cited eighty references to the Bible in the first treatise and twenty-two references to the Bible in the second. See William J. Federer, *America's God and Country Encyclopedia of Quotations* (St. Louis: Amerisearch, Inc., 2000), 397.

† Romans 13 is often used to justify total submission to civil authorities. See Q&A in the Appendix for a detailed explanation.

That which is to be drawn from Mans Reason, flowing from the true Current of that Faculty, when unperverted, may be said to be the Law of Nature; on which account, the Holy Scriptures declare it written on Mens hearts. For being indowed with a Soul, you may know from your self, how, and what you ought to act, Rom. 2:14.... He that intrudes upon [man's] Liberty, Violates the Law of Nature.... But in a more special meaning, this Liberty does not consist in a loose and ungovernable Freedom, or in an unbounded License of Acting.... Personal Liberty and Equality is to be cherished, and preserved to the highest degree, as will consist with all just distinctions amongst Men of Honour, and shall be agreeable with the publick Good.[86]

Wise argues personal that liberty—allowing people to go on their own faith journey—should "be cherished, and preserved to the highest degree." He advocates that people must have the liberty to ask faith-related questions and express personal beliefs, without being persecuted or coerced to believe state-sanctioned doctrines. But his call to personal liberty did not grant personal license. Wise put boundaries on personal liberty, limiting "ungovernable Freedom" that fails to support the public good.

Table 5.1 – The rediscovery of biblical principles for God's institution of civil government

1517	95 Theses, challenging the practices of the Catholic church and the divine right of the pope	Martin Luther
1579	God ordained the general institution of Government (Romans 13 as an affirmation of Genesis 9:5–6)	Philippe de Mornay
1620	Mayflower Compact, starting a community through a public covenant, supported by the Christian faith	Pilgrims

1638	"Fundamental Orders of Connecticut," declaring the foundation of government is laid in the free consent of the people	Thomas Hooker
1641	"The Body of Liberties" outlining our responsibility to God and our individual rights	Nathaniel Ward
1644	"Plea for Religious Liberty" and "Bloody Tenet of Persecution for Conscience Sake"; Coined phrases "Freedom of Conscience" and "Wall of Separation"	Roger Williams
1689	Two Treaties on Civil Government, promoted ideas of religious tolerance and social contract	John Locke
1717	"Vindication of the Government of New England Churches"; "personal Liberty and Equality is to be cherished, and preserved to the highest degree"	John Wise

In the years leading up to the Revolution, the colonists' dedication to the social contract was tested as the British began passing many laws that cut short their civil liberties without their consent. These views on liberty, shaped by Locke and enhanced by colonial pastors, were critical in convincing leaders that liberty was non-negotiable. The laws imposed on the colonists clearly violated the idea of consent of the governed, but was it enough reason for the colonists to separate from England?

THE GREAT AWAKENING

In the first approximately 150 years of colonial growth, God prepared the soil of independence as the founders explored, understood, and codified biblical principles to establish and maintain justice for all. This provided the rationale for the Revolution, but more would be required to stir hearts to have the conviction to stand up to England when the time came and see the business through.

The First Great Awakening started in the 1730s and lasted for several decades. Pastors like Jonathan Edwards, George Whitefield, and the evangelist brothers John and Charles Wesley were fueling a revival movement that swept across the New World. One longtime friend of Whitefield was Benjamin Franklin. In his autobiography, Franklin described the impact of George Whitefield's preaching:

> It was wonderful to see the change soon made in the manners of our inhabitants. From being thoughtless or indifferent about religion, it seemed as if all the world were growing religious, so that one could not walk thro' the town in an evening without hearing psalms sung in different families of every street.[87]*

The impact of the Great Awakening cannot be understated. It resulted in the founding of many universities—Brown, Columbia, Dartmouth, Rutgers, and Princeton—primarily dedicated to training ministers to preach the gospel. In the 1750s, these universities were training a new generation of colonial clergy who embraced the biblical foundations of civil government. These biblical foundations were taught as key Christian virtues needed for the preservation of a civil society.

This led to the tradition of *election sermons*, where pastors would remind their congregations of the role of civil government and the need for them to engage in the process of appointing godly leaders. One well-known example is Pastor Jonathan Mayhew of Boston (1720–1766), who preached a famous patriotic sermon in 1765 explaining that a king is not above the law and that he unseats himself if he violates the law:

> The king is as much bound by his oath not to infringe the legal rights of the people, as the people are bound to yield subjection to him. From whence it follows that as soon as the prince sets himself

---

* Franklin helped build an auditorium for Whitefield to preach in, which was later donated as the first building of the University of Pennsylvania. Franklin also printed Whitefield's journal and sermons, and because he (Franklin) was the postmaster in Philadelphia, he helped spread Whitefield's sermons through colonial America. Newspaper coverage, combined with spiritual revival, enabled an unprecedented level of understanding among the colonials in the New World. See William J. Federer, *America's God and Country Encyclopedia of Quotations* (St. Louis: Amerisearch, Inc., 2000), 245.

above the law, he loses the king in the tyrant. He does, to all intents
and purposes, un-king himself.[88]

Colonial pastors preaching liberty and just civil government were
so impactful that the British referred to them as the "Black Robed
Regiment."[89] This encouragement for the colonists to see their civil
duty as a key part of their faith was critical in creating a collective
resolve to stand up to King George the same way Daniel and his
friends stood up to their Babylonian captors (Dan. 3, 6).

The founding generation grew up during an era when revivalists
preached biblical repentance and pastors taught biblical citizenship
duty and the importance of defending their community. America's
founders were men and women who understood God's divine law, were
schooled in liberty, and viewed the defense of freedom as a Christian
virtue. They were experienced in reading and applying the word of
God to their situation and resolved to separate from England if God
ordained it. This resolve gave them the conviction to pledge their lives,
fortunes, and sacred honor as acts of worship.

KEY IDEAS FORMULATED IN COLONIAL AMERICA

The confluence of all these factors enabled and empowered the founding generation to take the bold step to separate from England. All these
events and experiences can be summarized by three primary points
that enabled the American struggle for independence to take place:

1. Thorough understanding of the theology surrounding justice,
   rights, liberty, and governing based on ideas refined through
   the Reformation and the colonial era.
2. Recognition of the citizenship duty all Christians have
   to establish and maintain civil justice, seeing defense as a
   Christian virtue.
3. Heart-felt conviction to follow God's plan for America—even
   in the face of insurmountable odds.

All they needed was a crisis to test the resolve of their faith—and King George's behavior and abuses gave them one.

CATALYST FOR THE AMERICAN FOUNDING

The first major military conflict in the American colonies was the French and Indian War (1754–1763). Officers like Colonel George Washington fought alongside their British counterparts, defending territories in western Virginia and Pennsylvania. The nine-year war depleted the English treasury, so the crown raised taxes on the colonies to help cover the cost of protecting colonial interests. But Parliament excluded the colonies from the decision-making and passed a number of oppressive regulations without their consent:

Table 5.2[90]– Summary of laws imposed on the colonies without their consent. The laws covered a range of issues and were the basis for the twenty-seven offenses listed in the Declaration.

1764	Currency Act—Regulated colonial money
1764	Sugar Act—Taxed sugar, certain wines, cloth, coffee, etc.
1765	Stamp Act—Taxed newspapers, legal and commercial documents
1765	Quartering Act—Forced colonists to house British soldiers
1766	Declaratory Act—Repealed Stamp Act but claimed absolute power to make laws and change colonial government
1767	Townshend Act—Paid salaries for governors loyal to the king
1773	Tea Act—Enabled the East India Company to ship tea duty-free from England, forcing the colonies to pay taxes on other tea
1774	*Boston Port Act*—Blockaded Boston Harbor in response to the Boston Tea Party
1774	*Justice Act*—Confirmed and secured British jurisdiction over the colonies
1774	*Massachusetts Government Act*—Gave the governor of Massachusetts greater powers, altering the colonial government without consent
1774	*Quartering Act*—Affirmed quartering of British troops, issued after the Boston Tea Party

---

* American Patriots referred to these *italicized* acts collectively as the "Intolerable Acts." These acts focused the national vision on separating from England.

1774	*Quebec Act*—Established principles of governing in Quebec and granted much of Ohio to Quebec, voiding previous land grants
1775	Proclamation of Rebellion—Declared the king's intent to use military force to deal with unrest in the colonies

The imposition of these laws without the colonists' consent was contrary to what they had become accustomed to, given what they learned and exercised as their biblical responsibility to govern themselves. Rather than continuing to give the colonists the autonomy to govern themselves and pass laws in harmony with the moral law, England began asserting more and more top-down oversight. This led to the steady usurpation of the rights of the colonists, who still considered themselves English citizens.

The colonists were not silent as these events unfolded. They sought redress through a variety of means, but each time the king put more pressure on the colonies to get them to comply. By June 1776, it became clear to the thirteen colonies that England planned to govern them as a police state, where none of their rights would be secure. The time had come to decide if they should submit to biblically unjust rule or to assert what they believed was their God-given right to be governed justly and to separate to form a new nation. They did not make this decision quickly or without debate. They were thirteen separate colonies that did not agree on all issues. But they could agree on the biblical basics of governing, which eventually allowed them to unify around separating from England.

They understood the biblical model for starting a new nation, specifically the need for a covenant where they would declare to God and the world their intentions. Given the seriousness of this action, they needed to explain their rationale for taking such a bold step and committing themselves to see it through. Most importantly, they understood they needed to acknowledge God in this endeavor and seek his help and divine protection. They believed in the truthfulness* of

---

* The word *rectitude* was used in the Declaration to refer to the truthfulness of their claim and the legitimacy of their conclusion to reject the civil rule of King George.

their cause and that God would help them see it through. Perhaps no speech illustrates this better than the one delivered by Patrick Henry on March 23, 1775, at the Virginia Convention, which was meeting in Richmond's St. John's Church due to British hostilities. In this speech he argued they should act because God would help them in their cause:

> Sir, we have done everything that could be done to avert the storm which is now coming on. We have petitioned; we have remonstrated; we have supplicated; we have prostrated ourselves before the throne, and have implored its interposition to arrest the tyrannical hands of the ministry and Parliament. Our petitions have been slighted; our remonstrances have produced additional violence and insult; our supplications have been disregarded; and we have been spurned, with contempt, from the foot of the throne.... There is a just God who presides over the destinies of nations, and who will raise up friends to fight our battles for us. The battle, sir, is not to the strong alone; it is to the vigilant, the active, the brave.... Is life so dear, or peace so sweet, as to be purchased at the price of chains and slavery? Forbid it, Almighty God! I know not what course others may take; but as for me, give me liberty, or give me death![91]

While this approach was biblical, proclaiming intent to separate in this way was a bold step and would require the colonies to stand up to the largest global empire at that time. There was a lot at stake, it would be difficult, and no one knew what the outcome would be. They needed a document to codify their mutual agreement, summarizing their belief in the purpose of civil government and their rationale for becoming an independent nation.

WRITING THE DECLARATION OF INDEPENDENCE

On June 11, 1776, a committee of five was appointed to draft the Declaration. Thomas Jefferson served as the lead writer, drafting the document over the course of several weeks. He combined the principles of biblical and political philosophers from previous generations as he sought to clearly state the colonists' understanding of the biblical purpose of civil government, along with the rationale for separation. After numerous revisions, the less-than-1,400-word Declaration was complete. The delegates adopted it on July 2 and added their signatures on July 4. The document follows this simple outline:

- There is a moral law that applies to all people and nations: the "Law of Nature and of Nature's God," to which all are obligated, and which all are entitled to live by.
- A summary of the purpose of civil government as protecting unalienable, God-given individual rights.

- Listing of King George's myriad violations of God's moral law.
- Summary of colonial attempts to reconcile.
- Declaration of the colonies' intentions to separate and their reliance on God to see it through.

THE THEOLOGY IN THE DECLARATION

The Declaration of Independence is a brilliant commentary on the theology of government—arguably the best written. All the principles we learned from Israel in previous chapters are included in the Declaration, as seen in Table 5.3. Note that everything needed for governing is provided in the Pentateuch delivered by Moses.

Table 5.3 – Mapping Scripture to concepts in the Declaration

Concept in the Declaration	Verses Where Delivered	Verses Where Clarified and Affirmed
A community or nation is established by a covenant.	Exod. 19:5–8; Lev. 26:3–5, 14–16	2 Chron. 7:14; Ps. 81:11–14
There is a Divine Law that applies to all individuals and nations at all times and is the standard for all lawmaking in the civil arena.	Exod. 20:1–17	Ps. 2:10–11, 66:7–9, 119:1–176, 138:4–5; Isa. 10:1–2; Matt. 5:19, 28:19; John 14:21; James 1:17
God provides individual rights and intends government to protect those rights through equal and impartial justice to all.	Gen. 9:5–6; Exod. 18:20–22; Deut. 16:18–20	Ps. 2:10–11, 66:7–9, 82:1–4, 138:4–5; Prov. 31:8–9; Isa. 10:2; Lam. 3:34–37; Mic. 6:8; Rom. 13:1–5
Critical rights include Life, Liberty, Pursuit of Happiness (and Property).	Life: Gen. 9:5–6; Exod. 20:13, 21:23; Lev. 24:17 Liberty: Gen. 2:15–17 Happiness: Deut. 7:12–16, 12:7, 28:1–6, 33:28–29 Property: Exod. 20:15	Life: Matt. 5:19, 28:19–20; Luke 18:20; John 14:21; 1 Tim. 2:1–4 Liberty: Ps. 81:11–14; Isa. 1:18; 1 Tim. 2:3–4; 2 Pet. 3:9; Rev. 20:7–8 Happiness: Eccles. 2:26, 3:12; Ps. 119, 144:15; Matt. 5:3–12 Property: Matt. 5:19, Luke 18:20

To protect these rights, governments are instituted among mankind. Civil leaders agree to govern according to the moral law (the "Social Contract").	Gen. 9:5–6; Exod. 18:20–22; Deut. 16:18–20	Ps. 82:1–4; Isa. 1:23; Jer. 22:15–16; Rom. 13:1–8; Titus 1:5–9
Legitimate governments derive their just powers through the consent of the governed.	Exod. 1:15–17, 18:20–22; Deut. 16:18–20	Dan. 3, 6; Acts 4:19, 5:29; Heb. 11; 1 Tim. 5:19–21; Titus 1:5–9; 1 Pet. 2:13
When government violates the moral law (especially over an extended period with no intent to adhere to it), it forfeits its God-given responsibility to govern. People of faith must resist as they are able, and act to restore justice, because God promises to judge the nation that dishonors him.	Lev. 26:3–5, 14–16; Deut. 28:15–68	Jer. 22:15–16; Dan. 3, 6; Amos 2:4–6; Mic. 6:8; Acts 4:19, 5:29; 2 Cor. 7:10–11; 1 Tim. 5:19–21; Titus 1:5–9; Heb. 11; 1 Pet. 2:13–17
When a nation acknowledges God in its founding covenant, he will bless that nation.	Exod. 23:3–8, 23:25; Deut. 7:11–15, 11:26–28, 28:1–14	Ps. 33:8–22, 66:7–9
When the people of a nation acknowledge and repent of their sins and call out to God for help, he will intervene on their behalf and restore their land.	Deut. 29:9, 30:2–10	2 Chron. 7:14

Several paragraphs of the Declaration are worth highlighting here, starting with the opening:

WHEN in the course of human Events, it becomes necessary for one People to dissolve the Political Bands which have connected them with another, and to assume among the Powers of the Earth, the separate and equal Station to which the Laws of Nature and of Nature's God entitle them, a decent Respect to the Opinions of Mankind requires that they should declare the causes which impel them to the Separation.

Here, the founders make several critical points:

- There is a timeless moral law known both through conscience and revealed to mankind through the Bible (Law of Nature and Nature's God).
- These laws set a standard for nations (powers of the earth) on how to govern their citizenry.
- All peoples are entitled (and have a God-given right) to expect to live by this standard.
- Rejecting this God-given responsibility should be explained to all nations, because it may appear to violate Romans 13.

The next section is the most quoted passage from the entire document:

WE hold these Truths to be self-evident, that all Men are created equal, that they are endowed by their Creator with certain unalienable Rights, that among these are Life, Liberty, and the pursuit of Happiness—That to secure these Rights, Governments are instituted among Men, deriving their just Powers from the Consent of the Governed.

This section is the most important, as it summarizes the founders' theology about civil government:

- Everyone is created equal before God. This means we are equally accountable to God, not that we will all have equal capabilities or material blessings in life.
- God is sovereign and gives everyone rights that cannot be taken away.
- We have a right to our lives, religious and civil liberty, and to pursue happiness.
- God instituted government based on the consent of the people electing their leaders.

The following section goes on to explain the rationale for separation:

… that whenever any Form of Government becomes destructive of these Ends, it is the Right of the People to alter or abolish it, and to institute a new Government, laying its Foundation on such Principles, and organizing its Powers in such Form, as to them shall seem most likely to affect their Safety and Happiness. Prudence, indeed, will dictate that Governments long established should not be changed for light and transient Causes; and accordingly all Experience hath shewn, that Mankind are more disposed to suffer, while Evils are sufferable, than to right themselves by abolishing the Forms to which they are accustomed. But when a long Train of Abuses and Usurpations, pursuing invariably the same Object, evinces a Design to reduce them under absolute Despotism, it is their Right, it is their Duty, to throw off such Government, and to provide new Guards for their future Security

This section explains the principle for when rebelling against a civil authority, which God has instituted, is warranted:

At some point, after many abuses, tyranny becomes despotism, crossing the biblical line of what a government is ordained to do.

The decision should not be made lightly, nor should citizens endure suffering indefinitely. When this occurs, it becomes the right and duty of the people to reject that tyrannical government and put a new one in its place.

The Declaration goes on to describe the repeated injuries by the king and lists twenty-seven examples of the immoral rule warranting separation. These include the rejection of colonial laws, forming illegal armies, trying to install his own governments, and imposing economic controls—all this without the colonies' representation.* In the end, the king had not only passed immoral laws but had also abused both the institution of the family and civil government.

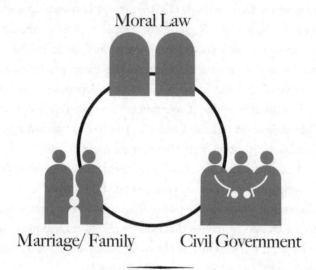

The final paragraph is also important:

We, therefore, the Representatives of the united States of America, in General Congress, Assembled, appealing to the Supreme Judge of the world for the rectitude of our intentions, do, in the Name, and by the Authority of the good People of these Colonies, solemnly publish and declare, That these United Colonies are, and of Right ought to be Free and Independent States; that they are Absolved from all Allegiance to the British Crown, and that all political connection between them and the State of Great Britain, is

---

* Taxation without representation was an example of imposing taxes without their consent. This was number seventeen on the list of twenty-seven. While taxation without representation has been pushed as *the reason* for the Revolutionary War, this is not accurate. This was only one of many immoral actions on the part of the king that were inconsistent with the colonists' biblical theology of civil government.

and ought to be totally dissolved; and that as Free and Independent States, they have full Power to levy War, conclude Peace, contract Alliances, establish Commerce, and to do all other Acts and Things which Independent States may of right do.

Here the founders firmly state their intent to separate and their conviction that God will agree with this action:

- They are appealing to the ultimate judge of the world based on their motives, which they believe are biblical and true (rectitude).
- They make their Declaration to form a new nation with all the privileges and responsibilities a legitimate nation should have.
- They stress this action is done by the consent of the representatives of the people.
- "Solemnly" implies this is a sacred action, "enjoined by religion … with a serious appeal to God; as a solemn oath."[92]
- They Declare separation as free and independent states with the rights of a free people (nation).

This last sentence affirms their reliance on God and their personal commitment:

And for the support of this Declaration, with a firm Reliance on the Protection of the divine Providence, we mutually pledge to each other our Lives, our Fortunes, and our sacred Honor.

Again, they state their reliance on God for protection as they proclaim their intent to separate from the most powerful empire on the planet. This simple act is as important as all the previous points in the Declaration—*calling out to God for help*:

- They are doing so with a reliance on God-given biblical guidance on the right of nations to govern themselves in a way that honors him.

- They pledge everything to see it through as an act of faith (lives, fortunes, sacred honor). Most of the founders suffered significant loss of property and/or experienced hardship as a result of this action.

So, we see the Declaration not only captured the theology for a just civil authority and the rationale for a legitimate and just separation, it also included a plea to God for help, for *surely they would need his help to be successful*. Knowing who won the war, it is easy to forget that the odds were significantly stacked against the colonists for the following reasons:

- They were a disorganized collection of colonies standing up to *the* global empire with nearly unlimited resources.
- They were starting without a navy and virtually no military, unlike the battle-hardened British regular troops, who were supported by a naval superpower.
- Roughly half of the colonial population was loyal to England and attempted to stop the separation. This meant the Patriots needed to be very careful whom they trusted. Many families were separated over the issue, including Ben Franklin and his son.

As soon as the Declaration was signed, copies were sent to General Washington, who immediately had it read to his troops. The Declaration had the intended effect of creating a clear and unifying message that inspired the founding generation in their struggle against the British.

THE IMPACT OF THE DECLARATION

The Declaration has historically been highly esteemed. Its language is lofty and complete, as Dr. Larry Arnn explains:

[The founders] made a series of demanding claims. Although they leave plenty of room for adaptation to transient things, their core meaning is said to be absolute and fixed. To believe them is to take on the obligation to obey them, and then one must live a certain way.[93]

In *Benjamin Franklin: An American Life*, Walter Isaacson describes the prestige of the Declaration of Independence, saying, "None of them realized that the document would eventually become viewed as a text akin to scripture."[94]

Though not Scripture, the Declaration of Independence includes phrases like "in the course of human events," asserting that its vision and principles are timeless and absolute. In the opening paragraph appears the phrase "Laws of Nature and of Nature's God," referring to a moral law that is neither up for debate nor subject to being rescinded.

In writing his Gettysburg Address, President Lincoln took from the Declaration to encourage battle-worn Union soldiers that they were fighting for a nation "conceived in Liberty, and dedicated to the proposition that all men are created equal." The Civil War tested whether a nation like this could long endure and proved it could. On the 150th anniversary of the Declaration, President Calvin Coolidge stated the following about the resiliency and permanence of the principles captured therein:

About the Declaration there is a finality that is exceedingly restful. It is often asserted that the world has made a great deal of progress since 1776, that we have had new thoughts and new experiences which have given us a great advance over the people of that day, and that we may therefore very well discard their conclusions for something more modern. But that reasoning cannot be applied to this great charter. If all men are created equal, that is final. If they are endowed with inalienable rights, that is final. If governments derive their just powers from the consent of the governed, that is final. No advance, no progress can be made beyond these propositions. If anyone wishes to deny their truth or their sound-ness, the only direction in which he can proceed historically is not forward, but backward toward the time when there was no equality, no rights of the individual, no rule of the people. Those who wish to proceed in that direction cannot lay claim to progress. They are reactionary. Their ideas are not more modern, but more ancient, than those of the Revolutionary fathers.[95]

Today, government officials tend to talk more about the Constitution, debating what it says we can and cannot do. But the Declaration *is the more important document*, as it articulates the foundation on which the Constitution rests. Proverbs 25:11 KJV says, "A word fitly spoken is like apples of gold in pictures of silver." President Lincoln used this verse to describe the Constitution as the frame for which the picture, the Declaration, is to be viewed:

The expression of that principle, in our Declaration of Independence, was most happy, and fortunate. Without this, as well as with it, we could have declared our independence of Great Britain; but without it, we could not, I think, have secured our free govern-ment, and consequent prosperity. No oppressed, people will fight, and endure, as our fathers did, without the promise of something better, than a mere change of masters. The assertion of that prin-ciple, at that time, was the word, "fitly spoken" which has proved an "apple of gold" to us. The Union, and the Constitution, are the picture of silver, subsequently framed around it. The picture was made, not to conceal, or destroy the apple; but to adorn, and preserve it. The picture was made for the apple—not the apple for the picture. So let us act, that neither picture, or apple shall ever be blurred, or bruised or broken.[96]

The Declaration is our national founding covenant. It calls out to every American citizen, proclaiming the vision for a just government. Every citizen is called to consider, reflect, and make a conscious choice to affirm these principles and live a life in harmony with them. Generations before us fought, sacrificing their lives, to preserve America's principles for government. Each new generation of Americans must carefully consider and resolve to defend these principles. This is the responsibility that comes with being an American citizen.

No other nation in history began this way, with the issuing of a Declaration containing the pretext, principles, and proclamation to form a new God-honoring nation—not even Israel. In that case, God called Abraham, and later Moses, to bring about a nation that would recognize his moral law and provide guidelines for civil justice. It was God who did the work of building the nation of Israel, often while the people were grumbling. In the American colonies, God was certainly orchestrating events leading up to 1776, but there was no audible voice or pillar of cloud like Israel had. Yet, the founders recognized God was blessing their efforts:

> There are instances of ... an almost astonishing Providence in our favor; our success has staggered our enemies, and almost given faith to infidels; so that we may truly say it is not our own arm which has saved us. The hand of Heaven appears to have led us on to be, perhaps, humble instruments and means in the great Providential dispensation which is completing.[97]
> —Samuel Adams, August 1, 1776

> The hand of Providence has been so conspicuous in all this (the course of the war) that he must be worse than an infidel that lacks faith, and more wicked that has not gratitude to acknowledge his obligations.[98]
> —George Washington, August 20, 1778

> I am sure that never was a people, who had more reason to acknowledge a Divine interposition in their affairs, than those of the United States; and I should be pained to believe that they have forgotten that agency, which was so often manifested during our

Revolution, or that they failed to consider the omnipotence of that God who is alone able to protect them.[99]
—George Washington, March 11, 1792

A coincidence of circumstances so wonderful gives confidence to the belief that the patriotic efforts of these illustrious men were Heaven directed, and furnishes a new seal to the hope that the prosperity of these States is under the special protection of a kind Providence.[100]
—John Quincy Adams, on the death of John Adams and Thomas Jefferson on the same day, July 4, 1826

The Declaration shows what these quotes prove is true: The founders performed their civic duty to establish a just government following the biblical template and trusted in God to bless it. The combination of duty and reliance on God was not only critical for America's founding, it is critical to sustaining the nation going forward—which we will further explore in later chapters.

QUESTIONS

Many questions arise when talking about the American founding, a few of which are captured below. These are discussed in detail in the Appendix.

• Did the Revolution violate Paul's call in Romans 13 for submission?
• Was America founded as a Christian nation?
• Were the founders deists?
• Are slavery and the three-fifths clause evidence America was founded on institutional racism?

SUMMARY

The Declaration of Independence was the product of 250 years of theological rediscovery, triggered by the Protestant Reformation. Having an

English Bible available to the masses with many bright minds studying and debating its application to the political arena led to a rediscovery of the theology of civil government. The settling of America provided the perfect environment to apply and refine these rediscovered principles to establish a just civil society. The tyranny of King George created the opportunity to follow the biblical template for starting a new nation with the colonists declaring their belief in the purpose of civil government, summarizing their rationale for separation, and stating their reliance on God to see the separation through. Against all odds, they prevailed, and the founders attributed this success to God's favor, which staked the whole effort on a national founding covenant. This template for starting a nation is available to any group wishing to govern God's way.

In recent history, America has gone on to create the greatest measure of freedom for its citizens. A simple question can then be asked: how is this freedom delivered? Many nations have attempted to create a free society but failed. It turns out there is a simple formula embedded in the Declaration of Independence and explicitly described in the Pledge of Allegiance that answers the freedom question. This is the topic of the next chapter.

SUMMARY POINTS

• The Declaration of Independence is the product of important historical events and theological break-throughs throughout the Church Age, especially since the Reformation.

• These events and doctrinal ideas applied to civil government were accomplished by pastors trying to implement concepts of self-government directly from the Bible.

• The American colonists had learned and embraced biblical principles of self-government in the 150 years leading up to the founding.

• After the French and Indian War, England began passing laws to collect taxes to help cover the war debt, but the colonists had no voice in the creation of these laws.

• After more than ten years of taxes and laws imposed by England taking away their right to self-govern, the colonists reasoned the king had forfeited his God-given responsibility to rule over them and that they had no choice but to separate.

• Knowing their decision to separate would be viewed as treasonous, they used the Declaration of Independence to document their belief in the purpose of civil government and rationale for separation.

• The Declaration of Independence captures the founders' theology of civil government, examples of the king's violations of these principles, and their solemn pledge to stand together in opposing the king's unjust rule.

• At the heart of the Declaration of Independence is a recognition of a timeless legal standard: the "Law of Nature and of Nature's God," otherwise known as the moral law and God-given unalienable rights.

- The development of the Declaration of Independence followed the timeless, biblically based blueprint for starting a community or nation.
- The founders did not incite an unjust revolution; they were acting on their deep personal faith and a biblical understanding of just government to separate from England and secure independence.
- These principles must be taught and celebrated if America is to remain free.

CHAPTER 6

THE FORMULA FOR FREEDOM

The American Covenant

Appoint judges and officials for each of your tribes in every town the LORD your God is giving you, and they shall judge the people fairly. Do not pervert justice or show partiality. Do not accept a bribe, for a bribe blinds the eyes of the wise and twists the words of the innocent. Follow justice and justice alone, so that you may live and possess the land the LORD your God is giving you.
—Deuteronomy 16:18–20

"Among the most inestimable of our blessings is that ... liberty to worship our Creator in the way we think most agreeable in His will; a liberty deemed in other countries incompatible with good government and yet proved by our experience to be its best support."
—Thomas Jefferson
November 18, 1807

CHAPTER 6

THE FORMULA FOR FREEDOM

The American Covenant

Appoint judges and officials for each of your tribes in every town the LORD your God is giving you, and they shall judge the people fairly. Do not pervert justice or show partiality. Do not accept a bribe, for a bribe blinds the eyes of the wise and twists the words of the innocent. Follow justice and justice alone, so that you may live and possess the land the LORD your God is giving you.
—Deuteronomy 16:18–20

"Among the most inestimable of our blessings is that ... liberty to worship our Creator in the way we think most agreeable in His will; a liberty deemed in other countries incompatible with good government and yet proved by our experience to be its best support."
—Thomas Jefferson
November 18, 1807

Ask the nations of the world what makes America unique, and the word you will hear most often is *freedom*. But how is freedom achieved? We tend to use the words *liberty* and *freedom* interchangeably. Do they mean the same thing? And how should we think about justice? Are concepts like social, racial, wage, and environmental justice biblical concepts? Add to all these questions the reality that the meaning of words evolves over time, and it is easy to have questions about "what the founders intended" when examining founding documents, speeches, and correspondence.

To properly navigate these questions, it is critical we understand how people in the founding era defined these key words.

Fortunately, in 1828, Noah Webster published the first American dictionary, which defined key words at the time of the founding.* The dictionary provides the necessary context to properly interpret the writings of the American founding and, subsequently, apply our understanding to the key principles that lead to freedom. In this chapter, I will clarify the meaning of these key words, highlight where they are in the Bible, and explain how they combine to create a formula that delivers freedom unique to America.

DEFINING FREEDOM

Webster defined *freedom* as "a state of exemption from the power or control of another; liberty; exemption from slavery, servitude or confinement. *Freedom* is personal, civil, political, and religious."[101] Freedom as an "exemption from the power or control of another" is the vision of freedom mankind has long struggled for.

Freedom is a result, not something achieved by simply declaring it to be. It is more like a scientific formula with several key variables required to produce an environment of freedom.

A concise statement of the formula for American freedom is in the final line of the Pledge of Allegiance, penned 116 years after America declared independence:

> I pledge allegiance to the Flag of the United States of America, and to the Republic for which it stands, one Nation under God, indivisible, with liberty and justice for all.†

---

* Noah Webster worked on his dictionary for twenty-six years, studying twenty different languages to fully understand and reflect the meaning of words in that era. (Rosalie J. Slater, "Noah Webster, Founding Father of American Scholarship and Education," Preface to American Dictionary of the English Language [1828] 25th pr. [San Francisco: Foundation for American Christian Education, 2016], 17.)

† Originally, the pledge read like this: "I pledge allegiance to my Flag and the Republic for which it stands, one nation, indivisible, with liberty and justice for all." See "The Pledge of Allegiance," UShistory.org, accessed December 30, 2020, ushistory.org/documents/pledge.htm?vm=r.

For *freedom* to exist, both *liberty* and *justice* must be present and equally applied to all, regardless of race or class. Removing or diminishing either of these variables erodes individual freedom. One more element is needed that provides context to what acceptable liberty and justice is. That element is the moral law described in chapter 3. Recognizing the need for liberty and justice based on the moral law, we can express the American formula for freedom in the following way:*

$$\frac{Liberty + Justice}{Moral\ Law} => Freedom$$

Exploring the biblical origin of these words will reveal the mindset of the founding generation and help us understand the principles they considered critical to begin a new nation.

THE FIRST VARIABLE: LIBERTY

Webster defines several categories of liberty, from general liberty to political, metaphysical, and journalistic liberty. He defines *natural liberty* as the following:

> Natural liberty consists in the power of acting as one thinks fit, without any restraint or control, except from the laws of nature.... This liberty is abridged by the establishment of government.[102]

In other words, citizens willingly give up some liberties as part of the social contract, in order to form a peaceful society in which they can enjoy the vast majority of their liberties. Governments will limit some natural liberty, but they should uphold religious and civil liberty, which Webster also defines:

> Civil liberty is an exemption from the arbitrary will of others,

---

*My technical colleagues pointed out that this equation mathematically shows that more of the moral law would result in less freedom. I recognize this algebraic conundrum and suggest this formula is viewed conceptually: the two numerators need to be *based* on the moral law, which yields freedom in fuller measure.

which exemption is secured by established laws, which restrain every man from injuring or controlling another.

Religious liberty, is the free right of adopting and enjoying opinions on religious subjects, and of worshiping the Supreme Being according to the dictates of conscience, without external control.[103]

Simply put, liberty exempts individuals from laws that prevent them from forming and expressing opinions on religious matters or that do not contribute to the good of society. As mentioned above, some limit on natural liberty is necessary for the good of society, but Webster points out that any unnecessary curtailment of liberty is nothing short of tyranny:

A restraint of natural liberty not necessary or expedient for the public, is tyranny or oppression.

Liberty was a bedrock concept at the time of the founding. Thomas Jefferson even put the phrase "resistance to tyrants is obedience to God" on his personal seal.

Since the time of Christ, Christians have faced persecution, execution, or attempted genocide—ironically, often in the name of defending the faith or protecting the state. The early Church was severely persecuted, and Christians were often in the Roman Colosseum offered as food for lions or executed for sport by gladiators. The medieval Church itself burned people at the stake for denying certain teachings. After the Reformation, British monarchs like ("Bloody") Mary Queen of Scots persecuted their subjects who dissented from tenets of the faith they deemed critical. These events led to a search for religious liberty and the eventual Pilgrim settlement in Plymouth.

Even in the American colonies, however, there was persecution of those who did not conform to colonial doctrine. Roger Williams was expelled by Puritan leaders of the Massachusetts Bay Colony for spreading "new and dangerous ideas."[104] His new idea was that the civil authority should be separate from the local church in order to prevent a conflict of interest across leadership. As a result of his expulsion, he fled south to found Providence in modern-day Rhode Island. This became the first colonial example of a leadership structure that separated the church and state.* A more familiar example of religious persecution was the Salem Witch trials. This led to the murder of several dozen people who did not embrace accepted doctrines at that time. Whether the state or church in Europe or America, there was a clear tendency for minorities to be persecuted.

In the 250 years leading up to the American Revolution, it became increasingly clear that liberty for all people was a critical element to achieve a civil society where no one was persecuted for his or her beliefs. As Lincoln stated in his Gettysburg Address, the American republic was "conceived in liberty" and was intended for all people. But where could the founders find the idea of liberty for all?

Our understanding of liberty for all comes from the Bible. God never forces himself on people but is always offering, sometimes pleading, that mankind repent. Throughout the Bible we see God presenting himself to mankind over and over, asking his hearers to choose to follow him. Note the passages from across the Bible that represent the liberty, or the volitional choice, God gives us to obey him:

> The LORD God took the man and put him in the Garden of Eden to work it and take care of it. And the LORD God commanded the man, "You are free to eat from any tree in the garden; but you must not eat from the tree of the knowledge of good and evil, for when you eat from it you will certainly die. (Gen. 2:15–17)

> "Come now, let us settle the matter," says the LORD. "Though your sins are like scarlet, they shall be as white as snow; though they are red as crimson, they shall be like wool."† (Isa. 1:18)

---

* This is different from the modern understanding of the term "separation of church and state." Williams was not arguing the church should be excluded from the business of governing, but that government leaders should be different from church leaders in order to prevent corruption.

† The English Standard Version even more clearly invites mankind to make the right, rational

Say to them, "As surely as I live, declares the Sovereign LORD, I take no pleasure in the death of the wicked, but rather that they turn from their ways and live. Turn! Turn from your evil ways! Why will you die, people of Israel?" (Ezek. 33:11)

This is good, and pleases God our Savior, who wants all people to be saved and to come to a knowledge of the truth. (1 Tim. 2:3–4)

The Lord is not slow in keeping his promise, as some understand slowness. He is patient with you, not wanting anyone to perish, but everyone to come to repentance. (2 Pet. 3:9)

From these verses we see that God grants everyone liberty as an unalienable right. The founding generation firmly embraced liberty as a God-given non-negotiable, and many of that generation wrote about it.

In January 1786, Thomas Jefferson wrote the "Virginia Statute of Religious Freedom" to disestablish the Church of England and guarantee freedom of religion to the people of Virginia.* The statute begins with these words:

Whereas, Almighty God hath created the mind free; that all attempts to influence it by temporal punishments … tend only to beget habits of hypocrisy and meanness, and are a departure from the plan of the holy author of our religion, who being Lord, both of body and mind yet chose not to propagate it by coercions on either, as was in his Almighty power to do, that the impious presumption of legislators and rulers, civil as well as ecclesiastical, who, being themselves but fallible and uninspired men have assumed dominion over the faith of others, setting up their own opinions and modes of thinking as the only true and infallible, and as such endeavouring to impose them on others, hath established and maintained false religions over the

choice: "Come now, let us reason together."

* Some historians argue that the church disestablishment movement was about barring the church from government, but that is untrue. It was about not having a state-sponsored church, like the Anglican Church in Virginia, to force a particular Christian sect on its citizenry.

greatest part of the world and through all time; that to compel a man to furnish contributions of money for the propagation of opinions which he disbelieves is sinful and tyrannical.[105]

Jefferson wrote this after the Revolution, but religious liberty and civil liberty were also central to the struggle for independence, finding prominence in the writings of the founders. He also wrote the following about the importance of religious liberty:

Among the most inestimable of our blessings is that ... liberty to worship our Creator in the way we think most agreeable in His will; a liberty deemed in other countries incompatible with good government and yet proved by our experience to be its best support. — Thomas Jefferson, November 18, 1807

In a letter to Johann Daniel Gros, George Washington wrote the following:

The establishment of Civil and Religious Liberty was the motive which induced me to the Field.... It now remains to be my earnest ... prayer, that the Citizens of the United States would make a wise and virtuous use of the blessings, placed before them."[106]

And who can forget the words Patrick Henry is reported to have said at the Second Virginia Convention on March 23, 1775, "Give me liberty or give me death!"

Synthesizing Webster, Jefferson, Washington, and the way the founders practiced liberty, we arrive at the following summary:

God's plan is that mankind has the free will (liberty) of adopting opinions on religious belief and the method of worshipping the Supreme Being, according to the dictates of their own conscience—exempt from the coercion of the state, institution, organization, or individual (freedom).

Ensuring citizens have the liberty to choose or reject God was a crucial principle in the American founding and is the first variable needed to deliver freedom.

THE SECOND VARIABLE: JUSTICE

Justice is the next important variable for freedom. Webster defined justice as the following:

> The virtue which consists in giving to every one what is his due; practical conformity to the laws and to principles of rectitude in the dealings of men with each other; honesty; integrity in commerce or mutual intercourse.[107]

Webster offered the following explanation:

> *Distributive justice* belongs to magistrates or rulers, and consists in distributing to every man that right or equity which the laws and the principles of equity require; or in deciding controversies according to the laws and to principles of equity. *Commutative justice* consists in fair dealing in trade and mutual intercourse between man and man.[108]

A simplified definition will serve our purposes:

> Justice is defending the rights of every individual according to the law.

In chapter 3 we summarized God's blueprint for governing. We also explored dozens of verses in both the Old Testament and New Testament where he commanded his people to live justly. The more Israel strayed from this design, the more he sent prophets to warn them.* In the following list, we see how God repeatedly focused on the establishment and maintenance of civil justice in the nation of Israel:

---

* God often referred to the nation of Israel as a "stiff-necked" people because of their cyclical refusal to follow his moral law. America appears to have the same tendency.

And he looked for justice, but saw bloodshed; for righteousness, but heard cries of distress. (Isa. 5:7)

Woe to those who make unjust laws, to those who issue oppressive decrees. (Isa. 10:1)

Their evil deeds have no limit; they do not seek justice. They do not promote the case of the fatherless; they do not defend the just cause of the poor. "Should I not punish them for this?" declares the LORD. "Should I not avenge myself on such a nation as this?" (Jer. 5:28–29)

"Does it make you a king to have more and more cedar? Did not your father have food and drink? He did what was right and just, so all went well with him. He defended the cause of the poor and needy, and so all went well. Is that not what it means to know me?" declares the LORD. "But your eyes and your heart are set only on dishonest gain, on shedding innocent blood and on oppression and extortion." (Jer. 22:15–17)

The people of the land practice extortion and commit robbery; they oppress the poor and needy and mistreat the foreigner, denying them justice. (Ezek. 22:29)

He has shown you, O mortal, what is good. And what does the LORD require of you? To act justly and to love mercy and to walk humbly with your God. (Micah 6:8)

The LORD within her is righteous; he does no wrong. Morning by morning he dispenses his justice, and every new day he does not fail, yet the unrighteous know no shame. (Zeph. 3:5)

This is what the LORD Almighty said: "Administer true justice; show mercy and compassion to one another. Do not oppress the widow or the fatherless, the foreigner or the poor. Do not plot evil against each other." But they refused to pay attention; stubbornly they turned their backs and covered their ears. They made their hearts as hard as flint and would not listen to the law or to the words that the LORD Almighty had sent by his Spirit through the earlier prophets. So the LORD Almighty was very angry. (Zech. 7:9–12)

You have wearied the LORD with your words. "How have we wearied him?" you ask. By saying, "All who do evil are good in the eyes of the LORD, and he is pleased with them" or "Where is the God of justice?" (Mal. 2:17)

God is clearly repulsed by injustice. In following God's blueprint, America's founders were infuriated by the protracted injustices of King George, which led to the struggle for independence (as summarized in chapter 5). As representatives in their respective colonies, these leaders perceived it their duty to confront injustice on behalf of those they represented. The standard by which they measured justice—or in this case, the *denial* of justice—rested in "the laws of Nature and of Nature's God," or the moral law.

THE THIRD VARIABLE: THE MORAL LAW

The moral law, discussed in chapter 3, operates as the timeless standard for lawmaking and the dispensing of civil justice for individuals. It is also intended to govern individual behavior, which means personal liberty does have boundaries. Because these boundaries can be broken, it is critical for governments to abide by the moral law to enable freedom for all. To better understand the mindset of the founders about government, we will review how the law was understood from before the time of Christ and through the American Revolution.

The equal application of justice to all—regardless of gender, race, or class—is unique to Judeo-Christian jurisprudence. As Americans, "liberty and justice for all" still rolls off the tongue easily because it is ingrained in our national culture. But in many cultures since the beginning of history, commoners did not possess the same rights as elites. Elites had their own law codes, and rights came with noble breeding; owning property brought power. The oldest known recorded law code is the "Code of Hammurabi," dating back to 1750 BC. This Babylonian document codifies justice in issues of contracts, wages, liability, marriage, and other areas—similar to the blueprint God gave Moses. The Babylonian code differs in one critical area: even-handed justice. It made distinctions between classes and genders: punishments and rewards were not extended equitably if you were a woman or a slave. Social stratification was embedded in the law.

God's blueprint, by contrast, levels all people under the rule of law, the moral law, without partiality:

> Appoint judges and officials for each of your tribes in every town the LORD your God is giving you, and they shall judge the people fairly. Do not pervert justice or show partiality. Do not accept a bribe, for a bribe blinds the eyes of the wise and twists the words of the innocent. Follow justice and justice alone, so that you may live and possess the land the LORD your God is giving you. (Deut. 16:18–20)

> Woe to those who make unjust laws, to those who issue oppressive decrees, to deprive the poor of their rights and withhold justice from the oppressed of my people, making widows their prey and robbing the fatherless. (Isa. 10:1–2)

> Cursed is anyone who withholds justice from the foreigner, the fatherless or the widow. (Deut. 27:19)

> Defend the weak and the fatherless; uphold the cause of the poor and the oppressed. (Ps. 82:3)

To apply the moral law as the standard to secure justice requires that civil leaders embrace and commit themselves to follow it. But faithful adherence to the moral law has ebbed and flowed across civilizations in the millennia that followed.* A famous example of the people addressing inequality under the law occurred at Runnymede, England, in 1215. Local barons (landowners) compelled King John to officially recognize certain rights of Englishmen, expressed in the Magna Carta. Although the Magna Carta was challenged and revised several times in subsequent years, its origination engraved in the governance code—and in history—the principle that the law should govern all men equally.† Justices to this day, including SCOTUS, routinely reference the Magna Carta as authoritative when delivering judicial rulings.[109]

As summarized in chapter 5, the Reformation in the 1500s led to a reexamination of church doctrine, including how the moral law was a key principle for governing. This is where John Locke's work had specific application. He influenced America's founders with the idea that the moral law is a timeless standard.‡ He defended the importance of the moral law in *The Reasonableness of Christianity as Delivered in the Scriptures* (1695), which provided the rationale for separating from England, captured eighty-one years later in the Declaration of Independence:

> It is plain, in fact, that human reason unassisted failed men in its great and proper business of morality. It never from unquestionable principles, by clear deductions, made out an entire body of the "law of nature." And he that shall collect all the moral rules of the philosophers, and compare them with those contained in the New

---

* The idea of the Ten Commandments as a reference for lawmaking was common through the Church Age because of leaders like St. Patrick and Alfred the Great.

† Interestingly, the Magna Carta was drafted by the local pastor, Stephen Langton. In the early 1600s, local pastors in New England continued to contribute their biblical viewpoints on politics. As mentioned previously, pastors Thomas Hooker and Nathanial Ward drafted the "Fundamental Orders of Connecticut" and the "Massachusetts Body of Liberties," respectively, to codify biblical principles of governing more fully. On matters of civil law, people knew to go to their spiritual leaders for guidance.

‡ Some historians claim Locke was a deist, and as mentioned in this book's Q&A, deists do not believe God is actively involved in the affairs of mankind. But the fact that Locke wrote a book defending Christianity strongly suggests he was a genuine Christian.

Testament, will find them to come short of the morality delivered by our Saviour, and taught by his apostles.[110]

In his "Second Treatise of Civil Government," Locke refers to the Law of Nature as "the eternal rule of all men" and as "the will of God." Paragraph 135 reads:

> Thus the Law of Nature stands as an Eternal Rule to all Men, *Legislators* as well as others. The *Rules* that they make for other Men's Actions, must, as well as their own and other Men's Actions, be conformable to the Law of Nature, *i.e.* to the Will of God, of which that is a Declaration, and the *fundamental Law of Nature* being *the preservation of Mankind*, no Humane Sanction can be good, or valid against it.[111]

To Locke, an undeniable influence on the founders, the moral law as revealed by the biblical God was the highest law, and civil laws contradicting it were invalid.

Faith had great effect on the founders leading up to America's founding. Theologians and politicians agreed the divine law governed the universe and must guide lawmakers. They saw this as both the natural and moral law. The Ten Commandments represented the rule of law—ordained by God for all eras and regions. This was the divine blueprint God gave to the Israelites through Moses, and it governed individual conduct as well as civil laws. This is the reason the Ten Commandments were displayed in virtually every school and courtroom in America until the latter part of the twentieth century. These visual representations reminded Americans that the personal code of conduct and the basis for lawmaking originates with God's blueprint. Even among citizens who do not embrace Christianity, the elevation of the moral code established a culture of "liberty and justice for all." Armed with an understanding of the moral law, citizens can govern their own conduct by a universal standard and will need less intervention by law enforcement.

From a biblical perspective, we know the removal of the moral law from the public square can only harm our culture as more people do what is "right in their own eyes" (Judges 21:25). Removing the moral law as the basis for justice has led to a cacophony of alternative justice theories centered on social, wage, and environmental justice but which often have little to do with justice, liberty, morality, or freedom. But any government action must ultimately be guided by the moral law to provide civil justice to the citizenry. We will explore this more in chapter 8.

PRINCIPLES APPLIED IN THE AMERICAN FOUNDING

The principles expressed by Blackstone and Locke were the fundamental building blocks our founders applied during our founding and early governance. James Otis (1725–1783) was a prominent Boston lawyer and representative of the Massachusetts General Court and influenced lawyers like John Adams. Otis argued in 1761, "There must be in every instance, a higher authority, viz. GOD. Should an act of parliament be against any of *his* natural laws, which are *immutably* true, their declaration would be contrary to eternal truth, equity and justice, and consequently void."[112]

James Wilson (1742–1798) was a signer of both the Declaration of Independence and the Constitution. He was the first law professor at the University of Pennsylvania (1789 to 1791), was a Supreme Court justice from 1789 to 1798, and wrote *Lectures on Law*, affirming the role of the moral law presented in the Bible:

> Law … communicated to us by reason and conscience … has been called natural; as promulgated by the Holy Scriptures, it has been called revealed…. But it should always be remembered, that this law, natural or revealed … flows from the same divine source; it is the law of God…. Human law must rest its authority, ultimately, upon the authority of that law, which is divine…. All men are equally subject to the command of their Maker.

Another key player in the American founding was John Jay (1745–1829). He was a New York delegate to the First Continental Congress, president of the Congress, author of five of *The Federalist Papers*, and the first chief justice of the Supreme Court of the United States. This makes him the only person in American history to serve in all three branches of our national government.* Jay also affirmed the importance of the moral law, writing, "Legal punishments are adjusted and inflicted by the law and magistrate, and not by unauthorized individuals. These and all other positive laws or ordinances established by Divine direction, must of necessity be consistent with the moral law."

Joseph Story (1779–1845) was on the Supreme Court from 1811 to 1845. He affirmed the role of the moral law in securing justice, attributing that role to the Christian faith:

"One of the beautiful boasts of our municipal jurisprudence is that Christianity is a part of the Common Law. There never has been a period in which the Common Law did not recognize Christianity as lying at its foundations."

The acknowledgment of the moral law as essential to America's governance has guided presidents from American's founding until well into the twentieth century. Consider the following words from presidents John Adams, Grover Cleveland, and Harry Truman:

We have no Government armed with Power capable of contending with human Passions unbridled by ... morality and Religion. Avarice, Ambition ... Revenge or Galantry, would break the strongest Cords of our Constitution as a Whale goes through a Net. Our Constitution was made only for a moral and religious

---

* John Jay served as a key negotiator and signer of the Treaty of Paris, which ended the Revolutionary War. He was the architect of the Jay Treaty when England threatened war during Washington's first administration. He served as governor of New York and president of the American Bible Society. But he was not viewed as a "founder," having not been present at the development or signing of either of the key three founding documents (Declaration, Articles of Confederation, and Constitution). Regardless of his absence from these momentous events, his contributions to the American founding cannot be overstated.

People. It is wholly inadequate to the government of any other.[113]
— John Adams

The strength, the perpetuity, and the destiny of the nation rest upon
our homes, established by the law of God, guarded by parental care,
regulated by parental authority, and sanctified by parental love.
These are not the homes of polygamy. The mothers of our land, who
rule the nation as they mold the characters and guide the actions of
their sons, live according to God's holy ordinances, and each, secure
and happy in the exclusive love of the father of her children.*
— Grover Cleveland

The fundamental basis of this Nation's law was given to Moses on
the Mount. The fundamental basis of our Bill of Rights comes from
the teachings which we get from Exodus and St. Matthew, from
Isaiah and St. Paul. I don't think we emphasize that enough these
days. If we don't have the proper fundamental moral background,
we will finally wind up with a totalitarian government which does
not believe in rights for anybody except the state.[114]
— Harry Truman

It is clear the moral law was pivotal in America's founding and
maintained respect through the twentieth century. It serves as the universal, timeless standard that will test the legitimacy of all other laws
and is vital to help deliver freedom.

So, we have a simple formula showing how to create freedom in a
community or nation:

$$\frac{\text{Liberty} + \text{Justice}}{\text{Moral Law}} => \text{Freedom}$$

* President Grover Cleveland defended the natural marriage of one man and one woman as prescribed by the Bible. See Grover Cleveland, First Annual Message (first term), December 8, 1885,
online by Gerhard Peters and John T. Woolley, The American Presidency Project, presidency.ucsb.
edu/node/204032.

Diminish or compromise any of these elements, and freedom will be compromised. The next step is putting the formula into practice and keeping it robust over time.

MAINTAINING THE FORMULA FOR FREEDOM

To bring this formula to life, it is critical to have a civil political body that aligns with these principles and establishes the means to secure liberty and justice for all on an ongoing basis. This is where politics comes in. For many Christians, politics is almost a four-letter word. It is as though one must sacrifice Christian integrity to be involved in politics. But the founding generation thought differently. For the founding generation, *politic* (a word obviously related to *politics*) was defined as follows:

1. Wise; prudent and sagacious in devising and pursuing measures adapted to promote the public welfare; *applied to persons...*
2. Well devised and adapted to the public prosperity; *applied to things...*
3. Ingenious in devising and pursuing any scheme of personal or national aggrandizement, without regard to the morality of the measure; cunning; artful, sagacious in adapting means to the end, whether good or evil.[115]

The first two definitions explain the execution of political action, the business of governing in a just way. Unlike the third, these two definitions come close to God's blueprint and require qualified leaders to understand the moral law and commit themselves to governing by it.

Webster shines more light on governance, defining *politics* this way:

The science of government; that part of ethics which consist in the regulation and government of a nation or state, for the preservation of its safety, peace and prosperity; comprehending the defense of its existence and rights against foreign control or conquest, the augmentation of its strength and resources, and the protection of its citizens in their rights, with the preservation and improvement of their morals.[116]

This more precise definition of politics not only clarifies the mission of government as America's founders understood it but also calls on political leaders to set a moral example for the citizens they govern. This moral example is informed by the moral law, not what culture says—either then or now.

Sadly, Webster's third definition of *politic* seems to have been prophetic of the modern perception of civic leaders. Many citizens today cringe at the mention of politics, seeing "scheme," "personal aggrandizement," "without regard to the morality of the measure," and "means to the end, whether good or evil" as the general standard. When civil leaders are elected who disregard or reject the moral law, they are more likely to conduct themselves in this way. Politicians operating with little regard for the moral law tend to deviate from the founding view of politics, eventually replacing the founders' intent with something else. History shows that leadership that ignores the objective standard provided by the moral law leads to corruption, in which dishonest citizens buy influence and civil leaders target their political opponents. It is not the faithful execution of governance summarized in God's blueprint, and it strays from the governing vision of America's founding generation.

As Christians rediscover God's call for a just society (first articulated in Genesis 9:5–6), examine the blueprint God gave Moses, and read the Declaration of Independence, they will discover a vision for our country in line with Webster's 1828 definition: "wise; prudent and sagacious ... measures adopted to promote the public welfare." The apostle Paul confirmed God's original design that "rulers hold no terror for those who do right, but for those who do wrong.... For the one in authority is God's servant for your good. But if you do wrong, be afraid, for rulers do not bear the sword for no reason. They are God's servants, agents of wrath to bring punishment on the wrongdoer" (Rom. 13:3–5). Politics, when practiced in a way that honors

God, is not antithetical to our Christian walk. On the contrary, our citizenship duty involves living according to God's moral law as a society and encouraging Christians with the gift and calling to serve in civil government to govern justly.

LIVING BY GOD'S MORAL LAW

The founders themselves championed the call for leaders to fear God, embrace Christianity, and demonstrate personal virtue which Webster defined as:

> (3) Moral goodness; the practice of moral duties and the abstaining from vice, or a conformity of life and conversation to the moral law.[117]*

When America was newly constructed, President George Washington in his Farewell Address spoke to the need for public virtue to ensure a just government:

> Of all the dispositions and habits which lead to political prosperity, Religion and morality are indispensable supports. In vain would that man claim the tribute of Patriotism, who should labour to subvert these great Pillars of human happiness, these firmest props of the duties of Men & citizens.... Let us with caution indulge the supposition, that morality can be maintained without religion.... Reason & experience both forbid us to expect that National morality can prevail in exclusion of religious principle.... 'Tis substantially true, that virtue or morality is a necessary spring of popular government. The rule indeed extends with more or less force to every species of free Government. Who that is a sincere friend to it can look with indifference upon attempts to shake the foundation of the fabric?[118]

John Adams echoed Washington's call in a letter to his cousin, Rev. Zabdiel Adams, on June 21, 1776:

---

* A simple definition of virtue is *the pursuit of moral living.*

Statesmen, my dear Sir, may plan and speculate for liberty, but it is Religion and Morality alone, which can establish the Principles upon which Freedom can securely stand. The only foundation of a free Constitution is pure Virtue, and if this cannot be inspired into our People in a greater Measure, than they have it now, they may change their Rulers and the forms of Government, but they will not obtain a lasting liberty.[119]

The founders were clear: America's survival has always hinged on her embrace of public virtue as defined by the moral law. This principle rings true throughout history: to reject the moral law is to reject God, and those who do so receive his judgment. In Paul's letter to the Romans, he describes what happens to people and societies when they do this:

> Furthermore, just as they did not think it worthwhile to retain the knowledge of God, so God gave them over to a depraved mind, so that they do what ought not to be done. They have become filled with every kind of wickedness, evil, greed and depravity. They are full of envy, murder, strife, deceit and malice. They are gossips, slanderers, God-haters, insolent, arrogant and boastful; they invent ways of doing evil; they disobey their parents; they have no under-standing, no fidelity, no love, no mercy. Although they know God's righteous decree that those who do such things deserve death, they not only continue to do these very things but also approve of those who practice them. (Rom. 1:28–32)

Rejection of the moral law for personal behavior and civil laws can lead only to decline. How do we prevent this from happening in the United States?

PREFERRING CHRISTIAN CIVIL LEADERS

If the formula for freedom is based on biblical principles, then we should be selecting leaders who believe in these principles. While a person can believe these principles and not be a Christian, it is also true that a person can claim to be a Christian and not align perfectly with these principles. Nonetheless, the odds a leader will follow biblical principles should improve if we elect people who are Christians, have the gift of leadership and administration, and feel called to serve in this area.

More than three decades after the United States declared independence, John Jay, in a letter to Jedidiah Morse on January 1, 1813, expressed concern for voting for those who reject Christianity:

> Whether our Religion permits Christians to vote for infidel rulers is a question which merits more consideration than it seems yet to have generally received, either from the clergy or the laity. It appears to me that what the prophet said to Jehoshaphat about his attachments to Ahab ("Shouldest thou help the ungodly and love them that hate the Lord?" 2 Chron. 19:2) affords a salutary lesson.... Public measures may not be a proper subject for the pulpit, yet, in my opinion, it is the right and duty of our pastors to press the observance of all moral and religious duties.[120]

In a letter to John Murray on October 12, 1816, John Jay clarified his call to elect Christians, writing "Providence has given to our people the choice of their rulers, and it is the duty, as well as the privilege and interest of our Christian nation to select and prefer Christians for their rulers."[121]

Noah Webster elaborated on the high stakes of fulfilling or neglecting this duty in his *History of the United States* (1832), warning that elected servants had a duty to secure public prosperity and happiness:

> When you become entitled to exercise the right of voting for public officers, let it be impressed on your mind that God commands you to choose for rulers just men who will rule in the fear of God.... The preservation of a republican government depends on the faithful discharge of this duty. If the citizens neglect their duty and place unprincipled men in office, the government will

soon be corrupted; laws will be made not for the public good so much as for the selfish or local purposes; corrupt or incompetent men will be appointed to execute the laws; the public revenues will be squandered on unworthy men; and the rights of the citizens will be violated or disregarded. If a republican government fails to secure public prosperity and happiness, it must be because the citizens neglect the divine commands and elect bad men to make and administer the laws.

While electing professing Christians does not guarantee virtuous political leadership, Christians bring two advantages over non-Christians: they are more likely to understand biblical principles for governing, and they are motivated by knowing they will give an account to God for their conduct, personally and professionally. Non-Christians can certainly serve in civil government with distinction, provided they embrace the principles of our founding covenant as they carry out their civil duties.

FREEDOM IS FRAGILE

God drew up his governance blueprint in Scripture, and America's founders embraced his design, laying a foundation for biblical governance. But once established, freedom is always challenged: oppression on one end and extreme personal liberty on the other. The twentieth century revealed what happens when tyrants come to power. Millions have lost their lives at the hands of nonbiblical civil governments that seek to silence their citizens. Millions more have died at the hands of doctors, as access to abortion is elevated to a personal liberty. America's future is incumbent on returning to the formula to ensure freedom. Civic leaders must understand the formula and teach it to the next generation. Ronald Reagan clarified this in a speech on March 30, 1961:

Freedom is never more than one generation away from extinction. We didn't pass it to our children in the bloodstream. It must be fought for, protected and handed on for them to do the same, or one day we will spend our sunset years telling our children and our children's children what it was once like in the United States where men were free.[122]

Freedom will endure only as long as present-day Americans preserve the key variables of the formula. Our civic duty is to pass it on.

SPIRITUAL FREEDOM

While the focus of this chapter has been on political freedom, spiritual freedom is also experienced when a person follows this formula to accept Jesus as his or her Savior. That happens when an individual realizes he or she can never keep the moral law perfectly, and breaking the moral law is the very definition of sin. This realization prompts individuals to make a choice, and liberty is what allows them to choose: will they accept God's gracious gift of salvation or continue living apart from him? Those who choose to repent and believe in the crucifixion and resurrection of Jesus will experience spiritual freedom. The Bible often speaks to this relationship between liberty and the resulting freedom that comes from justification:

I will always obey your law, for ever and ever. I will walk about in freedom, for I have sought out your precepts. I will speak of your statutes before kings and will not be put to shame, for I delight in your commands because I love them. (Ps. 119:44–47)

Whoever believes in him is not condemned, but whoever does not believe stands condemned already because they have not believed in the name of God's one and only Son. (John 3:18)

For if we have been united with him in a death like his, we will certainly also be united with him in a resurrection like his. For we know that our old self was crucified with him so that the body ruled by sin might be done away with, that we should no longer be slaves to sin—because anyone who has died has been set free from sin. (Rom. 6:5–7)

Very truly I tell you, whoever hears my word and believes him who sent me has eternal life and will not be judged but has crossed over from death to life. (John 5:24)

To the Jews who had believed him, Jesus said, "If you hold to my teaching, you are really my disciples. Then you will know the truth, and the truth will set you free." (John 8:31–32)

Jesus replied, "Very truly I tell you, everyone who sins is a slave to sin. Now a slave has no permanent place in the family, but a son belongs to it forever. So if the Son sets you free, you will be free indeed." (John 8:34–36)

It is for freedom that Christ has set us free. Stand firm, then, and do not let yourselves be burdened again by a yoke of slavery. (Gal. 5:1)

In him and through faith in him we may approach God with freedom and confidence. (Eph. 3:12)

But whoever looks intently into the perfect law that gives freedom, and continues in it—not forgetting what they have heard, but doing it—they will be blessed in what they do. (James 1:25)

This means seeking to govern according to God's design compels citizens to recognize that no one can measure up. In his letter to John Murray on April 15, 1818, John Jay reinforced this concept by stating "the law was inexorable, and by requiring perfect obedience, under a penalty so inevitable and dreadful, operated as a schoolmaster to bring us to Christ for mercy."[123] To become acquainted with the moral law is to come face to face with one's own unrighteousness. Any individual can be set free from the bondage of sin if he or she repents, accepting Christ's atoning death on the cross. This means the maintenance of liberty and justice based on the moral law is not only critical for civil order but also an enabler of evangelism in a community. The administration of liberty and justice for all is a timeless part of God's evangelistic plan. If our rights are protected, we are free to declare the gospel to our fellow citizens, sharing how they can be free.

SUMMARY

In this chapter we discussed the following key terms and discovered how the founders defined them. These definitions help us understand the founders' intention for how the American government should work:

Liberty: The ability to have and express opinions
Justice: Protecting individual rights as defined by the moral law
Moral law: Individual standard of behavior toward God and your neighbor
Freedom: Not being under the control of another person or institution
Politics: The business of governing justly to deliver freedom
Virtue: The pursuit of moral living

We unearthed a formula any nation can use to deliver freedom to her people. The best chance of forming a nation that will long endure is to elect virtuous leaders, people who consciously acknowledge God's moral law and feel bound to live by it. Heightened by accountability to God, virtuous leaders will view serving in civil government as a sacred duty, knowing God will hold them accountable for their conduct in this life. In the next chapter, we will focus on what the founders believed citizens should do with their freedom.

SUMMARY POINTS

- To achieve freedom, the civil government must provide liberty, which is the ability to have and express opinions.
- Civil government must also secure justice for the citizenry to achieve freedom.
- This civil justice must be based on the moral law, as summarized by the Ten Commandments.
- The highest order of law is the divine law, which is in effect at all times and in all places and must be respected as the standard for civil justice.
- The founders believed that all laws must be in harmony with God's moral law.
- The founders believed that any law in conflict with God's moral law was illegitimate, null, and void.
- The most effective way to ensure freedom for all is to elect civic leaders who believe in biblical principles of governance, especially the idea that the moral law is the standard for justice and lawmaking.
- Civil leaders act as God's servants to establish and maintain liberty and civil justice for all.
- The founders believed that the citizenry should prefer leaders who fear God and seek to live virtuous lives.

Chapter 7

The Pursuit of Happiness

Objective of the American Covenant

Praise be to you, Lord; teach me your decrees. With my lips I recount all the laws that come from your mouth. I rejoice in following your statutes as one rejoices in great riches. I meditate on your precepts and consider your ways. I delight in your decrees; I will not neglect your word.
—Ps. 119:12–16

We hold these Truths to be self-evident, that all Men are created equal, that they are endowed by their Creator with certain unalienable Rights, that among these are Life, Liberty, and the pursuit of Happiness.
—Declaration of Independence
July 1776

CHAPTER 7

THE PURSUIT OF HAPPINESS

Objective of the American Covenant

Praise be to you, Lord; teach me your decrees. With my lips I recount all the laws that come from your mouth. I rejoice in following your statutes as one rejoices in great riches. I meditate on your precepts and consider your ways. I delight in your decrees; I will not neglect your word.
—Ps. 119:12–16

We hold these Truths to be self-evident, that all Men are created equal, that they are endowed by their Creator with certain unalienable Rights, that among these are Life, Liberty, and the pursuit of Happiness.
—Declaration of Independence
July 1776

Many of us can recite these iconic words from the Declaration of Independence. The phrase "Life, Liberty, and the pursuit of Happiness" is ingrained in the mind of practically every American. Life and liberty are easy enough to understand, but what exactly is meant by *the pursuit of Happiness*?

The typical explanation of *pursuit of Happiness* is that it refers to the accumulation of possessions or experiences we believe will make us happy in the moment. Americans have pursued this type of happiness by acquiring everything from stylish cars to fresh-looking hairdos.

Advertisers know our weaknesses; they prey on this desire for tempo-rary gratification. But temporal pleasure is transient by definition, and many Americans live in the disappointing pursuit of the next object they believe will bring happiness.

Pastors correctly point out that this is the great lie that so many people fall for: believing they can find happiness in things that give them temporary pleasure. People buy things, and for a while they are happy, but soon the newness wears off and they are unsatisfied. The modern pastor points out that people should instead pursue joy, which is a mental assent to the truth that Christians are eternally secure rest-ing in the grace and love of God. People who embrace the Christian faith understand this to be true.

The modern historical narrative of the founding is that the found-ers were a product of the enlightenment, and when they used the phrase *pursuit of Happiness*, the founders were indicating the great aim of life is to pursue temporal materialistic pleasures; i.e., to "eat, drink and be merry." Not only is this pursuit *not* a noble end, it reinforces the narrative that the founders may have rejected the faith altogether. Unfortunately, this narrative on the founders' view of pursuit of hap-piness has been embraced and reinforced by many pastors.

A well-known pastor once gave a message from Matthew 5 enti-tled "Life Outside the Amusement Park." He opened with this:

> [Happiness] is an American thing. Can you believe it? When you stop and think about it, it's kind of silly, isn't it? Right alongside life and freedom, we put in our Declaration of Independence "the pursuit of happiness."[124]

He quoted Malcolm Muggeridge, an English journalist and sati-rist, who wrote *Conversion: A Spiritual Journey*, where he included the following:

> Of all the different purposes set before mankind, the most disas-trous is surely "the Pursuit of Happiness", slipped into the American

Declaration of Independence, along with "Life and Liberty" as an inalienable Right, almost accidentally, at the last moment."[125]

The clear implication of Muggeridge and of the pastor quoting him was that the insertion of this phrase into the Declaration was not only ill advised but also counter to the Christian faith. But is this what the founders intended when they wrote the phrase into the Declaration?

In this chapter I will illustrate happiness according to the Bible, show how the founding generation understood happiness, and highlight the connection between "pursuit of happiness" and the ability to accumulate and manage property.

WEBSTER'S DEFINITION OF HAPPINESS

We turn again to Noah Webster's 1828 dictionary to understand what the word *happiness* meant in the founding era:

> The agreeable sensations which spring from the enjoyment of good; that state of a being in which his desires are gratified, by the enjoyment of pleasure without pain; felicity.... *Happiness* is comparative.... *Happiness* therefore admits of indefinite degrees of increase in enjoyment, or gratification of desires. Perfect *happiness*, or pleasure unalloyed with pain, is not attainable in this life.[126]

This suggests *happiness* is connected to the "enjoyment of good," a state in which "desires are gratified." Webster noted, and the founders agreed, that a person cannot attain perfect happiness in this life, no matter how diligently he or she pursues it. So, how should we understand this happiness the founders wanted people to pursue?

Webster's definitions for the adjective *happy* provide insight into what the founders believed would make people happy:

1. Lucky; fortunate; successful....
2. Being in the enjoyment of agreeable sensations from the possession of good; enjoying pleasure from the gratification of

202

appetites or desires. The pleasurable sensations derived from the gratification of sensual appetites render a person temporarily *happy*; but *he only can be esteemed really and permanently happy, who enjoys peace of mind in the favor of God.* To be in any degree *happy*, we must be free from pain both of body and of mind; to be very *happy*, we must be in the enjoyment of lively sensations of pleasure, either of body or mind....

3. Prosperous; having secure possession of good.[127]

These definitions clarify *happiness* as the securing of something good. Webster illustrates his definitions with two biblical references to illustrate this kind of happiness:

Happy am I, for the daughters will call me blessed. (Gen. 30:13)

Happy is that people whose God is Jehovah. (Ps. 144:15)

Based on Webster and several Bible references, we conclude the key to long-lasting happiness is having favor with God.

HAPPINESS ACCORDING TO SCRIPTURE

Let's leave the founders in the eighteenth century for a moment to answer an ultimate question according to the Bible: how does one obtain happiness and find favor with God? Earlier, we discussed that humans are separated from God because of their sin, which breaks the moral law. But God sent Jesus, who kept the moral law perfectly, to be crucified on the cross, paying our penalty and satisfying his wrath against our sin.* All one has to do to be saved from eternal judgment is acknowledge that he or she has violated God's moral law, repent, and accept Jesus as having paid the debt. In doing this, an individual secures salvation and becomes a follower of Christ.† When this occurs,

---

* The theological word for this is *propitiation* (pro-pih-shee-AY-shun), which means "to satisfy God's wrath against sin." Jesus was the propitiation for our sins.

† Salvation means God has pardoned them, and they will be found not guilty at the coming judgment. For those who have *not* accepted Jesus, who died on the cross in our place, they will be

that person has found favor with God.

When individuals exercise their liberty to choose to follow Christ, they find true happiness in their union with him. Their happiness, joy, and delight continues to increase as they strive to live in harmony with God's moral law. This is seen in a number of verses:

> To the person who pleases him, God gives wisdom, knowledge and happiness, but to the sinner he gives the task of gathering and storing up wealth to hand it over to the one who pleases God. (Eccles. 2:26)

> Blessed is the one who does not walk in step with the wicked or stand in the way that sinners take or sit in the company of mockers, but whose delight is in the law of the LORD, and who meditates on his law day and night. (Ps. 1:1–2)

> The law of the LORD is perfect, refreshing the soul. The statutes of the LORD are trustworthy, making wise the simple. The precepts of the LORD are right, giving joy to the heart. The commands of the LORD are radiant, giving light to the eyes. The fear of the LORD is pure, enduring forever. The decrees of the LORD are firm, and all of them are righteous. They are more precious than gold, than much pure gold; they are sweeter than honey, than honey from the honeycomb. By them your servant is warned; in keeping them there is great reward. (Ps. 19:7–11)

> Though rulers sit together and slander me, your servant will meditate on your decrees. Your statutes are my delight; they are my counselors. (Ps. 119:23–24)

> Your faithfulness continues through all generations; you established the earth, and it endures. Your laws endure to this day, for all things serve you. If your law had not been my delight, I would

---

found guilty. The Bible describes their fate as a lake of fire where they will be tormented forever. This is why Christians are so concerned about evangelism. They long to share the good news about Jesus so people do not have to endure this future judgment.

have perished in my affliction. I will never forget your precepts, for by them you have preserved my life. (Ps. 119:90–93)

Blessed are those who are persecuted because of righteousness, for theirs is the kingdom of heaven. Blessed are you when people insult you, persecute you and falsely say all kinds of evil against you because of me. Rejoice and be glad, because great is your reward in heaven, for in the same way they persecuted the prophets who were before you.* (Matt 5:10–12)

You have loved righteousness and hated wickedness; therefore God, your God, has set you above your companions by anointing you with the oil of joy. (Heb. 1:9)

But the fruit of the Spirit is love, joy, peace, forbearance, kindness, goodness, faithfulness, gentleness and self-control. Against such things there is no law. (Gal. 5:22–23)

Looking at these verses that span the Old and New Testaments, it is clear that understanding and seeking to live inside the boundaries of the moral law is the key to the pursuit of happiness.†

God has established a connection between Christians who strive to live inside his moral law and general happiness, but obedience does not guarantee that the journey will be without disappointment, grief, or hardship. Yet even in hardship, Jesus told his disciples, "Do not let your hearts be troubled. You believe in God; believe also in me" (John 14:1). Moses also spoke of God's presence in difficult times, saying, "Be strong and courageous. Do not be afraid or terrified because of them, for the LORD your God goes with you; he will never leave you nor forsake you" (Deut. 31:6). All these verses show that a person who charts a path according to God's

---

* The Beatitudes, from Jesus's Sermon on the Mount, affirm the connection between serving God and being blessed, which means "happy" (Matt. 5:3–12).

† Reading all of Psalm 119—the longest Old Testament psalm—will deepen your understanding for how appreciating God's moral law leads to happiness.

moral law will find true happiness (joy from within) more than if he or she ignores God's call and pursues fleeting happiness (external pleasures) instead.

Now, were America's founders to read this explanation of "the pursuit of happiness," would they agree or object?

HAPPINESS ACCORDING TO THE FOUNDERS

We know what the founding generation believed by looking at documents they authored, debated, and signed. We can study their speeches and dissect their personal correspondence. Hundreds of these artifacts point to one conclusion: our forefathers—and the sages they learned from—believed the "pursuit of happiness" was inextricably connected to the freedom to pursue and know God based on one's individual conscience.

William Blackstone's *Commentaries on the Laws of England* captured his perspective on how to apply God's moral law in the civic arena. Notice how he explains that the law comes from God and is intended for the well-being of mankind:

> As therefore the creator is a being, not only of infinite power, and wisdom, but also of infinite goodness.... For he has so intimately connected, so inseparably interwoven the laws of eternal justice with the happiness of each individual, that the latter cannot be attained but by observing the former; and, if the former be punctually obeyed, it cannot but induce the latter. In consequence of which mutual connection of justice and human felicity [intense happiness], he has not perplexed the law of nature with a multitude of abstracted rules and precepts, referring merely to the fitness or unfitness of things, as some have vainly surmised; but has graciously reduced the rule of obedience to this one paternal precept, "that man should 'pursue his own happiness.'" This is the foundation of what we call ethics, or natural law.[128]

In other words, human happiness is bound up with justice, which is itself bound up with keeping the moral law.

Blackstone connects striving to keep the "laws of eternal justice" with the surest way to secure a happy life.[129] Blackstone's impact on the founding generation was profound: his published commentaries were recognized as the definitive source of Common Law, and knowledge of them was a prerequisite to becoming a lawyer. These concepts found their way into the Declaration of Independence in two places (italicized):

> We hold these Truths to be self-evident, that all Men are created equal, that they are endowed by their Creator with certain unalienable Rights, that among these are Life, Liberty, and the *pursuit of Happiness*, That to secure these Rights, Governments are instituted among Men, deriving their just Powers from the Consent of the Governed ... that whenever any Form of Government becomes destructive of these Ends, it is the Right of the People to alter or abolish it, and to institute a new Government, laying its Foundation on such Principles, and organizing its Powers in such Form, as to them shall seem *most likely to effect their Safety and Happiness*.

On what did such happiness depend, according to the founders? They frequently identified "religion and morality" as key supports, which the following examples demonstrate.

In 1778 Congress passed a resolution directed to the states that encouraged their citizens to be virtuous.[130] While this resolution may be overly controlling by today's standards, it clearly illustrates their belief that genuine happiness depended on religion and morality:

> Whereas true religion and good morals are the only solid foundations of public liberty and happiness:
>
> Resolved, that it be, and it is hereby earnestly recommended to the several States, to take the most effectual measures for the encouragement thereof, and for the suppressing of theatrical

entertainments, horse racing, gaming, and such other diversions as are productive of idleness, dissipation, and a general depravity of principles and manners.[131]

With the Declaration in place, states started writing their own Constitutions and statutes concerning religious liberty. Roger Sherman was involved in this task for the state of Connecticut in 1783. Sherman has the distinction of being the only founder who helped draft and sign the Declaration and Resolves (1774), the Articles of Association (1774), the Declaration of Independence (1776), the Articles of Confederation (1777, 1778), and the US Constitution (1787).[132] He was regularly appointed to key committees and helped draft the Bill of Rights, including the First Amendment, which focuses on protecting religious liberty. If anyone understood the connection between religion, morality, and happiness, it would be he. Of particular interest is the statute Sherman drafted to protect religious liberty*:

> As the happiness of a people, and the good order of civil society, essentially depend upon piety, religion, and morality, it is the duty of the civil authority to provide for the support and encouragement thereof; so as that Christians of every denomination ... may be equally under the protection of the laws ... and ... may enjoy free liberty of conscience.[133]

In 1785, the Maryland House of Delegates proposed a general assessment bill that began with the following resolution:[134]

> That in the opinion of this house, that the happiness of the people, and the good order and preservation of civil government, depend upon morality, religion, and piety; and that these cannot be generally diffused through a community, but by the public worship of Almighty God.[135]

---

* Sherman's language also shows the founders' belief that the civil authority should in fact be directly involved in teaching religion and virtue to preserve a civil society. This is the complete opposite of what modern progressives believe with respect to "separation of church and state."

In 1785, Georgia drafted a statute entitled "For the Regular Establishment and Support of the Public Duties of Religion," with the following preamble:[136]

As the knowledge and practice of the principles of the Christian religion tends greatly to make good members of society, as well as good men, and is no less necessary to present, than to future happiness, its regular establishment and support is among the most important objects of legislature determination; and that the minds of the citizens of this state may be properly informed and impressed by the great principles of moral obligation and thus be induced by inclination furnished with opportunity, and favored by law to render public religious honors to the Supreme Being.[137]

In 1787, new American laws reinforced principles from the Declaration of Independence and summarized how the new nation was to expand. The "Northwest Ordinance" (1787, 1789) provided guidelines for states being admitted to the Union. Notice the hints of the founders' thinking in the following:

"Religion, morality, and knowledge being necessary to good government and *the happiness of mankind*, schools and the means of education shall forever be encouraged."[138]

Near the end of his life, on February 3, 1790, Ben Franklin petitioned the new Congress to abolish slavery. Despite being a part of the 1787 Constitutional Convention where they agreed not to attempt to pass federal legislation ending slavery for twenty years, Franklin appealed to Congress nonetheless with this declaration:

That from a regard for the happiness of Mankind an Association was formed several years since in this State by a number of her Citizens of various religious denominations for promoting the Abolition of Slavery.... That mankind are all formed by the same

Almighty being, alike objects of his Care & equally designed for the Enjoyment of *Happiness* the Christian Religion teaches us to believe & the Political Creed of America fully coincides with the Position....[139]

In George Washington's Farewell Address (1796), he highlighted the objective of happiness and its relation to religion and morality:

Of all the dispositions and habits which lead to political prosperity, Religion and Morality are indispensable supports. In vain would that man claim the tribute of Patriotism, who should labor to sub-vert these great Pillars of human *happiness.*

On June 12, 1817, Thomas Jefferson wrote a letter to John Manners, who had inquired about the origin of American religious and civil liberties. Jefferson explained where religious liberty comes from, arguing for freedom of worship based on "pursuing happiness" as a foundational truth universally understood and accepted:

Our right to life, liberty, the use of our faculties, the pursuit of happiness, is not left to the feeble and sophistical investigations of reason but is impressed on the sense of every man. [W]e do not claim these under the Charter of kings or legislators; but under the king of kings[.] [I]f he has made it a law in the nature of man to pursue his own happiness, he has left him free in the choice of place as well as mode.[140]

On November 20, 1825, James Madison wrote to Frederick Beasley on the need for a moral order to enable happiness in the citizenry:

This belief in a God Allpowerful [*sic*] wise & good, is so essential to the moral order of the world & to *the happiness of man*, that arguments which enforce it can not be drawn from too many sources.[141]

In 1833, Rev. Jasper Adams wrote a sermon entitled "The Relation of Christianity to Civil Government in the United States," which bolstered the connection between religion and happiness. On May 9, 1833, Chief Justice John Marshall responded,

> I am much indebted to you for the copy of your valuable sermon on the relation of Christianity to civil government preached before the convention of the Protestant Episcopal Church in Charleston, on the 13th of Feby. last. I have read it with great attention & advantage. The documents annexed to the sermon certainly go far in sustaining the proposition which it is your purpose to establish. One great object of the colonial charters was avowedly the propagation of the Christian faith. Means have been employed to accomplish this object, & those means have been used by government. No person, I believe, questions the importance of religion to the *happiness of man* even during his existence in this world. It has at all times employed his most serious meditation, & had a decided influence on his conduct.[142]

President William Henry Harrison reinforced the connection between Christianity and lasting happiness in his inaugural address (1841), saying,

> I deem the present occasion sufficiently important and solemn to justify me in expressing to my fellow-citizens a profound reverence for the Christian religion and a thorough conviction that sound morals, religious liberty, and a just sense of religious responsibility are essentially connected with all true and lasting *happiness*.[143]

In 1892, one hundred years after the Constitution was written, Supreme Court Justice David Josiah Brewer wrote an opinion in *Holy Trinity Church v. United States*. He cited numerous documents in America's history that all affirmed America's Christian heritage, one of which is the Massachusetts Constitution of 1780. This document shows what the founding generation envisioned for the purpose of civil government and its connection to the pursuit of happiness and morality:

> Or like that in articles 2 and 3 of part 1 of the constitution of Massachusetts, (1780), "It is the right as well as the duty of all men in society publicly, and at stated seasons, to worship the Supreme Being, the great Creator and Preserver of the universe.... As the *happiness of a people* and the good order and preservation of civil government essentially depend upon piety, religion, and morality.... And as these cannot be generally diffused through a community but by the institution of the public worship of God and of public instructions in piety, religion, and morality: Therefore, to promote their *happiness*, and to secure the good order and preservation of their government, the people of this commonwealth ... authorize ... the several towns, parishes, precincts ... to make suitable provision ... for the institution of the public worship of God and for the support and maintenance of public Protestant teachers of piety, religion, and morality."[144]

Even one of the first progressive presidents, Woodrow Wilson, connected truth and duty to happiness. In 1917, during World War I, Wilson penned a foreword for a pocket Bible that was given to thousands of American soldiers:

> The Bible is the word of life. I beg that you will read it and find this out for yourselves ... and the more you read the more it will become plain to you what things are worth while and what are not, what things make men *happy*; - loyalty, right dealing, speaking the truth, readiness to give everything for what they think their duty.... When you have read the Bible you will know it is the Word of God, because you will have found it the key to your own heart, your own *happiness*, and your own duty.[145]

America's founders—and civic leaders who followed them—left documents, legislation, speeches, and personal correspondence that point to their belief that pursuing God leads to happiness. Our forefathers believed people would achieve happiness by keeping his moral law and living in harmony with this design. They understood the Christian faith started with accepting Christ as Lord. Furthermore, being a Christian meant they had a duty to help establish and maintain liberty and justice for all. They saw this as allowing everyone to exercise liberty of conscience, going on a self-paced personal faith journey. They understood stepping forward and serving in this capacity (including law enforcement, military, and first responders) was not optional for those with the gift and calling in this area. While difficult at times, serving God in these areas enabled the happiness of the citizenry, as well as personal fulfillment on their part.

LIFE, LIBERTY, AND PROPERTY

When the founders used the phrase *pursuit of happiness*, they were also concerned about the protection of a person's property, as this supports the practical realities of living in community with other people. In the colonial era, laws protecting civil liberties protected citizens' ability to secure their lives, have and express opinions, and accumulate and manage property. Again, they were following the ideas of John Locke, who described the interplay between life, liberty, and property in his *Two Treatises of Civil Government*:

> The *State of Nature* has a Law of Nature to govern it, which obliges every one: And Reason, which is that Law, teaches all Mankind, who will but consult it, that being all equal and independent, no one ought to harm another in his Life, Health, Liberty, or Possessions.... When his own Preservation comes not in competition, ought he, as much as he can, *to preserve the rest of Mankind*, and may not unless it be to do Justice on an Offender, take away, or impair the life, or what tends to the Preservation of the Life, the Liberty, Health, Limb or Goods of another."[146]

Given the concern with property, it is noteworthy that the founders did not put the word *property* in the Declaration. We know this idea of life, liberty, and property was widely understood to be the litmus test for true freedom during the founding era. Note the language George Mason used for the Virginia Declaration of Rights just as Jefferson was drafting the Declaration of Independence:

> That all men are by nature equally free and independent, and have certain inherent rights, of which, when they enter into a state of society, they cannot, by any compact, deprive or divest their posterity; namely the enjoyment of life and liberty, with the means of acquiring and possessing property, and pursuing and obtaining happiness and safety.[147]

The similarities between the Virginia Declaration and the Declaration of Independence are obvious, yet Jefferson did not include the word *property* as an unalienable right. Perhaps it was because everyone connected the phrase *pursuit of happiness* with God's moral law after Blackstone's explanation that protection of property was clearly implied in the commandment not to steal. We can only speculate as to why Jefferson, and the full assembly reviewing his draft, did not include the word *property*, but the use of *pursuit of happiness* implies property rights are among the unalienable rights all individuals should enjoy.

Interestingly, we know the importance of being able to manage one's property extended into the nineteenth century. The clear evidence of this is after the Civil War when the Fourteenth Amendment was added to the Constitution. This amendment clarified that freed slaves had the same rights as everyone else, especially relating to their ability to acquire and manage property:

> nor shall any State deprive any person of life, liberty, *or property*, without due process of law; nor deny to any person within its jurisdiction the equal protection of the laws. [emphasis added]

Given the issue of the day, the word *property* was used to help ensure the full rights of American citizenship to former slaves. Having protections for personal property was deemed necessary for realizing true freedom. Congress put this amendment in place to guarantee the former slaves' civil liberty according to the vision set forth in the Declaration, but unfortunately many former slaves did not experience this protection. For many blacks, it would take another century until civil rights were addressed.

SUMMARY

America's founders believed the ultimate object of freedom was the liberty to pursue God as one's conscience dictates, which is the "pursuit of happiness." This phrase did not refer to the pagan or Enlightenment idea of focusing on material pleasure. It centered on their belief that true happiness occurs inside the boundaries of God's moral law. Living within the boundaries of a universal code of conduct does not impose Christianity on the citizenry. The moral law provides an authoritative framework that is mutually beneficial for the community as well as the individual, regardless of faith. Among those benefits are the protection of life, liberty, and property.

When we read the Bible alongside historic documents, we see how philosophers during the Revolutionary era arrived at this conclusion about what enables mankind to be happy. From earlier chapters, we have seen how other biblical principles for governing informed America's vision for government in our Declaration of Independence and Constitution. Sadly, many of our contemporaries have abandoned these principles and vision for American government. Having rejected the Christian faith, they have chosen a path away from God—one caught in chaos, dissension, division, and unhappiness. They have rejected God's blueprint, proposing their own design: a secular model called *progressivism*, which we will explore in the next chapter.

SUMMARY POINTS

• The common modern narrative about the phrase *pursuit of happiness* is that it was from the Enlightenment and meant accumulation of possessions or experiences we believe will make us happy.

• Many in the church today think the founders believed in this secular definition of the phrase *pursuit of happiness*.

• In the founding era, *happiness* connoted deep and permanent joy derived from upholding the moral law, not temporal pleasure derived from possessions or activities.

• The *pursuit of happiness* connoted securing individual religious liberty to pursue God as one's conscience dictated.

• The founders believed the best way to discover happiness is by living inside the boundaries of God's moral law.

• A community can achieve general happiness when those called to public service understand the moral law, step forward to serve following the biblical template for governing, and are supported by the local church.

CHAPTER 8

THE PROGRESSIVE BLUEPRINT FOR CIVIL GOVERNMENT

Challenging the American Covenant

Samuel told all the words of the LORD to the people who were asking him for a king. He said, "This is what the king who will reign over you will claim as his rights: He will take your sons and make them serve with his chariots and horses, and they will run in front of his chariots.
—1 Samuel 8:10–18

I could not put it more accurately than to repeat: "Men have forgotten God; that's why all this has happened."
—Aleksandr Solzhenitsyn
1983

CHAPTER 8

THE PROGRESSIVE BLUEPRINT FOR CIVIL GOVERNMENT

Challenging the American Covenant

> Samuel told all the words of the LORD to the people who were asking him for a king. He said, "This is what the king who will reign over you will claim as his rights: He will take your sons and make them serve with his chariots and horses, and they will run in front of his chariots. Some he will assign to be commanders of thousands and commanders of fifties, and others to plow his ground and reap his harvest, and still others to make weapons of war and equipment for his chariots. He will take your daughters to be perfumers and cooks and bakers. He will take the best of your fields and vineyards and olive groves and give them to his attendants. He will take a tenth of your grain and of your vintage and give it to his officials and attendants. Your male and female servants and the best of your cattle and donkeys he will take for his own use. He will take a tenth of your flocks, and you yourselves will become his slaves. When that day comes, you will cry out for relief from the king you have chosen, but the LORD will not answer you in that day."
> —1 Samuel 8:10–18

I have spent well-nigh 50 years working on the history of our revolution; in the process I have read hundreds of books, collected hundreds of personal testimonies, and have already contributed eight volumes of my own toward the effort of clearing away the

rubble left by that upheaval. But if I were asked today to formulate as concisely as possible the main cause of the ruinous revolution that swallowed up some 60 million of our people, I could not put it more accurately than to repeat: "Men have forgotten God; that's why all this has happened."[148]
—Aleksandr Solzhenitsyn
1983

In previous chapters, we explored the biblical principles rediscovered during the Reformation, debated in colonial America, and codified through the signing of the Declaration of Independence in 1776. Eighty-seven years later, in his Gettysburg Address, Abraham Lincoln stated that the United States was "engaged in a great civil war, testing whether that nation, or any nation so conceived and so dedicated, can long endure." Battle lines were clearly drawn between North and South, and the Confederacy nearly succeeded in severing the nation— but the Union endured.

Over the last century, new battle lines have been drawn with the introduction of a secular humanistic civil government instead of one based on transcendent truths and God-given rights. This opposing form of government is based on progressivism and seeks to fundamentally transform America. Progressives are opposed by conservatives, many of whom are Christians and want to maintain America's founding principles.* The two sides have been battling over the future of America, one fighting for the timeless ideals in our national founding covenant, and the other arguing that America was built on institutional racism and must be completely remade into a secular state led by a better political class.

Progressives have historically had a broad following and, in recent years, have made significant progress in infiltrating key American institutions, including public schools, universities, corporations, civil authorities, and even churches. Many are earnestly looking to improve

---

*This is generally the definition of being conservative—wanting to conserve the founding principles established in 1776 with the Declaration of Independence.

the human condition and are concerned about social issues such as a fair wage and health care. But there is also a subset of the progressive movement, the proponents of which have pushed God completely out of the governing equation. This "Far-Left" progressive group has adopted Marxist teachings and is most at odds with the American founding. This group has an increasingly large voice in the Democratic Party and is pushing hard to fundamentally transform America into a socialist/communist state. It is the ideology and actions of this Far-Left progressive group that contrasts with America's founding covenant.

In this chapter I will describe the origins of the modern progressive movement and how it evolved over time. I will compare its ideology to our original founding covenant, and we will look at nations that have embraced this approach and the ensuing results. Lastly, we will look at the strategies and methods the modern Far-Left progressive movement uses as its playbook to entice and nudge Americans away from our founding national covenant.

PROGRESSIVISM DEFINED

Progressivism originated in the late 1800s and evolved over time. Early Progressives* believed mankind has an obligation to advance the human condition, leveraging the latest advances in science and technology. Progressives generally addressed inequality and oppression across race, gender, and class lines. The early Progressives were in step with the Judeo-Christian thinking, and the church has a long history of applying their biblical worldview to alleviate the needs of their fellow citizens. Motivated by Christian beliefs, many private organizations were born in the Progressive Era, the late 1800s and early 1900s, to help underserved citizens. These organizations included the Benevolent Empire (Charles Finney), the Salvation Army (William Booth), the YMCA or Young Men's Christian Association (George Williams), and Alcoholics Anonymous (Bill Wilson and Bob Smith). These organizations promoted the application of Christian principles to those in

---

* When referring to the early Progressive movement, I capitalize *Progressive*. I do not capitalize modern progressivism.

need. Each of these influential private enterprises was designed to lend people a hand in different areas of life, not a handout. They mirrored the work of the earliest Christians, in the first-century church:

> All the believers were one in heart and mind. No one claimed that any of their possessions was their own, but they shared everything they had. With great power the apostles continued to testify to the resurrection of the Lord Jesus. And God's grace was so powerfully at work in them all that there were no needy persons among them. For from time to time those who owned land or houses sold them, brought the money from the sales and put it at the apostles' feet, and it was distributed to anyone who had need. (Acts 4:32–35)

Today's progressivism has deviated drastically from these Christian-oriented roots.

HOW EVENTS LED TO THE MODERN FAR-LEFT PROGRESSIVE MOVEMENT

In chapter 1, I summarized how the Progressive worldview evolved and advanced through pivotal court cases, but social factors also played a role in the movement's growth. The Industrial Revolution, with its advancements in technology, sparked a need for reforms in areas like child labor and working hours. During this period, women's suffrage also gained more traction. To address some of the issues that America's founders could not have anticipated, politicians began calling for the federal government to play a greater role.

Prior to the Civil War, states operated autonomously. But in order to save the Union, President Lincoln exercised his power as commander-in-chief to take unilateral action such as suspending the writ of habeas corpus.* While done in an extreme war time situation, this

---

* *Habeas corpus* is a Latin term meaning "you shall have the body." It describes the legal principle that a person cannot be unlawfully imprisoned. Tyrannical governments often arrest and imprison those who oppose them without going before a judge to confirm the lawfulness of the detention. These actions would be a violation of habeas corpus. Lincoln suspended this protection during the Civil War to detain those disloyal to the Union.

action created a precedent: the federal government can intervene to address a legitimate crisis. For those insisting the federal government play a greater role in addressing social issues, all they needed was a leader who would embrace this new precedent. They needed someone who would exercise federal control beyond the established boundaries of presidential authority during *non*-wartime conditions. Republican Theodore Roosevelt proved to be that man when he became president after the assassination of President William McKinley in 1901.

President Roosevelt was a take-charge person who believed in the original blueprint for America. He also perceived a unique opportunity for the federal government to address injustices created by the abuses of power in business and industry, but how could this expansion in peacetime be justified?

In 1902, a coal miners' strike threatened the nation with a coal shortage that would not only impact commerce but would also deprive many people of heat in the winter. Roosevelt took advantage of the impasse by threatening to dispatch federal troops to bring coal operations back to normal if "big coal" would not do it themselves. This intervention led to an agreement that averted the strike and increased miners' pay while reducing their hours.

Roosevelt's actions set a precedent for an expanded role of the executive branch. He was motivated by several important factors: big business's inordinate power, underpaid workers, and the potential for Americans to be cold because business owners refused to negotiate with their workers. Success with the coal strike fueled Roosevelt's desire to further take on big business in order to help the common man. This led to his iconic "Square Deal" and the beginning of the federal government's expanded role. This program focused on several areas like consumer protection, control of corporations (trust busting), and conservation (establishment of national parks). These programs had many positive effects across America, making it hard to argue with the idea of increased presidential authority.

As a result of Roosevelt's success, presidential interventions in situations like the coal miners' strike evolved from rare to commonplace.

Increased government oversight showed up in 1906 with the Hepburn Bill (establishing railroad rates), the Meat Inspection Act, and the Pure Food and Drug Act. Originally, the objective was to protect the public, but questions arose concerning how much authority the federal government should have to address moral issues and force the citizenry to do the right thing. Would the federal officials whom the citizens elected stay true to the founding American covenant?

Roosevelt's actions paved the way for his successors to expand the power of the presidency well beyond the boundaries the founders intended. Woodrow Wilson continued the federal government's expansion, and what began as accountability to reign in big business evolved into a stark new reality for America. In some cases, federalized social reform could expand liberty and justice to all; in other cases, it would take it away. In 1920, the Nineteenth Amendment gave women the right to vote, increasing their liberty to take part in America's governance. That same year, liberty was restricted with Prohibition, a nationwide ban on the production, importation, transportation, and sale of alcoholic beverages. This federal overreach was so extreme that the policy lasted only thirteen years. However, this new Progressive operational vision was still widely accepted, and the office of the president continued to evolve. Instead of serving citizens just as the overseer of the faithful execution of the law, the president became the CEO of the country, with a similar approach to exercising power.

Not everyone embraced this new approach. After Wilson, Presidents Coolidge and Hoover showed lackluster enthusiasm for expanding the role of government. But when President Franklin D. Roosevelt moved into the White House under the backdrop of the Great Depression, he brought the promise of the "New Deal." President Roosevelt advanced this federalized governing vision by taking advantage of the economic and social impacts of the Great Depression.* His expansions still echo in mandates like minimum wage, farm subsidies, and Social Security. Even more sweeping was his claim that Americans needed an "economic

---

* One of the strategies modern progressives use to effect change is to take advantage of crises. Their reasoning is that people will be much more open to embrace change, and even to compromise their values or give up their liberty, to neutralize a threat they perceive to be imminent.

Bill of Rights," in which he proposed that the government was responsible to provide the following:

- employment with a living wage
- housing
- medical care
- food, clothing, and leisure
- education
- freedom from unfair competition and monopolies

FDR's economic Bill of Rights codified an emerging progressive vision: people could and should expect the federal government to guarantee their standard of living. In so doing, he became a hero of the Progressive movement.

Although in numerous speeches FDR recognized the importance of Christianity in Western civilization, his appointments to the Supreme Court enabled greater progress toward the secular Progressive vision for America. His court presided over the 1947 case of *Everson v. Board of Education*, the decision that claimed a constitutional principle of "separation of church and state."* This decision led to school prayer (1962) and Bible readings (1963) being declared unconstitutional. After more than 300 years of the Judeo-Christian God being recognized in the public square in the New World, it became illegal to recognize him in publicly funded schools, buildings, and institutions. As a result, references to the Bible, including plaques and monuments of the Ten Commandments, have slowly been removed in the name of defending the Constitution. The impact has been subtle but profound.

These alterations to American culture were not accomplished by amending our founding covenant or the Constitution with the approval of the people. It was accomplished by a handful of jurists who chipped away at the foundational principles of America's founding covenant through court rulings in which they redefined constitutional interpretation. The founders built the American standard for all

* See Appendix for further explanation of "separation of church and state."

lawmaking on the foundation of "the Laws of Nature and of Nature's God." Rather than teaching the biblical origins of the American founding and acknowledging God in school prayer, as was the practice for centuries, these judges declared these activities as unconstitutional—a violation of separation of church and state. As a result of these changes, Far-Left modern progressives have marginalized Christian dissent and are actively working to transform all areas of society in order to realize their utopian, godless vision for America.

COMPARING PROGRESSIVISM TO THE MORAL LAW

I have made the claim throughout this book that the moral law is foundational to biblical principles of governing (and evangelism) and was the catalyst for the American founding. While many individuals viewing themselves as progressive (in one or multiple aspects)* embrace elements of the moral law, the Far-Left progressive movement mostly rejects the notion of an objective, universal moral standard. In fact, the movement takes a political position counter to every one of the Ten Commandments as seen in Table 8.1. While those holding the Judeo-Christian and more moderate progressive worldview disagree on many points, they can live at peace with one another. But the Far-Left progressives are not content respecting individual liberty. Their aim is to fundamentally transform America by any means possible.

Table 8.1

Commandment	Judeo-Christian Position (Biblical)	Far-Left Position (Secular)
Have no other gods.	Trust exclusively in the Judeo-Christian God.	Reject the idea of a single, all-powerful God and substitute other things as supreme.
Worship no graven image.	Worship God only and do not distort who he is.	Substitute idols (money, education, sports, power, science, technology, etc.), in place of God.

---

* An example: Christians often say they are fiscally conservative but more progressive on social issues.

Commandment	Judeo-Christian Position (Biblical)	Far-Left Position (Secular)
Do not take the Lord's name in vain.	Use God's name in ways that honor him.	Profanity or vulgarity is acceptable. Pay little regard to the offense to God and Christians.
Keep the Sabbath holy.	Set aside time to rest and meditate on the goodness of God.	Treat Sunday like any other day.
Honor mother and father.	Respect and obey your parents and the traditional family unit.	Dilute the role of mother and father by accepting no-fault divorce (uncoupling), and alternative lifestyles. Claim masculinity is toxic and support gender reassignment.
Do not murder.	Respect all human life. Protect the innocent (especially the unborn), who cannot defend themselves.	Protect abortion on demand up to and after the moment of birth (partial birth abortion or other full-term abortive procedures). Elevate importance of animal life to be equal to human life.
Do not commit adultery.	Respect God's design for marriage between a man and woman and the family unit as the critical building block of a civil society. Seek to avoid divorce.	Promote sexual promiscuity, sex between unmarried people, same-sex unions, and redefinition of the family unit.
Do not steal.	Do not take what belongs to others.	Legalize through the tax code the redistribution from the "haves" to the "have nots." View this as necessary to achieve equality of means and "social justice."
Do not lie.	Be honest in all situations and in all dealings.	Advocate deception and lying if it is required to advance an agenda ("ends justify the means") or to implement critical programs and policies (e.g., universal health insurance as a human right).
Do not covet.	Be content with what you have instead of always comparing yourself to others.	Feed covetous attitudes by telling the poor that they deserve what the rich have or that the rich stole from the poor. Pit the classes against each other to foment anger and the demand for social and economic equality.

The Far Left has been successful in removing the moral law from the public square. Stripped of the moral law, American culture is vulnerable to a competing secular worldview that contradicts nearly every major aspect of the moral law. When contrasting the Judeo-Christian worldview with that of the progressive Far-Left ideology, the differences between these two worldviews becomes clear. For example, the 2020 Democratic Party platform illustrates the conflict with the Ten Commandments on numerous points. By far, the most troublesome position is for abortion on demand through late-term pregnancies, including partial-birth abortion, which conflicts with the command "Do not murder." The 2020 platform document affirms that "every woman should be able to access high-quality reproductive health-care services, including safe and legal abortion."[149] We know from their actions and statements that this includes late term and partial birth abortions, and there is no intent to moderate even the most extreme position.[150]

Progressives have a range of beliefs about God, but they generally claim the following with regard to governing:

- God is not relevant and may not even exist.
- Mankind can live and thrive without God.
- Rights come from the state, not from God's moral law.
- Traditional morality is outdated and leads to intolerance in an evolving culture.
- It is possible to improve the human condition through government administration of the economy, as opposed to God enabling individuals through personal responsibility.

While some progressives assert belief in God—even embracing the faith of a Christian denomination—the stark differences make the Judeo-Christian and progressive worldviews mutually exclusive. This is because it is not possible for someone to worship God at church and ban him from the framework of governing in the public square. Christians understand they may live under the jurisdiction of a leader who may not be a Christian. But they also understand the moral law is always in force and should be followed. In fact, recognizing the moral law as God's standard is central to becoming a Christian. It is at work, informing a Christian's personal conduct and puts boundaries on civil leaders who attempt to pass immoral laws. The progressive worldview does not hold the moral law with the same regard. This allows their policies to be unconstrained by any moral framework and can go in any direction that popular opinion, or those in charge, may take it.

With the rejection of moral law, Far-Left progressives have basically rejected the God of the Bible. This leads to a difference in worldviews that is the most concerning—that in a secular state, citizens are ultimately at the mercy of the state instead of the mercy of God. It is the state (i.e., the ruling class) that determines legitimate rights and laws, which means whoever holds political power gets to determine right and wrong. In the Judeo-Christian worldview, which informed the American founding, all citizens—and all mankind—are accountable to and at the mercy of God who gave us the moral law.

Since God does not change (James 1:17), we know his moral law does not change. The idea of a fixed legal standard to which we all subscribe should bring great comfort to citizens. In a nation where the state decides what is legal, no one is safe. The two views are contrasted below:[151]

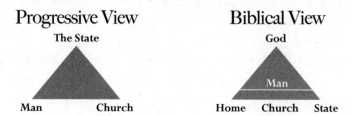

The practical effect of these different worldviews was made clear during COVID-19 pandemic-related closures. From a progressive worldview, it made perfect sense that abortion clinics and casinos were essential, and yet the church, where people simply gather to sing and pray, would not be essential. From a biblical worldview, it is obvious that our devotion to God is *the* most important thing, and so, church services would be the last thing to cancel.

History shows it is just a matter of time until someone or some group takes charge and uses political power to enslave or persecute those who oppose them. This is why it is so important to keep God and his moral law preeminent in civil government. Furthermore, the

Bible clearly warns us of the negative effects of having a single person in charge. In 1 Samuel, we see God's warning after the Israelites asked for a king so they could be like neighboring nations:

> Samuel told all the words of the LORD to the people who were asking him for a king. He said, "This is what the king who will reign over you will claim as his rights: He will take your sons and make them serve with his chariots and horses, and they will run in front of his chariots. Some he will assign to be commanders of thousands and commanders of fifties, and others to plow his ground and reap his harvest, and still others to make weapons of war and equipment for his chariots. He will take your daughters to be perfumers and cooks and bakers. He will take the best of your fields and vineyards and olive groves and give them to his attendants. He will take a tenth of your grain and of your vintage and give it to his officials and attendants. Your male and female servants and the best of your cattle and donkeys he will take for his own use. He will take a tenth of your flocks, and you yourselves will become his slaves. When that day comes, you will cry out for relief from the king you have chosen, but the LORD will not answer you in that day." (1 Sam. 8:10–18)

America has experienced a modern-day version of what Samuel warned against. Through his word, God told us that if we give power to a person or handful of unelected people not accountable to anyone, they will slowly take away our civil liberties. This is especially true when those leaders do not believe in the "Laws of Nature and of Nature's God."

REDEFINING WORDS TO PURSUE DIFFERENT POLICIES

This fundamental difference in worldviews has led Far-Left progressives to pursue very different policies from what America embraced for its first 200 years. In the process, these progressives began to redefine common terms, the meanings of which are critical to understanding

America's founding principles. When progressives use these terms in political discourse, many Americans assume they are affirming traditional American values. However, Far-Left progressives mean something very different, often concealing their true intentions (see Table 8.2). This redefining of words leads to further confusion as voters try to discern what these Far-Left progressives honestly believe and intend to do if given political power.

Table 8.2

Topic	Biblical principles incorporated in the American founding documents	Progressive evolving principles informing the transformation they seek for America
Liberty	• Freedom to have and express opinions • Freedom from coercion • Christians seek tolerance and forgiveness to prevent generational bitterness	• Freedom of speech and opinion should be restricted to foster tolerance and ensure no minority is offended • Views not in line with those in power may be canceled to prevent intolerant views from being expressed
Law	• God's moral law is timeless • Laws incongruent with the moral law are invalid.	• Laws evolve with society • There is no timeless, objective standard to use to evaluate a proposed law
Rights	• Come from God • Are universal • Cannot be revoked • Follow from the moral law	• Come from government • Evolving and can be extended or restricted to address inequality
Justice	• Applies to every citizen • Individuals are responsible for their own behavior • Punishment should match the level of the crime	• Use the legal system as a lever for change rather than protecting individual rights • Social justice is required to right past wrongs • Apply the intersectionality principle to establish victim classes who deserve greater measures of restitution*

* The intersectionality principle is that there are different dimensions of discrimination (racism, sexism, classism, etc.), and a person can experience a combination (intersection) to create greater degrees of discrimination. This idea opens the door to the imposition of any penalty or settlement progressive judges decide is proper for a combination of injustices that occurred in the past.

Along with redefining the meaning of key words central to the American founding, Far-Left progressives have begun reshaping public policy to match the direction they feel society is evolving. They have started reshaping everything from the purpose of civil government down to how we should educate our children. When advancing these positions in the public square, they often use the keywords above that make them sound like they are in sync with traditional American values, but their track record clearly shows this is not the case (see Table 8.3).

Table 8.3

Policy	Biblical Worldview	Far-Left Progressive Worldview
Purpose of government	• Create a free and orderly society • Keep evil in check • Protect religious liberty to allow everyone to pursue happiness	• Lead society mores as the state evolves, based on the vision of the political elite • Control the means of production as the political class thinks best
Mission of government	• Protect individual liberties and rights • Secure justice for all citizens • Develop laws harmonious with God's moral law • Provide for the public defense to promote national sovereignty	• Seek economic and social justice through policies that redistribute property • Identify and grant new rights • Seek harmony and jurisdictional alignment with other nations of the world (globalism)
Responsibility of leaders	• See public service as a personal ministry and way of serving God • Honor God by governing according to his moral law • Help citizens live moral and ethical lives	• Address social, economic (wage), and property (equal outcomes) inequality • Pass laws to address inequities proportional to victim class intersectionality

Policy	Biblical Worldview	Far-Left Progressive Worldview
National sovereignty	• Have a right to exist • Defend borders • Promote liberty and justice for all • Are blessed when obedient • Are judged when they stray	• Should yield to a common global vision for governing • Promote open borders as a means to achieve global equality • Perceive America as an illegitimate country that has bullied and pillaged other nations • Believe this must be corrected through any means possible
Economy	• Free enterprise under liberty and justice for all • Encourages citizens to identify, cultivate, and apply their talents to provide for themselves and family • Individuals with a strong work ethic can supply goods and services that meet consumer needs and create wealth at the same time	• Believe central planners should control the economy through mandates • Prevent wage and property inequality • Federal regulations enforce their utopian vision of economic equality • Believe wealth is fixed and must be redistributed to achieve equality
Wealth and property	• Accumulated through hard work and perseverance • Each individual has the right to accumulate property and manage it as he or she sees fit	• Perceive American wealth as achieved by greed and bullying • Seek to redistribute wealth to those without, who claim to have been victimized • Redistribution at government leaders' discretion
Education	• "The fear of the Lord is the beginning of knowledge" (Prov. 1:7) • Bible is source of Christian worldview • Bible contains the blueprint for law and order in a society • Hard sciences reveal God as the creator, and studying creation is studying God's handiwork • A biblical moral compass improves the human condition • Everyone is born with different talents and gifts, which are cultivated through education	• Reject the Bible as providing the key context for learning • Embrace Darwinian evolution with no moral absolutes • Believe the goal is equal outcomes where students are tested on facts and compliance to the Far-Left progressive worldview • Focus on boosting test scores instead of recognizing the different and unique ways students learn and tailoring education accordingly

Given the differences in the meaning of words and policies, Far-Left progressives and conservative Americans are working out of a different dictionary. With these differences in the definitions of common words and the concepts behind them, it is easy to see how their discussions often result in confusion, contention, and hostility. But during much of the twentieth century, progressive candidates were very careful when articulating their policy positions. Their soft-pedaling convinced compassionate Americans to believe that progressives espoused traditional American values.

THE FAR-LEFT PROGRESSIVE IMPACT

Far-Left progressives are working to transform America into a godless state where the ruling elite determines legitimate rights and cancels those who disagree. Their argument is that America was founded illegitimately on racism and built on stolen land. Their solution is for individuals to give up their liberties and turn power over to them. This is their solution because they believe having the elite dictate politically correct thought and distribute property across the citizenry is a far more equitable governing vision. In the end, they advocate for state control instead of individual freedom.

To understand the impact of fully embracing progressivism here in America, we simply need to look at other nations that have headed down this same path. Specifically, we want to look at nations that have turned away from God and the notion of individual rights and instead have a political class ruling over the citizenry. The transition typically starts as socialism but ends up progressing to communism or some other form of totalitarian government.

The twentieth century provides a number of examples to learn from, including Russia, Germany, China, Cuba, and Venezuela. In each case, we see how oppression led to a revolution, which led to an authoritarian regime that used force to gain and maintain power. All these countries abandoned God and religion as the unifying glue that fostered a free and prosperous society—and all of them have had disastrous results.

Soviet Union—The Russian revolution started in 1917, with the Bolsheviks coming to power in 1923. The state-controlled economy crumbled, and between starvation and executions, it is estimated that 40–70 million people were killed.[152]

Nazi Germany—The Nazis also put socialism into practice in the years leading up to WWII. Although the German government did not own the means of production (as a communist state would have), it controlled who did. Hitler's Nazis murdered between 11 and 20 million people.

China—The civil war started in 1946 and ended in 1949, resulting in the formation of the People's Republic of China. As with Russia, China's economic central planners caused a food shortage that killed up to half the population in some villages. In the 1960s, more than 65 million people were murdered under Communist leader Mao Zedong alone.*

Cuba—Fidel Castro came to power in 1959, promising socialism would lead to widespread equality and prosperity. However, Cuba followed the same predictable course once he gained power. Estimates of Cuban Communism's victims range from 11,000 to 110,000 souls.†

Venezuela—Hugo Chavez came into power in 1999 and implemented the "widespread nationalization of private industry, currency and price controls, and the fiscally irresponsible expansion of welfare programs."[153] These actions destroyed production due to the government's inability to manage complex businesses and the incentive to hire employees to secure political support. "Food production fell 75 percent," and inflation increased due

---

* Lee Edwards, "The Legacy of Mao Zedong Is Mass Murder," The Heritage Foundation, February 2, 2010, https://www.heritage.org/asia/commentary/the-legacy-mao-zedong-mass-murder.

† Mary Anastasia O'Grady "Counting Castro's Victims," The Wall Street Journal, December 30, 2005, https://www.wsj.com/articles/SB113590852154334404

to printing more currency to support growing welfare.[154] As a result, "Venezuela went from being one of the wealthiest countries in South America—one rich in natural resources—to a country where people are literally fighting for scraps of food."[155]

We do not have to wonder if these same results will happen in America if we follow the socialistic path that has already been tried elsewhere and remains in effect in many countries today.

The common thread behind every nation that has brutalized their citizenry is that they turned their back on God. This was something Aleksandr Solzhenitsyn, a Russian dissident, was well aware of. In a 1983 speech he warned:

> I have spent well-nigh 50 years working on the history of our revolution; in the process I have read hundreds of books, collected hundreds of personal testimonies, and have already contributed eight volumes of my own toward the effort of clearing away the rubble left by that upheaval. But if I were asked today to formulate as concisely as possible the main cause of the ruinous revolution that swallowed up some 60 million of our people, I could not put it more accurately than to repeat: "Men have forgotten God; that's why all this has happened."[156]

His own experience led Solzhenitsyn to single out the fundamental cause of Soviet Communism and the misery that followed: marginalizing God from the governing process. When this happens, the moral law is discarded. History warns that secularized attempts at governing lead to an extreme, communist left or fascist right. The best possible position on the political spectrum is the common-sense center—the moral center.

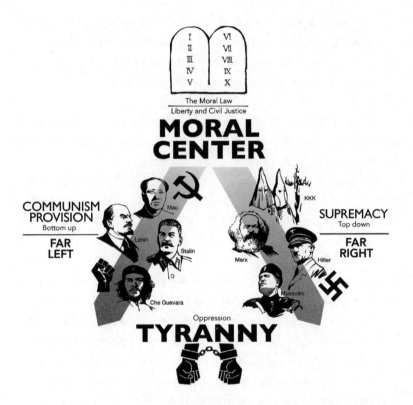

This moral center is the original American vision captured in our national covenant. We have never totally achieved this timeless vision, but it continues to be the "north star" we strive for. To achieve the moral center requires a majority of society to take responsibility for themselves, their families, and their communities. They are to seek to live under the standard of liberty and justice as individuals and members of their community in keeping with our national covenant. This call to the moral center is what John Adams meant when he said "Our Constitution was made only for a moral and religious people. It is wholly inadequate to the government of any other."[157]

Progressives, on the other hand, tend not to strive toward the moral center. They are working toward a secular America that limits God-given liberties to establish their own preconceived notions of morality and justice. As Adams indicated, the Constitution was not meant for a nation run by progressives rejecting our moral center, especially those who are Far-Left and set God aside. Yet more and more, that seems to be the direction our nation is going.

THE FAR-LEFT PROGRESSIVE LONG-TERM GAME PLAN

Unlike contemporary progressives, the first Progressives faced stiffer headwinds in getting Americans to reject their "freedom-based" governing blueprint. To make significant progress, they needed a strategy to challenge America's founding covenant. Over the last century, progressives coalesced around the following strategies in their quest to transform America:

1. Recast the founders and their intentions with the American founding.
2. Move away from an originalist interpretation of the founding documents, which limits the scope of the federal government and states that rights come from God.
3. Use the courts to re-interpret and remove key founding principles.
4. Rebrand progressive policies to distract from their intentions.
5. Embrace dirty politics to neutralize or remove political opponents.

STRATEGY #1 – RECAST THE FOUNDERS AND THEIR INTENTIONS

Progressives realized it would be difficult to shift from the founding vision and structure for governing when respect for the founders was so strong. For the first two centuries, Americans revered the sacrifice of the founders, given they pledged their lives, fortunes, and sacred honor to establish America. The founders did not declare independence for a better life or to keep their property. "They had everything to lose.... Of the fifty-six [signers of the Declaration of Independence], few were long to survive. Five were captured by the British and tortured before they died; twelve had their homes from Rhode Island to Charleston sacked, looted, occupied by the enemy, or burned; two lost their sons in the army; one had two sons captured; nine of the fifty-six died in the war."[158] Because of the founders' sacrifice, many Americans had a love for the founding generation that endured for many years.

The only way to undercut this patriotic love for the founding generation was to discredit their motives or question their values. To do this, progressives rewrote the founding narrative. History was recast to portray America's founders as slave-holding bigots who were deists—not Christians. According to this new narrative, the founders' greed drove them to revolt to avoid paying higher taxes. The progressives' aim was to delegitimize the claim that America was a unique and great nation with a superior vision for governing.

Over the last fifty years, progressives altered public school curriculum, college instruction, and began incorporating the new narrative into television and film. Today, alterations from the Far Left have been accepted as an unchallenged narrative. The new curriculum ignores the overwhelming body of evidence that refutes it. Table 8.4 lists some of the more common assertions about the founders, many of which have been addressed in earlier chapters.

Table 8.4

Far-Left Progressive Claim	Rebuttal
The Europeans should have never come to colonize the New World and steal lands from the indigenous peoples.	If the official position of the colonizing Europeans was to pillage and eradicate the indigenous population, then this claim would be valid. But that was not the intent of many of the settlers. Importantly, the official position of many of the colonial leaders, including the Continental and US Congress, was that no lands could be taken from the Native Americans without negotiation (Northwest Ordinance of 1787, 1789). Additionally, Matthew 28 commands Christians to go throughout all the earth and share the gospel message. For believers not to have come would have been to deny their faith. There are accounts of evangelizing the Native Americans, with many converting to Christianity, including Pocahontas.
The founders were deists, not orthodox Christians.	From the Declaration itself, and many examples from speeches and private correspondence, it is clear they believed in a God who would come to their aid and frequently acknowledged his hand in helping them secure independence.

Jefferson rejected the established church and wrote his own Bible.	Jefferson completed several studies summarizing the moral philosophy of Jesus as a reference for evangelizing the Kaskaskia Indians (1804, 1819). He never called it a Bible.[159] This reference originated later, after his manuscript was acquired by the National Museum in 1895 from his grandson. Beginning in 1904 up until the 1950s, a copy was given to new members in Congress. Over time, it became known as the "Jefferson Bible," but it was nothing more than his attempt to arrive at a biblical answer to a question about the philosophy taught by Jesus (much like this book addresses questions of civil government but is not the "Burrell Bible").
America was not founded as a Christian nation.	The full body of evidence shows Christian principles informed the founding, and that the founders, and generations that followed, viewed America as a Christian nation. (More explanation in the Appendix.)
The founders intended for a separation of church and state.	They were against creating a national Christian church based on one sect but felt the state should never control the church. They believed Christian principles were critical for good government, not that they should be prohibited from influencing civil government. This is explained further in chapter 10.
America's founding was fundamentally flawed and needs to be transformed.	The vision for governing in the Declaration, the protection of inalienable rights of Life, Liberty, and the Pursuit of Happiness, is the most benevolent model for civil government in the modern era. Where applied faithfully, it has produced the greatest level of human flourishing and supported the greatest improvement of the human condition ever.
The intent of the phrase "pursuit of happiness" meant to pursue temporal pleasure or material things.	Explained in chapter 7. In that era this phrase was coupled with the idea that individuals should be able to pursue God as their conscience dictated.
The founders believed slaves were worth only three-fifths of a person.	The founders' objective was to limit the legislative power of the South by apportioning fewer representatives to slaves. This recognized them as people but limited the South's ability to protect slavery in the new federal congress. It also provided an incentive to slave states to abolish slavery, as they would immediately gain more power in the federal government. Frederick Douglass supported this view.
America was built on systemic racism (the "1619 Project").	While America inherited slavery as part of British rule, the Northern colonies actively rejected it. While the Southern colonies accepted it (starting in Jamestown in 1619), significant and consistent effort was made to end the practice during the founding era. The vision captured in the Declaration clearly excluded slavery, but providing full civil rights was consistently hampered by Democratic opposition in the South, which led up to the Civil War and to the modern era.

This Far-Left progressive strategy took clear aim at the Christian community, asserting "separation of church and state" meant they had no business imposing Christian principles in the public arena.* By convincing Christians of this new narrative, Far-Left progressives neutralized much of their political opposition.

* More on "separation of church and state" in chapter 10 and in the Appendix.

Progressive ideology has also infiltrated many churches. Many of today's pastors affirm this altered narrative and are caught up in the social justice movement, which further discredits the faith and motives of our founders. Sincere Christians are then sidelined, because they conclude that active public service is not as important as evangelism or service-oriented ministry, since that is all most pastors talk about. Into this vacuum Far-Left activists eagerly step, with little opposition.

Far-Left progressives employ several approaches to shift the narrative of the American founding (Table 8.5). One such approach is deconstructionism, which is a steady constant flow of negative criticisms about aspects of the founding. There is also minimalism, which simplifies complex issues to short catch phrases that do not accurately represent a particular situation. For instance, saying "they maintained slavery" does not come close to describing the combined efforts of many people trying to find a way to abolish or limit slavery during the founding era.* Americans need to learn to spot these techniques and do their own research to come to a more balanced view on contentious issues.[160]

Table 8.5[161]

Historical Academic Approach	Description (*Example*)
Deconstructionism	Steady flow of negative criticism to demean the founding (*They were deists, not genuine Christians, they rebelled to protect slavery, they were racists.*)
Minimalism	Reduces complex situations to one-line characterizations; oversimplifying (*They maintained slavery, thought slaves were three-fifths of a person.*)
Academic Collectivism	Relies on opinions or claims of others to discern the truth instead of original documents and context (*Secular academia has concluded the founders were racists and separated to protect their property, namely their slaves.*)
Modernism	Examines how people might have lived based on today's values instead of using the context of their times and recognizing the barriers preventing certain changes (*They should have abolished slavery immediately.*)
Poststructuralism	Rejects absolutes (*moral law*) and argues that each person must judge for him- or herself how to interpret events (*We must accept other people living out their truth, having concluded the founders were racists and America is systemically racist.*)

* More on actions to abolish slavery in the Appendix.

STRATEGY #2 – MOVE AWAY FROM AN ORIGINALIST INTERPRETATION OF FOUNDING DOCUMENTS

Darwin's *On the Origin of the Species* (1859) suggested humans evolved over time instead of being created by God, winning an early following with the academic elite of his day. Evolution offered a scientific alternative to the biblical account of God's creation. Embracing Darwin's theory opened the door to peripheral arguments, including how to think about the law. If humans evolved over millions of years, then rights are not natural, unalienable, timeless, or God-given. Instead, rights evolve as society does. Therefore, the law and government must also evolve along with people's rights. As discussed in chapter 1, the theory of evolution provided the ideological catalyst to refute natural rights theory and replace it with legal realism. Armed with this new approach, judges adjusted their focal point: they looked forward to where an evolving society was headed rather than looking to the historical documents and legal doctrines of the past. They abandoned the view that the moral law was the ultimate arbiter of justice. A new authoritative voice evolved: the "living Constitution." Judges embracing this evolutionist view began transforming rights through judicial rulings.

This evolutionary view also allowed progressives to recast our national covenant, the Declaration of Independence, to an interesting but obsolete document—written in an era when people thought differently. President Woodrow Wilson offered this explanation for why the Declaration of Independence was no longer relevant for an America in the middle of the Industrial Revolution: "The old political formulas do not fit the present problems; they read now like documents taken out of a forgotten age. The older cries sound as if they belonged to a past age which men have almost forgotten."[162] Wilson and later proponents have successfully recast the Declaration of Independence from a timeless exposition of biblical truths informing our national covenant to a malleable charter that can be edited to suit changing opinions about our rights and from where they originate.*

---

* Those who hold to the original belief that rights come from God are now labeled as part of the

Strategy #3 – Use the Courts to Re-Interpret and Remove Key Founding Principles

The original intent of the Supreme Court was to determine if laws violated the moral law and the specific parameters of the Constitution. The idea of a living Constitution laid the groundwork for an evolving interpretation and application. Just as societal evolution happens in steps, judges began issuing rulings that created precedents that would allow society to evolve in any direction. This empowered the courts to change our founding principles through a series of rulings. As cited earlier, the 1947 *Everson v. Board of Education* case ruled that the church must be separate from the state, laying the groundwork to prohibit school prayer in 1962 and Bible readings in school in 1963. These and other rulings evolved into declaring any presentation of the Ten Commandments on public property unconstitutional. Overnight, moral education in public schools was deemed harmful and contrary to the Constitution. This sea change contradicts the advice of George Washington, who, in his farewell address, warned of the importance of religion and morality for just government:

> Of all the dispositions and habits which lead to political prosperity, religion and morality are indispensable supports. In vain would that man claim the tribute of patriotism who should labor to subvert these great pillars of human happiness—these firmest props of the duties of men and citizens. The mere politician, equally with the pious man, ought to respect and to cherish them. A volume could not trace all their connections with private and public felicity. Let it simply be asked, Where is the security for property, for reputation, for life, if the sense of religious obligation desert the oaths which are the instruments of investigation in courts of justice? And let us with caution indulge the supposition that morality can be maintained without religion. Whatever may be conceded to

---

extreme Right. In 2008, President Barack Obama cited this group that is frustrated with how America has evolved as "clinging to their guns or religion." (Barack Obama, "Obama: 'They Cling to Guns or Religion,'" *Christianity Today*, April 13, 2008, christianitytoday.com/news/2008/april/obama-they-cling-to-guns-or-religion.html.)

the influence of refined education on minds of peculiar structure, reason and experience both forbid us to expect that national morality can prevail in exclusion of religious principle.

It is substantially true that virtue or morality is a necessary spring of popular government. The rule indeed extends with more or less force to every species of free government. Who that is a sincere friend to it can look with indifference upon attempts to shake the foundation of the fabric?[163]

Washington perceived religion and morality as underpinnings of a just government, but the Supreme Court removed America's moral foundation. With no moral law as an objective standard, judicial activism can advance in any direction. In recent years, SCOTUS chipped away at the Defense of Marriage Act (DOMA) in the 2013 *United States v. Windsor* case. This paved the way for the 2015 *Obergefell v. Hodges* case that declared same-sex marriage a constitutional right.* This redefinition of morality has been accomplished by a handful of jurists whose progressive ideology led them to believe they were acting in the best interests of the evolving society. Thomas Jefferson confronted this threat in a letter to William Jarvis, writing on September 28, 1820, "You seem … [to] consider the judges as the ultimate arbiters of all constitutional questions; a very dangerous doctrine indeed, and one which would place us under the despotism of an oligarchy."

Jefferson's prophecy seems to be coming true in the modern era. When SCOTUS strikes down a statute, in whole or in part, it is widely accepted that the inverse becomes law. In other words, SCOTUS has assumed the authority to create laws, not simply interpret them. The *Obergefell* ruling is an example of this. Far-Left progressives immediately asserted that same-sex unions met the definition of marriage, and same-sex marriage became the law of the land. No legislation had been passed, rather, just a Supreme Court ruling advanced by five justices. This is the oligarchy Jefferson warned of. Rather than the court

---

* The majority on the Supreme Court cited the Due Process and Equal Protection clauses from the Fourteenth Amendment. This amendment was passed to ensure the rights of freed blacks but has become a catalyst for progressive change well beyond its original intention.

evaluating the laws passed by Congress and comparing the legislation to the Constitution, previous approved statutes, and the moral law, the court has seized power to determine what is lawful. This power circumvents the legislative branch altogether, which is exactly what Jefferson was concerned about.

In a system built on checks and balances, there is no check when the courts, especially the Supreme Court, have arrogated to themselves such authority. The proliferation of the secular mindset has granted SCOTUS a substantive impact on advancing the Far-Left progressive ideology through judicial activism. This is why, in 2021, progressives felt so threatened with the conservative-leaning Supreme Court, given that the Trump administration appointed three originalists. They talked openly about adding more justices, clearly their attempt to regain a majority to prevent rulings that would slow or reverse their agenda. [164]

STRATEGY #4 – REBRAND POLICIES TO DISTRACT FROM THEIR TRUE INTENTIONS

Earlier we talked about how progressives redefine words and policy. They have been very effective in reframing hot-button issues by rephrasing positions with words that have a traditional, reasonable, or sympathetic ring to them. Unfortunately, as with any good long-term marketing campaign, this strategy works. Compassionate people sometimes fail to see this tactic and are manipulated. Below is a short list of current Far-Left progressive wording, often used on the campaign trail to mask true intentions.

Table 8.6

Traditional Wording	Far-Left Progressive Rebranding
Abortion	Reproductive rights, women's reproductive health care
Pro-Life	Anti-Abortion
Taxes	Investments
National debt	Paying-for problem

Gun control, gun seizure from law-abiding Americans	Common sense gun safety
Equal opportunity, equal justice under the law	Pursuit of equal outcomes, wealth redistribution*
Illegal aliens	Economic refugees
Granting amnesty to those who have come to America illegally	Sanctuary cities where those who violated immigration laws will not be prosecuted
Laws ensuring free and fair elections	Voter suppression laws
Government-run health care	Health care is a basic human right. Universal health care
Embracing moral and ethical principles	Needing to recognize individual bias to be more inclusive of those living out their own truth
Intolerant: not respecting people's right to hold and express views others disagree with	Intolerant: not endorsing what a person declares to be true of himself or herself

Far-Left progressives have no problem attempting to rebrand policies they wish to pursue, even if it means deceiving the public from their true intentions. Many of them earnestly believe this approach is justified in order to achieve their ends, which they believe serve a greater good. History shows, however, that socialism fails wherever it is tried. Sadly, many Christians are swayed by this approach and end up supporting policies at odds with their faith. Christians need to understand this strategy and learn to recognize when they are not being told the truth.

---

* Ironically, socialism was tried early in the Plymouth settlement. Pilgrim Governor William Bradford described the attempt in his book *Of Plymouth Plantation*, stating the sharing of "all profits & benefits ... in [the] common stock," regardless of how hard each individual worked was a failure. The failure of that experiment of communal service, which was tried for several years by good and honest men, proves the emptiness of the theory of Plato and other ancients—that the taking away of private property and the possession of it in community by a commonwealth would lead to happiness and flourishing; as if they were wiser than God.... "So, every family was assigned a parcel of land, according to the proportion of their number.... This was very successful.... It made all hands very industrious ... and gave far better satisfaction." (Verna M. Hall, *The Christian History of the Constitution of the United States of America* [Chesapeake, VA: Foundation for American Christian Education, 2006], 212, 213.)

STRATEGY #5 – EMBRACE PARTISAN (DIRTY) POLITICS TO DEFEAT POLITICAL OPPONENTS

One of the reasons many Christians have disengaged from politics is the division and deception that swirls around it. Who is to blame for this? Many in the church assert both sides are complicit, even those who are fighting to protect our founding principles. Certainly, there are people on both sides of the spectrum who do not conduct themselves above reproach. But the Far-Left progressives' consistent attempt to erode our founding principles is the root cause of our country's political dissention. Far-Left activists use dirty politics to pull America away from our founding covenant. It is a Marxist approach to drive the political change they seek.

One of the pioneers in the advancement of these tactics was Saul Alinsky, who wrote *Rules for Radicals.** This handbook is a kind of operational manifesto for Far-Left activists and revolutionaries. In it, Alinsky details strategies to drive political change, including the following examples:

- Power is not only what you have but what the enemy thinks you have.
- Make the enemy live up to its own book of rules.
- Ridicule is man's most potent weapon.
- Keep the pressure on.
- If you push a negative hard and deep enough, it will push through into its counterside (a positive).
- Pick the target, freeze it, personalize it, and polarize it.[165]

The central part of the Far-Left progressive playbook is to isolate and attack political opponents by any means necessary.† Such was the strategy during the confirmation process of Justice Brett Kavanaugh. The Far Left understands the importance of maintaining a left-leaning

---

* In the foreword, Alinsky acknowledges the rebellious angel Lucifer as "the first radical known to man."

† It is true both sides of the aisle engage in negative discourse. My assertion is that the Far Left initiates this acrimony by intentionally applying Alinsky tactics in an ongoing and organized way to create conflict in order to achieve their political goals.

court, and his appointment was going to create a conservative majority. To derail the appointment, Kavanaugh's opponents focused on
uncorroborated accusations of rape thirty years in the past. The strategy failed to block the confirmation, but it showed their desperation
to achieve their objective.

In observing today's political fray, it is easy to spot these antago-
nistic Marxist tactics being applied and the divisive impact they have.
These tactics are not coming from those who believe in liberty and
justice for all. They are not coming from those who wish to honestly
engage in transparent political debates to constructively effect change.
They are coming from a group committed to transform America away
from our founding principles through any means necessary.

Divisive approaches like these violate God's desire for civil discourse and explain why Washington is in legislative gridlock. These
Marxist approaches also seek to pit different groups against each other.
For instance, even though Christians believe differently from members
of the LGBTQ community on marriage and gender assignment, there
is no reason why these groups cannot respect each other's opinion as
long as they agree to respect life, liberty, and the pursuit of happiness. Liberty should be respected both ways, but the Far Left is seeking to criminalize those who do not agree with the LGBTQ agenda.
Examples include Jack Phillips and Barronelle Stutzman.

Jack Phillips is the owner of Masterpiece Cake Shop in Lakewood,
Colorado, and has been making beautiful custom wedding cakes for
years. In 2012, when a homosexual couple asked him to make a wedding cake for them, he politely declined. One state official said he was
using religious freedom "to justify discrimination." He was ordered by
the government to teach his employees (family members and others)
that he was wrong to operate his business consistent with his convictions. This resulted in a lawsuit going all the way to SCOTUS, where,
in a 7-2 ruling, the court supported his religious liberty.[166*]

Barronelle Stutzman, who is 77 years old, is the owner of Arlene's

---

*Since then, Phillips's religious freedom has been attacked by the critical gender theory movement
and remains in court. ("*Scardina v. Masterpiece Cakeshop*," Alliance Defending Freedom, last modified August 8, 2021, https://adflegal.org/case/scardina-v-masterpiece-cakeshop.)

Flowers in Richland, Washington. She has served and employed people who identify as LGBTQ for her entire professional life. Despite this, the American Civil Liberties Union and the Washington attorney general claim that she is guilty of unlawful discrimination when she acted consistent with her faith and declined to use her floral skills to celebrate the same-sex wedding ceremony of a long-time customer, Robert Ingersoll. Alliance Defending Freedom asked the court to dismiss the attorney general's lawsuit and filed a countersuit against him. They also asked the court to protect Barronelle from personal attacks from the ACLU and the state and restrict the lawsuits to her business, Arlene's Flowers. The court ruled against Barronelle and ordered her to pay penalties and attorneys' fees.[167]

Christians must learn to spot these dirty political activities and not be swayed by them. They should speak out when fellow Christians are attacked for exercising their faith. Importantly, they must not group those fighting back against these tactics alongside Far-Left activists creating the division in the first place. Instead, Christians must support those in the political arena fighting back to preserve the biblical values our nation was founded on. They can do this while still offering the gospel.

COMPARING THESE WORLDVIEWS

When comparing these two worldviews it is easy to see they are diametrically opposed. First, they have different objectives. The goal in America's founding covenant is freedom, while the Far-Left progressive goal is equality of outcomes.

Second, progressives operate under completely different formulas.

$$\frac{\text{Liberty} + \text{Justice}}{\text{Moral Law}} = \text{Freedom}$$

$$\frac{\text{PC Speech} + \text{Social Justice}}{\text{Subjective Truth}} = \text{Equality}$$

Notice the key variables are different in the Far-Left progressive formula. In this second worldview, liberty is compromised and replaced with the imposition of "politically correct" speech, where people are bullied or "cancelled" when they fail to comply. Rather than advocating civil justice, which is what the Bible teaches, Far-Left progressives use different qualifying terms that create completely different concepts and resulting policies. The most common term used today is *social justice*, which is the focus on fair or equal distribution of wealth among individuals in society to achieve equality.[168] When used in this context, the concept implies that civil authority has a responsibility to create this equality of outcomes rather than just focusing on protecting individual rights and ensuring fair and impartial civil justice for all. The Bible certainly talks about the need to address social issues and for the civil authority to provide a safety net for folks who are struggling, but it does not teach the notion that a society must ensure equal outcomes for all beyond the notion of equal civil justice for all. Wealth distribution by the civil authority is stealing and is an attempt to legalize plundering from the citizenry.

Third, the philosophical fork in the road is the rejection of a moral law to which mankind must submit. The problems created by rejecting this moral standard cannot be overstated. Taking the rejection of the moral law to its logical conclusion means there can be no constraints on human behavior, nor on the government if enough people in power believe a particular behavior to be acceptable. Furthermore, rejecting the moral law as Truth means there is no such thing as objective truth. Without objective truth, there is no way to reach any kind of political compromise, because of the subjective criteria for measuring arguments. By rejecting the biblical idea of what is good and true, Far-Left progressives can cancel any person they disagree with, even if they present a logical and reasoned argument.

In his book *What Do White Americans Owe Black People?* Jason D. Hill explains how postmodernism has changed the very means that we use to determine truth. According to postmodernism, "truth claims are discriminatory and oppressive on the grounds that they are totalizing, hegemonic, and definitive."[169] In other words, the Far Left accuses those who use logic, facts, and reason as guilty of having accepted a worldview invented by imperialist male white supremacists. This means those making a logical argument (like me in this book), are racist and bigoted, nullifying their argument from the start. Instead of facts, Far-Left progressives believe feelings are what determine what is True and Good.

Furthermore, they feel that asserting these feelings is the way a person asserts his or her very identity. So, to dismiss a person's feelings, even if those feelings are contrary to facts, denies a person identity.[170] This philosophical twister leads to an impasse when a person with the traditional American worldview tries to find common ground with a person holding this Far-Left progressive worldview. Hill summarizes the result of this worldview:

By default and by design, the end result of this philosophy is nihilism and political or psychological anarchy. Today, in the form of not just these but in manifestations of cancel culture, endless accusations of cultural appropriation, and successful efforts to suppress offending speech, we are witnessing the wholesale death of our civilization.[171]

THE FAR-LEFT PROGRESSIVE VIEW: A REJECTION OF AMERICA'S FOUNDING COVENANT

A thorough comparison of the Far-Left progressive worldview shows this group has completely rejected America's national founding covenant. While there are constant calls for bipartisan cooperation, the comparison shows there is little in common between Americans who believe in our founding covenant and those of the Far Left who want to fundamentally transform it. People who call for bipartisan cooperation either do not understand how deep the divide is or they are willfully supporting the rejection of our national covenant. Like all problems mankind experiences when attempting to live in community, this is not new. In Psalm 55:20–21, David writes of a fellow citizen, saying, "My companion attacks his friends; he violates his covenant. His talk is smooth as butter, yet war is in his heart; his words are more soothing than oil, yet they are drawn swords."

Furthermore, what we see from the last fifty years is a steady but clear push to eliminate our natural God-given individual rights. If you hold the traditional American worldview and believe in our founding covenant, then there can be no more concessions, as the intentions of the Far Left have become crystal clear: they will stop at nothing to take America away from our national founding covenant. If they are successful, we will lose our civil and religious liberties, along with any reliable civil justice.

THE CHOICE BEFORE US

Those wishing to preserve America's founding principles of life, liberty, and the pursuit of happiness are finding themselves in a position where there can be no more negotiations. We are approaching a tipping point where America will either embrace man's approach to governing as driven by the Far Left or return to God's approach to governing as captured in our national covenant.

The situation today is eerily similar to what the founders faced in 1776. As the Continental Army prepared for the Battle of Long Island, George Washington stated the following:

> The time is now near at hand which must probably determine, whether Americans are to be, Freemen, or Slaves; whether they are to have any property they can call their own; whether their Houses, and Farms, are to be pillaged and destroyed, and they consigned to a State of Wretchedness from which no human efforts will probably deliver them. The fate of unborn Millions will now depend, under God, on the Courage and Conduct of this army—Our cruel and unrelenting Enemy leaves us no choice but a brave resistance, or the most abject submission; this is all we can expect—We have therefore to resolve to conquer or die.[172]

Our situation is also similar to what it was during the Civil War, when Southern states were so determined to defend their right to maintain slavery, they seceded from the Union. The difference now in the conflict is not regional; it is throughout America. Americans wanting to preserve our Union will have to do it state by state, through the political system.

To defend our national covenant, we will need every person who loves freedom to step forward, especially Christians. Christians are the ones entrusted with the word of God and therefore are able to explain what is going on and show the way forward. In the first five chapters of this book, I laid out the case for active Christian citizenship not only as a duty but as a means to evangelize. As Jesus said in Matthew 5:13, we are to be salt and light in a dark world.

In his First Inaugural Address (March 4, 1817), President James Monroe argued that Americans must remain informed and committed if the American experiment is to continue:

> What raised us to the present happy state?… The Government has been in the hands of the people. To the people, therefore, and to the faithful and able depositaries of their trust is the credit due.… It is only when the people become ignorant and corrupt, when they degenerate into a populace, that they are incapable of exercising the sovereignty. Usurpation is then an easy attainment, and an usurper soon found. The people themselves become the willing instruments of their own debasement and ruin.… If we persevere in the career in which we have advanced so far and in the path already traced, we can not fail, under the favor of a gracious Providence, to attain the high destiny which seems to await us.[173]

While the political arena is intimidating, those who love America, especially Christians, must band together to resist the Far-Left progressive movement in their attempts to fundamentally transform America away from its founding covenant. Christians should work to maintain a government that respects and protects the liberty of all citizens, whether they accept or reject the Christian faith. The ultimate victory will be determined by the governing vision that citizens embrace.

SUMMARY

The greatest threat to Christian-centered "liberty and justice for all" is the modern progressive movement, driven by the Far Left, who want to transform America into a socialist/communist state. While this movement claims to support the disadvantaged, it is built on a worldview opposed to God's moral law and his blueprint for a just civil authority—a worldview that makes this ideology diametrically opposed to America's founding covenant.

This Far-Left version of progressivism's reach has devastated American culture. This godless system of governing has used the judicial system to impose a new vision for America that would not have been passed through the constitutional legislative process. Americans must realize this Far-Left group is not trying to govern sincerely but rather is seeking to transform America into a nation that rejects God. Instead of engaging in political debate to seek compromise, they attack and condemn anyone who stands in the way of their new world order.

Christians must become educated in this worldview, discerning when positions are diametrically opposed to biblical principles for governing. They should support leaders who commit to governing according to our national founding covenant, acting as God's servants to do good as defined by the moral law. In the next chapter we will explore specific citizenship responsibilities all Christians have in the communities in which they live: ensuring liberty and justice for all, while enabling every individual to go on his or her personal faith journey.

SUMMARY POINTS

- The alternative to a Judeo-Christian model for civil government is a secular, humanistic model in which a respect for God and his governing principles are not part of the vision or governing structure.
- The early Progressive movement focused on helping the oppressed and needy, and sincere Christians supported these efforts.
- Once Darwin's theory of evolution became popular, the Progressive movement became more secular and veered away from its Christian roots.
- The Industrial Revolution led to a more complex economy and the assertion that the federal government should take a more active role in running the national economy.
- Over time, secular progressives gained control of political, educational, and social institutions and began pushing America away from its Christian governing values.
- The modern progressive equation for governing removes liberty and justice based on an objective moral standard and replaces it with politically correct thought/speech, social, environmental, and economic justice—all based on moral relativism. Instead of seeking freedom, progressivism seeks equality of outcomes.
- While progressives claim their vision will lead to a fair and just society, history demonstrates that when this approach is followed, it is only a matter of time until people lose their liberty and freedom to state control.
- Progressives have been following a clear strategy for transitioning America to their progressive model: recast the founding in a negative light, disparage the founders and their motives, and suggest the Declaration and Constitution are outdated and need to evolve.

- Progressives redefine wording to appear to support the disadvantaged, but in the end, they are striving to advance a godless agenda.
- Progressives have infiltrated both major parties in America but have taken over the Democratic Party, which is now being led by Far-Left radicals who are fully committed to transforming America away from its Christian roots.
- If this transition occurs, it will hamper the advance of the gospel and lead to the oppression of millions in America and around the globe.

Chapter 9

Christian Citizenship

Maintaining the Covenant

Godly sorrow brings repentance that leads to salvation and leaves no regret, but worldly sorrow brings death. See what this godly sorrow has produced in you: what earnestness, what eagerness to clear yourselves, what indignation, what alarm, what longing, what concern, what readiness to see justice done. At every point you have proved yourselves to be innocent in this matter.
—2 Cor. 7:10–11

These are the times that try men's souls. The summer soldier and the sunshine patriot will, in this crisis, shrink from the service of their country; but he that stands by it now, deserves the love and thanks of man and woman.
—Thomas Paine
Common Sense, December 1776

CHAPTER 9

CHRISTIAN CITIZENSHIP

Maintaining the Covenant

> Godly sorrow brings repentance that leads to salvation and leaves
> no regret, but worldly sorrow brings death. See what this godly
> sorrow has produced in you: what earnestness, what eagerness to
> clear yourselves, what indignation, what alarm, what longing, what
> concern, what readiness to see justice done. At every point you
> have proved yourselves to be innocent in this matter.
> —2 Cor. 7:10–11

> These are the times that try men's souls. The summer soldier and the
> sunshine patriot will, in this crisis, shrink from the service of their
> country; but he that stands by it now, deserves the love and thanks
> of man and woman. Tyranny, like hell, is not easily conquered; yet
> we have this consolation with us, that the harder the conflict, the
> more glorious the triumph. What we obtain too cheap, we esteem
> too lightly.... Heaven knows how to put a price upon its goods;
> and it would be strange indeed if so celestial an article as freedom
> should not be highly rated.
> —Thomas Paine
> *Common Sense*, December 1776

No matter how brilliant and robust the American founding covenant is, it takes a concerted effort to maintain it over generations. Without this ongoing focus, it would be forgotten, cast aside, and replaced. To prevent this, successive generations must learn about it, commit themselves to it, and defend it against all enemies, foreign or domestic. This is the goal of Christian citizenship, to first establish liberty and justice for all, and then maintain it using the biblical principles covered in earlier chapters.

For America's first two centuries, citizens understood and defended our national founding covenant, in large part due to its emphasis in the church. Citizenship duty was conveyed as an expression of the Christian faith and a critical area of discipleship. However, over the last fifty years, the relentless cry for *separation of church and state* by progressives has convinced most churches across America to disengage from the political arena. Without the church filling this stewardship role, it is nearly impossible to maintain commitment to our national covenant. Christians need to rediscover the biblical principles that informed the American founding and re-embrace our citizenship responsibilities to help reestablish liberty and justice for all.

In this chapter I will describe the basic citizenship responsibilities all Christians have, present guidelines for choosing civil leaders, and share a simple model to help all Americans internalize the duty they have in the communities in which they live. I will begin our discussion of Christian citizenship and patriotism by defining key words, turning again to Noah Webster's 1828 dictionary.

CITIZENSHIP DEFINED

In his 1828 dictionary Noah Webster provides the following definitions that should inform our attitudes about Christian citizenship:

citizen (noun): The native of a city, or an inhabitant who enjoys the freedom and privileges of the city in which he resides.[174]

citizenship (noun): The state of being vested with the rights and privileges of a citizen.[175]

patriot (noun): A person who loves his country, and zealously supports and defends it and its interests.[176]

patriotism (noun): Love of one's country; the passion which aims to serve one's country, either in defending it from invasion, or protecting its rights and maintaining its laws and institutions in vigor and purity. Patriotism is the characteristic of a good citizen, the noblest passion that animates a man in the character of a citizen.[177]

Webster's definitions lead to several conclusions, all of which are consistent with what the Bible teaches about our citizenship duties and what the founders believed:

- Being a citizen means having the ability to enjoy a community's rights and privileges. This presupposes there are rights and privileges of mutual benefit to citizens.
- A good citizen not only serves his or her country but is passionate about maintaining its laws and institutions, defending it from domestic and foreign enemies.
- Citizens can sustain this patriotic ideal by maintaining the founding principles of their country.

In July 1776, while commanding the Continental Army, George Washington conveyed these sentiments in the following order:

The General hopes and trusts, that every officer, and man, will endeavour so to live, and act, as becomes a Christian Soldier defending the dearest Rights and Liberties of his country.[178]

Some argue that Christians should withhold their patriotism if their nation rejects Christian principles for governing, and just focus on evangelism, but Genesis 9:5–6 does not allow for ignoring civic duty just because a community is unjust. On the contrary, this passage is meant to spur mankind on to provide justice, especially to motivate people of faith. The Bible calls us to both establish justice and evangelize in our communities. This is always to be our joint pursuit.

Our bigger problem today is that it has become popular to

propagate American shame, not patriotism. Over the last fifty years, progressives have pushed a negative narrative of America at all levels of education. They point to issues like slavery and the treatment of Native Americans, asserting America was flawed from the very beginning.* But, as we have shown, historical documents demonstrate the founders embedded their vision of judicial equality and natural rights *for all* in the Declaration of Independence. The flaws came when state and national leadership suppressed the universal implementation of God's blueprint, which the Declaration itself affirmed. We are to learn from these failures and fully implement the vision in our Declaration instead of being paralyzed by shame because of those who disregarded this vision years ago.

America's present imperfections lead to a clear solution: elect leaders who will not abuse their civil authority but will govern according to the founders' vision. When elected officials embrace and defend biblical principles of justice and governance, the founding vision can be achieved, but they must be able and willing to defend these principles against counterfeit ideas that are branded as just and equitable. For a nation to have these virtuous leaders, citizens must be aware of these principles and elect leaders who will defend them. Good citizenship and patriotism are linked to the citizenry understanding and defending these biblical principles.

KEY CITIZENSHIP RESPONSIBILITIES

Citizens living in community have a variety of responsibilities, which, if faithfully executed, lead to a productive society. There are two general categories of citizenship: personal/familial, and public/civic. Christians need to embrace both categories as they steward their liberty.

---

* See Q&A in Appendix for a detailed explanation.

Individual Responsibilities	Community Responsibilities
• Educate yourself and your family on how to be a responsible citizen. • Develop a vocation to provide for yourself and your family. • Take care of your family. • Operate with the highest integrity. • Forgive individual offenses.	• Be involved in elections. • Be involved in public discourse. • Serve and volunteer in community or government organizations. • Give generously. • Ensure the government provides for common defense for all. • Serve if gifted and called; otherwise, support those serving with prayer, encouragement, and financial resources as they seek to be ministers of God.

Individual Responsibilities

Individual responsibilities include taking care of yourself and your family. This requires maintaining good standing as productive members of your community and doing your best to take care of yourself and your family. Good standing is achieved by the following:

Educating yourself and your family on how to be a responsible citizen

American culture prioritizes education for all citizens: male and female; black, brown, white, and other; rich and poor. For Christian families, the Bible presents the framework for education as it presents God's view of truth and history. Scripture urges believers to approach learning with a desire to extract principles for all areas of living. God wants his children to begin learning when they are young and continue learning throughout their lives so they can be equipped to handle anything life throws at them. One can fully tap into the blessings of liberty and freedom when one learns *how to think* and then establishes a lifelong pattern of learning. This is a constant theme throughout the Bible:

> Only be careful, and watch yourselves closely so that you do not forget the things your eyes have seen or let them fade from your heart as long as you live. Teach them to your children and to their children after them. (Deut. 4:9)

Show me your ways, LORD, teach me your paths. Guide me in your truth and teach me, for you are God my Savior, and my hope is in you all day long. (Ps. 25:4–5)

The fear of the LORD is the beginning of knowledge, but fools despise wisdom and instruction. (Prov. 1:7)

Start children off on the way they should go, and even when they are old they will not turn from it. (Prov. 22:6)

Fathers, do not exasperate your children; instead, bring them up in the training and instruction of the Lord. (Eph. 6:4)

Developing a vocation to provide for yourself and your family.
In a free-market economy, individuals may decide what skills they want to develop, based on their natural talents and society's need for products and services. The Old and New Testaments give a sampling of vocations believers pursued: Adam and Eve tended the Garden of Eden; Joseph and David shepherded flocks; Peter and Andrew caught fish; Luke cared for his patients; Matthew was a tax man; Paul made tents; Jesus was a carpenter. Even our biblical heroes who spent most of their waking hours in ministry jobs had vocations capable of providing gainful employment. Solomon reinforces the virtue of hard work, contrasting the lazy with the diligent:

Lazy hands make for poverty, but diligent hands bring wealth. He who gathers crops in summer is a prudent son, but he who sleeps during harvest is a disgraceful son. (Prov. 10:4–5)

The vast majority of modern citizens have the wherewithal to support themselves, which Paul stresses in 2 Thessalonians as a primary individual responsibility:

In the name of the Lord Jesus Christ, we command you, brothers
and sisters, to keep away from every believer who is idle and dis-
ruptive and does not live according to the teaching you received
from us. For you yourselves know how you ought to follow our
example. We were not idle when we were with you, nor did we eat
anyone's food without paying for it. On the contrary, we worked
night and day, laboring and toiling so that we would not be a bur-
den to any of you. We did this, not because we do not have the
right to such help, but in order to offer ourselves as a model for you
to imitate. For even when we were with you, we gave you this rule:
"The one who is unwilling to work shall not eat." (2 Thess. 3:6–10)

If someone is unable to work or may become incapacitated due to
injury or protracted illness, the church should step in:

In those days when the number of disciples was increasing, the
Hellenistic Jews among them complained against the Hebraic
Jews because their widows were being overlooked in the daily
distribution of food. So the Twelve gathered all the disciples
together and said, "It would not be right for us to neglect the
ministry of the word of God in order to wait on tables. Brothers
and sisters, choose seven men from among you who are known to
be full of the Spirit and wisdom. We will turn this responsibility
over to them." (Acts 6:1–3)

Religion that God our Father accepts as pure and faultless is this: to
look after orphans and widows in their distress and to keep oneself
from being polluted by the world. (James 1:27)

Taking care of your family, providing for your children, and honoring your father and mother

When a man and woman marry, they vow to take care of each other
"in poverty and riches, in sickness and in health." If children expand
the family, the obligation to care for them is a logical extension of the

wedding vows. God's blueprint extends the obligation in the other direction, too. If one's parents become infirm, adult children are to take care of them; this is part of the biblical mandate to "honor your father and mother" (Exod. 20:12). Good citizens meet these family responsibilities to the degree they are able. This is God's original blueprint described in the Old Testament and affirmed in the New:

> Stand up in the presence of the aged, show respect for the elderly and revere your God. I am the LORD. (Lev. 19:32)

> Honor your father and your mother, as the LORD your God has commanded you, so that you may live long and that it may go well with you in the land the LORD your God is giving you. (Deut. 5:16)

> Give proper recognition to those widows who are really in need. But if a widow has children or grandchildren, these should learn first of all to put their religion into practice by caring for their own family and so repaying their parents and grandparents, for this is pleasing to God. The widow who is really in need and left all alone puts her hope in God and continues night and day to pray and to ask God for help. But the widow who lives for pleasure is dead even while she lives. Give the people these instructions, so that no one may be open to blame. Anyone who does not provide for their relatives, and especially for their own household, has denied the faith and is worse than an unbeliever. (1 Tim. 5:3–8)

> "Honor your father and mother"—which is the first commandment with a promise—"so that it may go well with you and that you may enjoy long life on the earth." (Eph. 6:2–3)

If the family is unable to provide for its own, the church should step in to provide relief (Acts 2:42–47). The local civil authority should provide care only when all other options are exhausted.

Operating with the highest integrity in all your dealings
Productive citizens exemplify biblical virtues in honesty and loyalty.
God's call to personal integrity is consistent throughout Scripture.

> The integrity of the upright guides them, but the unfaithful are
> destroyed by their duplicity. (Prov. 11:3)

> Let your eyes look straight ahead; fix your gaze directly before you.
> Give careful thought to the paths for your feet and be steadfast in
> all your ways. Do not turn to the right or the left; keep your foot
> from evil. (Prov. 4:25–27)

> He must manage his own family well and see that his children
> obey him, and he must do so in a manner worthy of full respect.
> (1 Tim. 3:4)

**Forgiving individual offenses and letting civil authorities
secure justice**
In earlier chapters I explained how civil government is to secure justice when an individual breaks the law. In all cases, however, the one
offended is instructed to forgive the offender. Forgiveness and recon-
ciliation are key parts of the Judeo-Christian faith. These actions are
required not only to prevent the rampant interpersonal conflict that
existed prior to the flood but they are also critical in order for believers
to achieve true inner peace, as Solomon and Moses tell us:

> Do not testify against your neighbor without cause—would you
> use your lips to mislead? Do not say, "I'll do to them as they have
> done to me; I'll pay them back for what they did." (Prov. 24:28–29)
> If your enemy is hungry, give him food to eat; if he is thirsty, give
> him water to drink. (Prov. 25:21)

> Do not seek revenge or bear a grudge against anyone among your peo-
> ple, but love your neighbor as yourself. I am the LORD. (Lev. 19:18)

In the Sermon on the Mount, Jesus reaffirmed how important for-giveness is, setting a lofty standard to not only forgive personal injury but also to love our enemies:

> You have heard that it was said, "Eye for eye, and tooth for tooth." But I tell you, do not resist an evil person. If anyone slaps you on the right cheek, turn to them the other cheek also. And if anyone wants to sue you and take your shirt, hand over your coat as well. If anyone forces you to go one mile, go with them two miles. (Matt. 5:38–41)

> But I tell you, love your enemies and pray for those who persecute you. (Matt. 5:44)

Later, Peter asked Jesus how many times one should forgive an offender:

> Then Peter came to Jesus and asked, "Lord, how many times shall I forgive my brother or sister who sins against me? Up to seven times?" Jesus answered, "I tell you, not seven times, but seventy-seven times." (Matt. 18:21–22)

In Romans 12, Paul also stressed the need to forgive:

> Do not repay anyone evil for evil. Be careful to do what is right in the eyes of everyone. If it is possible, as far as it depends on you, live at peace with everyone. Do not take revenge, my dear friends, but leave room for God's wrath, for it is written: "It is mine to avenge; I will repay," says the Lord. On the contrary: "If your enemy is hungry, feed him; if he is thirsty, give him something to drink. In doing this, you will heap burning coals on his head." Do not be overcome by evil, but overcome evil with good. (Rom. 12:17–21)

Last, there may be occasions where the justice system fails. In this case Christians are certainly allowed every legal remedy, but God tells us *he* will ultimately secure justice:

It is mine to avenge; I will repay. In due time their foot will slip; their day of disaster is near and their doom rushes upon them. (Deut. 32:35)

These five building blocks are the foundation of a just nation. As Christians adhere to God's original blueprint regarding issues of personal and familial responsibilities, it becomes possible for a just and productive community to emerge. When it does, the responsibilities of Christians expand in order for a community to establish enduring freedom for its citizens.

COMMUNITY RESPONSIBILITIES

Once people have prioritized their personal and familial responsibilities, they should fulfill their community responsibilities in several basic areas. Their goal is to be a model citizen not only to fulfill biblical citizenship duties but also to set an example for others to see and aspire to emulate.‾

Being involved in the election process

Free nations—where the people can elect their civil leaders—have been the exception, not the norm, throughout history. In America, free elections reach back to the earliest settlements. Since God's blueprint elevates the responsibility of all citizens to appoint capable, godly leaders, all Christians should engage in the election process. Model citizens do not simply vote; they vote *responsibly* to appoint capable leaders in all levels of civil government who understand, can articulate, and can defend biblical principles found in our national founding covenant. Again, both the Old and New Testaments speak to the involvement of the individual in the selection of responsible leaders:

But select capable men from all the people—men who fear God, trustworthy men who hate dishonest gain—and appoint them as officials over thousands, hundreds, fifties and tens. (Exod. 18:21) Choose some wise, understanding and respected men from each of your tribes, and I will set them over you. You answered me, "What you propose to do is good." So I took the leading men of your tribes, wise and respected men, and appointed them to have authority over you—as commanders of thousands, of hundreds, of fifties and of tens and as tribal officials. And I charged your judges at that time, "Hear the disputes between your people and judge fairly, whether the case is between two Israelites or between an Israelite and a foreigner residing among you." (Deut. 1:13–16)

These were the men appointed from the community, the leaders of their ancestral tribes. They were the heads of the clans of Israel. (Num. 1:16)

Brothers and sisters, choose seven men from among you who are known to be full of the Spirit and wisdom. We will turn this responsibility over to them. (Acts 6:3)

Paul and Barnabas appointed elders for them in each church and, with prayer and fasting, committed them to the Lord, in whom they had put their trust. (Acts 14:23)

The reason I left you in Crete was that you might put in order what was left unfinished and appoint elders in every town, as I directed you. (Titus 1:5)

These verses cover a variety of situations where individuals appoint leaders of a new or expanding community. Often the existing leadership selects its replacement, but in communities where the general citizenry is allowed to engage in the election process, Christians should exercise the opportunity to elect their leaders. They should do so as a solemn responsibility, understanding the election of godly leaders is critical for their own spiritual journey as well as the liberty to share their faith with unbelievers.

Some Christians may feel called to go door to door, attend rallies, or serve on their local election board. The church should encourage such involvement, training believers in the principles for governing and how to conduct themselves in a manner that will honor God.

Being involved in public discourse regarding policies and laws that are just, equitable, and provide for the common good
Mature Christians learn to spot laws that contradict God's moral law and make them known to voters committed to preserving America's founding covenant. Laws that infringe on liberty and freedom should be scrutinized and opposed if they allow the government to slowly erode individual rights. Laws must also be uniformly applied without preference, regardless of social standing, race, or religion. Christians who study the Bible learn biblical principles of rights, justice, and governance. They must also learn to articulate these truths to maintain a just society.* Again, the Bible is filled with verses calling for this active engagement:

> So justice is driven back, and righteousness stands at a distance; truth has stumbled in the streets, honesty cannot enter. (Isa. 59:14)
> The people of the land practice extortion and commit robbery; they oppress the poor and needy and mistreat the foreigner, denying them justice. "I looked for someone among them who would build up the wall and stand before me in the gap on behalf of the land so I would not have to destroy it, but I found no one." (Ezek. 22:29–30)

> Who will rise up for me against the wicked? Who will take a stand for me against evildoers? Unless the LORD had given me help, I would soon have dwelt in the silence of death. (Ps. 94:16–17)

---

* As mentioned in chapter 3, understanding what just laws look like in the public arena will also help governing within the home.

He rules forever by his power, his eyes watch the nations—let not the rebellious rise up against him. Praise our God, all peoples, let the sound of his praise be heard; he has preserved our lives and kept our feet from slipping. (Ps. 66:7–9)

For lack of guidance a nation falls, but victory is won through many advisers. (Prov. 11:14)

Now Herod had arrested John and bound him and put him in prison because of Herodias, his brother Philip's wife, for John had been saying to him: "It is not lawful for you to have her." Herod wanted to kill John, but he was afraid of the people, because they considered John a prophet. (Matt. 14:3–5)

If anyone, then, knows the good they ought to do and doesn't do it, it is sin for them. (James 4:17)

John the Baptist set the example in this area, confronting the immorality of Herod, a civil leader who had married his brother Phillip's wife. John was imprisoned and eventually murdered because of his stand against the immorality of the leader of his civil government. His example refutes the notion that Christians should remain silent for fear of offending others. Jesus bolsters the argument, explaining that living out one's faith will often make them unpopular at home or in their community. Regardless, he encouraged his disciples to speak out:

You must be on your guard. You will be handed over to the local councils and flogged in the synagogues. On account of me you will stand before governors and kings as witnesses to them. And the gospel must first be preached to all nations. Whenever you are arrested and brought to trial, do not worry beforehand about what to say. Just say whatever is given you at the time, for it is not you speaking, but the Holy Spirit. Brother will betray brother to death, and a father his child. Children will rebel against their parents and have them put to death. Everyone will hate you because of me, but the one who stands firm to the end will be saved. (Mark 13:9–13)

Serving in public organizations established to help improve the general morality and/or welfare of a community

Establishing and maintaining just societies is hard work. Faith-based groups should take the lead to establish ongoing support organizations for the betterment of the local community. When needs cannot be met by families or ministries, then, and only then, should the government step in. America has a rich history of promoting the general welfare through Christian ministries like Matthew 25 Ministries, the Salvation Army, and crisis pregnancy centers. Establishing service-related ministries is based on scriptures like the following:

At the end of every three years, bring all the tithes of that year's produce and store it in your towns, so that the Levites (who have no allotment or inheritance of their own) and the foreigners, the fatherless and the widows who live in your towns may come and eat and be satisfied, and so that the LORD your God may bless you in all the work of your hands. (Deut. 14:28–29)

Give proper recognition to those widows who are really in need. But if a widow has children or grandchildren, these should learn first of all to put their religion into practice by caring for their own family and so repaying their parents and grandparents, for this is pleasing to God. The widow who is really in need and left all alone puts her hope in God and continues night and day to pray and to ask God for help. But the widow who lives for pleasure is dead even while she lives. Give the people these instructions, so that no one may be open to blame. Anyone who does not provide for their relatives, and especially for their own household, has denied the faith and is worse than an unbeliever. (1 Tim. 5:3–8)

Giving generously to those in need

The Bible calls on Christians to give generously to help others who are in need. This should be viewed as an active part of practicing the faith and done cheerfully as shown by the following verses:*

> Remember this: Whoever sows sparingly will also reap sparingly, and whoever sows generously will also reap generously. Each of you should give what you have decided in your heart to give, not reluctantly or under compulsion, for God loves a cheerful giver. And God is able to bless you abundantly, so that in all things at all times, having all that you need, you will abound in every good work. As it is written:
>
> "They have freely scattered their gifts to the poor; their righteousness endures forever."
>
> Now he who supplies seed to the sower and bread for food will also supply and increase your store of seed and will enlarge the harvest of your righteousness. You will be enriched in every way so that you can be generous on every occasion, and through us your generosity will result in thanksgiving to God. (2 Cor. 9:6–11)

> What good is it, my brothers and sisters, if someone claims to have faith but has no deeds? Can such faith save them? Suppose a brother or a sister is without clothes and daily food. If one of you says to them, "Go in peace; keep warm and well fed," but does nothing about their physical needs, what good is it? In the same way, faith by itself, if it is not accompanied by action, is dead. (James 2:14–17)

Ensuring that government provides for local and national defense

Civil government bears the responsibility to provide for both individual protection and the defense of the community. Jesus affirmed the right to bear arms when he told his disciples, "But now if you have a

---

* The general principle for giving is the tithe: 10 percent of one's gross income. The Bible encourages believers to give well beyond that, establishing the expectation that Christians should be among the most generous people in society.

purse, take it, and also a bag; and if you don't have a sword, sell your cloak and buy one" (Luke 22:36). From earliest history, cities were protected by a physical barrier like a moat or a wall. The following Old Testament references represent the norm:

> Now the gates of Jericho were securely barred because of the Israelites. No one went out and no one came in. (Josh. 6:1)

> Then I said to them, "You see the trouble we are in: Jerusalem lies in ruins, and its gates have been burned with fire. Come, let us rebuild the wall of Jerusalem, and we will no longer be in disgrace." I also told them about the gracious hand of my God on me and what the king had said to me.
>
> They replied, "Let us start rebuilding." So they began this good work. (Neh. 2:17–18)

Many nations described in the Bible also maintained armies to deal with foreign enemies. These nations included Israel, the Philistines, the Assyrians, and the Babylonians. America faces similar needs along its international borders, especially the southern border, because of the historic flow of immigrants who enter illegally and the flow of illegal drugs. These challenges threaten the well-being of our citizens, which should concern all Americans, especially Christians. As a sovereign nation with the responsibility to protect her citizens, America must have leaders who will provide for national protection.

Serving in public office as one feels led and supporting those who serve

As Exodus 18 and Deuteronomy 1 record, God instructed the people to select leaders at the local level to rule over them. These individuals were to come from the ranks of the citizens—not aliens or outsiders. They were ordinary citizens, who believed in Israel's national covenant and who were called to serve in the civil arena. In doing so, they fulfilled their citizenship duty.

Church leaders must encourage capable congregants to consider civil leadership as a valid and critical extension of their church's ministry. Christian individuals who are gifted in leadership and qualified biblically (see Romans 12, 1 Corinthians 12, and Ephesians 4) should be urged and supported to seek election. Israel's history represents a succession of rulers and judges—some faithful, others not. Many times, God has called everyday citizens to restore justice, as in Hebrews 11, where he commends those who honored God through their civil leadership:

> And what more shall I say? I do not have time to tell about Gideon, Barak, Samson and Jephthah, about David and Samuel and the prophets, who through faith conquered kingdoms, administered justice, and gained what was promised; who shut the mouths of lions. (Heb. 11:32–33)

God called these individuals because civil leaders had turned their backs on him. The writer of Hebrews mentions both the spiritual and civil leaders of Israel's past because both are needed to establish a godly nation based on God's blueprint to protect rights and administer justice. The people commended in Hebrews were people of faith called to lead in troubled times.

As long as human governments exist, the need for responsible, godly citizens and civil leaders remains. In the Old Testament, God gave community elders the responsibility to train these civil leaders, so they could fulfill their responsibility. In the modern era, church leaders and mature believers assume this stewardship role, to remind believers of their responsibility to their families and duty to their local community.

BIBLICAL VIRTUE AND CITIZENSHIP

At the core of being a model citizen is pursuing a virtuous life. In chapter 6 we stated that virtue was the pursuit of moral living. Noah Webster provides more context in the third definition of *virtue* in his 1828 dictionary:

Virtue (noun): Moral goodness; the practice of moral duties and the abstaining from vice, or a conformity of life and conversation to the moral law. In this sense, *virtue* may be, and in many instances must be, distinguished from religion. The practice of moral duties merely from motives of convenience, or from compulsion, or from regard to reputation, is virtue, as distinct from religion. The practice of moral duties from sincere love to God and his laws, is *virtue* and religion.[179]

Webster illustrates his definition, quoting from Timothy Dwight: "Virtue is nothing but voluntary obedience to truth." Dwight goes on to say, "Error, on the contrary, is the foundation of all iniquity. It leads the soul only away from duty, from virtue, from salvation, and from God.[180] In his farewell address, George Washington elevated personal virtue as foundational for America to find success in the form of government outlined in the Constitution, saying,

> 'Tis substantially true, that virtue or morality is a necessary spring of popular government.... Observe good faith & justice [towards] all Nations[;] cultivate peace & harmony with all—Religion & morality enjoin this conduct; and can it be that good policy does not equally enjoin it? ... Can it be, that Providence has not connected the permanent felicity of a Nation with its virtue?[181]

The founders understood the critical connection between having biblical virtue and the ability to establish and maintain a just and stable nation with "liberty and justice for all." Devoid of personal virtue, a nation would need an aggressive police force to maintain order, but a nation where citizens are taught and exemplify virtue will need minimal policing. In William Bennett's *Book of Virtues*, he provides a solid list of biblical virtues Christians should pursue:[182]

Self-discipline: Instructing, educating, informing the mind to govern oneself

Compassion: Suffering with another by the distress or misfortunes of another
Responsibility: Being accountable to an obligation
Friendship: Showing favor, support, and personal kindness to an intimate acquaintance
Work: Laboring in the achievement of a task to its completion
Courage: Facing danger or difficulties with firmness and resolve
Perseverance: Pursuing what one undertakes
Honesty: Applying justice and moral principles in all social conditions
Loyalty: Demonstrating allegiance to another individual
Faith: Believing in the veracity of the Bible and the God it declares

On the surface, some of these have no connection to religion, but all are critical aspects of the Christian faith and are reinforced throughout the Bible. A society with citizens who embrace and value these virtues will be just and stable. A society that does not value nor instill these virtues in their citizens will be dangerous and require much more law enforcement.

A SIMPLE MODEL: THE FIVE MARKS OF A CHRISTIAN PATRIOT

We have covered a lot of ground in this book describing biblical principles for civil government and the many citizenship responsibilities Christians have. This information can be overwhelming. To help distill these principles, I offer a simple model you can apply to your life and teach others. These five things describe well the life of a Christian patriot who honors God:

Covenant: Keep your covenants (civil, marital, personal).
Honor: Live in harmony with the moral law (virtue).
Protection: Protect your family, local community, and nation.
Justice: Ensure equal and impartial justice for all.
Liberty: Promote and defend liberty for all.

These concepts are all vital to preserving a God-honoring nation and are covered in earlier chapters. Note also that the Far Left described in the previous chapter fundamentally rejects each of these. In contrast, the mature Christian exemplifies all of these qualities in his or her everyday life. Mastering these concepts also prepares Christian patriots for one of their most important duties: to choose leaders.

CHOOSING LEADERS WHO EXEMPLIFY THE 'THREE CS'

A primary responsibility Christian citizens have is to appoint worthy civil leaders who exemplify the "Three Cs": they are *committed*, are *competent*, and exhibit godly *character*. In earlier chapters we extracted the Bible's charge that government is to protect the safety and well-being of a community. We now turn to applying those principles to learn how to evaluate candidates as we exercise our right and duty to vote. This is where Christians must weigh the most critical traits among the candidates in keeping with biblical values. In some cases, these values are black and white, and in some cases they are not. This is ultimately a matter of conscience, and there are often reasonable points of disagreement faithful Christians may have. The Bible provides important filters, however, to aid in vetting candidates of their *commitment, competence*, and *character*. And the best candidate might be competent and committed yet not a Christian.

In non-political areas, we rely all the time on committed, competent non-Christians. We place our children in the care of committed, competent coaches; we entrust our automobiles or homes to qualified mechanics and tradesmen; we even feel comfortable placing our lives in the hands of a surgeon who may believe differently than we do. But we do not go in blind: we evaluate training, experience, and record of success—without ever inquiring about spiritual condition. If we discover a committed, competent coach, mechanic, builder, doctor, etc., who is also an active follower of Christ, our choices are much simpler. But the candidate pool usually requires that we make tradeoffs.

Applying the filters of *commitment, competence*, and *character* becomes clearer for us by looking back at Israel's history in the Old Testament. In the book of Judges, God called ordinary citizens like Deborah, Gideon, and Samson to point the nation in the right direction. Eventually, Israel asked God to appoint a human king. God called Samuel to warn the people of how a king would oppress them, but they persisted in their request, and Samuel installed King Saul. Saul showed commitment and competence to lead, but he lacked godly character. The Lord removed him, calling a common shepherd, David, to serve as Israel's second king. David was committed and competent—and his character earned him the God-given title "a man after God's own heart." But David was not perfect. As king, he struggled with adultery and tried to cover that sin with murder, but God promised that David's dynasty would last forever, even though he had significant moral baggage.

Solomon succeeded David, and he asked God for wisdom instead of wealth and power. God used Solomon to elevate Israel to unparalleled success. But even the great Solomon had a weakness: adding many wives to his wealth. He was lured into worshipping the foreign gods of his wives. After Solomon's reign, Israel went into decline: national division broke the kingdom into ten northern tribes and two southern. The lack of unity and a downward spiral into idolatry led to the Babylonian invasion, and the finest young men of Israel were taken into exile. One of the prominent exiles was Daniel, a man whose natural commitment, competence, and character made him a perfect fit for Nebuchadnezzar's leadership team. In the book of Daniel we see a godly leader (Daniel) who worked for a pagan king who suffered bouts of insanity, but Daniel—like Joseph, who hundreds of years earlier served a pagan pharaoh—served with distinction.

Joseph, Daniel, Solomon, David, Saul, and so many others all accepted God's call to serve. Some served in periods of unprecedented national success; others served as exiles for pagan invaders. All brought strengths and weaknesses to their positions, but God called them and empowered them for "such a time as this" (Esther 4:14).

Christians today can draw insights from these biblical accounts of ordinary citizens whom God called into extraordinary service. Consider the following observations we can distill from Israel's successes and failures:

- God calls godly and ungodly individuals to rule nations (Joseph and Pharaoh in Genesis 41; Daniel and Nebuchadnezzar in Daniel 1–4).
- Some respect God and uphold his moral law; some do not (Josiah in 2 Kings 22–23; Manasseh in 2 Kings 21).
- God calls ordinary citizens to positions of leadership (Othniel in Judges 3; Gideon in Judges 6–7; Jephthah in Judges 11).
- God calls men *and* women to be leaders (David in 2 Samuel 2; Daniel in Daniel 1–4; Deborah in Judges 4; the queen of Sheba in 1 Kings 10).
- God calls flawed people to serve (Samson in Judges 14; Saul in 1 Samuel 13; David in 2 Samuel 11).
- God may call Christians to serve leaders who are ungodly in their governance. The Christian should strive to live according to God's moral law and support the pagan leaders as conscience dictates, helping the leader to rule in a way that honors God (Joseph in Genesis 41; Daniel in Daniel 1–4).
- When leaders (godly or not) pass decrees that violate God's moral law, Christians should resist as they feel led (Daniel in Daniel 1 and 6; Shadrach, Meshach and Abednego in Daniel 3).

As we can see, the Bible provides us with an array of civil leaders to learn from, taken from various points in Israel's history. All of these serve as examples for us living today of how we should conduct ourselves as citizens in whatever circumstances we find ourselves. When living in a country where citizens are permitted to vote, Christians must make every attempt to vote according to the Three Cs.

APPLYING THE 'THREE Cs'

Knowing the Three Cs and applying them to a list of potential candidates requires that we process each candidate through each filter, one at a time. The order is critical, as the first filter can disqualify candidates. That first C is for *commitment*.

The commitment that is most important, and is a deal-breaker if not met, is a candidate's *commitment to the moral law*. We have stressed in earlier chapters the critical role of the moral law in the just governing of a society and in the life of the Christian. It is the lens through which Christians should conduct themselves, lawmakers should make laws, and judges should render verdicts. If a candidate rejects the moral law or suggests the moral law is for the private faith of Christians and not the public square, then no citizen can rely on that individual to support policies or pass laws that are in harmony with the moral law. This also means a person rejecting the moral law has fundamentally rejected America's founding covenant, since the whole action of separating from England was based on the long-term immoral actions of the king. The result of electing a person with this worldview would be a nation that dishonors God and slowly usurps the rights of the citizens. This is exactly what has happened in America.

The most egregious example of rejecting the moral law is the support of abortion,[183] some states now allowing abortion through full-term pregnancies.[184] In Genesis 9:5–6, in which God ordained civil government, the infraction for which he was *demanding* justice was the taking of an innocent life. Is there any other example of a life being taken where the victim is more innocent than an unborn baby? This is where the Far Left of the Democratic Party has taken the nation and proves their utter and complete contempt for the moral law. Those with this worldview, who reject the moral law as the legal standard, are immediately disqualified from civil service, given America's national founding covenant.

While this may seem like an extreme position to take in politics, consider the situation when a Bible-believing evangelical church is looking for a pastor or electing an elder. Would that congregation for one minute consider a candidate who did not believe the Bible to be inspired by God and authoritative on all matters of faith and practice?

Of course not! Then why would Christians vote for political candidates who are contemptuous of the moral law—which is the bedrock foundation of America's government and the Christian faith? Note that a person who is not a Christian but agrees with and defends the moral law as the legal standard could be preferable even over a Christian candidate, if he or she excels in the next filter—*competence*.

We can gauge a person's competence to hold a particular office by evaluating his or her previous experience. A candidate running for county coroner requires a different work history than someone running for mayor; a person who was a great county commissioner may lack competence to be governor or president. Each elected office has certain skills that candidates should have demonstrated to be positioned for success. Christians should consider what each candidate has done to give evidence that he or she will be competent and successful if elected. This, too, is exactly what a church considers when evaluating a person to fulfill the role of pastor or elder—that he will be competent in providing spiritual leadership for their church.

Candidates who pass the first two filters should be evaluated against the third C: *character*. The virtue of a person should be considered, as described previously. There should be clear examples of integrity that a political candidate can use to substantiate that he or she has operated and will operate with integrity, if elected.

In the case of America, there is one final test. *Does the candidate truly agree with and commit him- or herself to the American founding covenant?* Does he or she support the principles set forth in the Declaration of Independence based on the "Laws of Nature and of Nature's God" (i.e., the moral law)? Any candidate who rejects the moral law rejects the Declaration. He or she does not accept that rights come from God and instead believes that rights come from the state. Anyone who embraces politically correct speech and "cancel culture" rejects liberty. All of this also disqualifies anyone from consideration for any office in America.

The last forty years have also revealed that party platforms clarify the vision for where that party wants to take the country. As detailed

CHAPTER 9 : CHRISTIAN CITIZENSHIP

in chapter 8, the modern-day Democratic Party has been taken over by the Far Left and has demonstrated hostility to the moral law on every point. I am not asserting that all Democrats subscribe to the current anti-God platform, but it is crystal clear where the party itself stands relative to God and the Christian faith. Christians voting for modern-day Democrats need to understand this is a vote for a platform that is inconsistent with the bedrock principles of Scripture, the Christian faith, and what God demands from all civil authorities on earth.

Careful analysis based on these filters will generally identify the best candidate and disqualify others. It is actually not that difficult to select candidates to vote for once Christians understand and put into practice the concepts covered in this book. This is Christian citizenship: realizing and embracing our duty to maintain our national governing covenant.

A LESSON FROM HISTORY

We know all too well the result when Christians disregard their citizenship role and allow people who do not meet the criteria above to take charge. In Nazi Germany, the church remained silent during Hitler's rapid rise to power. In the early 1930s, two-thirds of the German people were in the German Evangelical Church. In an effort to establish absolute power, Hitler attempted to direct the church to steer clear of politics, essentially telling religious leaders to be concerned only with getting people to heaven. *He* would take care of governing them on earth. The nearly 45 million churchgoers could have curbed Hitler's power grab, but only a few church leaders spoke up. Among the most prominent were Dietrich Bonhoeffer and Martin Niemöller. These two courageous men worked to awaken other church leaders. One of Bonhoeffer's most timeless quotes that speaks to today's Christian is this:

Silence in the face of evil is itself evil: God will not hold us guiltless. Not to speak is to speak. Not to act is to act.[185]

Bonhoeffer and Niemöller urged believers to stand on the ultimate authority of the church, but they were unsuccessful. Bonhoeffer was jailed and then executed in the final days of the war. Niemöller survived seven years in Sachsenhausen and Dachau concentration camps, much of that time in solitary confinement. Once liberated, he helped in the reconstruction of Germany. In postwar speeches he reflected on the rise of concentration camps in the 1930s and the general silence from the church:

> First they came for the socialists, and I did not speak out—because I was not a socialist. Then they came for the trade unionists, and I did not speak out— because I was not a trade unionist. Then they came for the Jews, and I did not speak out—because I was not a Jew. Then they came for me—and there was no one left to speak for me.[186]

Immediately following the war, Niemöller helped initiate the "Stuttgart Declaration of Guilt." In the following words, the Council of the Evangelical Church of Germany publicly confessed it did not do enough to oppose Hitler:

> With great pain we say: By us infinite wrong was brought over many peoples and countries. That which we often testified to in our communities, we express now in the name of the whole Church: We did fight for long years in the name of Jesus Christ against the mentality that found its awful expression in the National Socialist regime of violence; but we accuse ourselves for not standing to our beliefs more courageously, for not praying more faithfully, for not believing more joyously, and for not loving more ardently.[187]

Hitler's reign demonstrates how an ungodly ruler can murder millions if the church remains passive or disengaged in politics. While the declaration allowed Christians to acknowledge the role their inactivity played, their confession came too late for the 11 million murdered Jews and other people groups. Modern church leaders need to learn from those who lived through political oppression and train their congregations in the biblical principles of just governance. In this way, the church can become the moral compass for society and resolve to resist evil civil leaders when they abuse their God-given authority to govern justly.

A PRACTICAL CITIZENSHIP ROADMAP

The place to start is in building your own personal knowledge. Your goal is not to become an expert but to confirm your own beliefs and be able to explain the basics of the American founding and your citizenship responsibilities. We must first get honest with our experiences, beliefs, and biases around our responsibility toward civil government. How do your personal beliefs line up with the theology presented in this book? Where do you still have questions or doubts? Much of what I have presented is new to many Christians, so it is important to review this material several times to see the Bible's broad theology regarding civil government and how this theology informed the American founding. I recommend revisiting the history behind the founding, looking at it through a biblical lens. You could start with these resources[*]:

- American Minute, a website by Bill Federer, makes available his many DVDs and books describing all of church history in addition to American history. Federer also has a daily email that explains important events across history. This is an excellent way to learn a little history every day. Many Christian radio stations also carry his daily *American Minute* (one-minute) program. **Americanminute.com**
- WallBuilders is an organization founded by David Barton, another excellent American historian, who also has many books and DVDs worth having in your library. Mr. Barton has the largest private collection in the world of original documents from America's founding era. WallBuilders has a daily 30-minute radio program (carried by many Christian stations), which emphasizes responsible Christian citizenship. **WallBuilders.com**

---

[*] I recommend several books by these authors, which are listed in the bibliography.

The next thing you might do is look up incorporation or charter documents for your state and nearby municipalities, both original and current. Then find out who your representatives are and visit their web pages. Get to know these representatives and the issues they stand for. Attend your city council meetings and school board meetings to learn more about how these organizations operate and what they are working on. Let your representatives know you expect them to support our national founding covenant and operate within the parameters of the Constitution as originally intended. At city council meetings and school board meetings, "citizen speakers" may speak on any issue, so speak up! Let your respectful and winsome voice be heard! Make yourself known in these meetings as a knowledgeable, engaged, and interested citizen!

I encourage you to consider how you might support those in office, especially where there are issues pulling us away from our founding principles. Often just showing up at city council meetings where people share concerns can have a big impact. The saying "all politics are local" is true, and this is the first place to make your views known to have a positive impact on your local community. This is one critical way you can impact the local culture for Christ.

Of course, you should also pray for all those in authority over you, that they may have the wisdom and conviction to govern justly and honor God in all they do.

MODELING BIBLICAL CITIZENSHIP

When I moved my family to Cincinnati in the summer of 2001, I began learning about the rich history of the area. One Civil War story grabbed my attention, as it exemplifies the biblical idea of citizenship. David Mowery captures the story's details in *Cincinnati in the Civil War: The Union's Queen City*. [188] Mowery describes how Cincinnati was made aware of the threat of Confederate attack and responded in the late summer of 1862. In August Major General Edmund Kirby Smith defeated Union forces only ninety miles away from Cincinnati at Richmond, and the possibility of an attack on the city became real. Amazingly, 60,000 local citizens assembled along with 2,300 reserve militia and 22,500 soldiers to prepare defenses on the Kentucky border spanning nearly eight miles. In early September, General Henry Heth approached Cincinnati with 8,000 Confederate soldiers. Heth saw the defenses the citizens built and a militia force roughly ten times the number of his force, and he decided not to attack. On September 14, the *Cincinnati Gazette* wrote, "Thanks to the promptitude of Generals Wright and Wallace,* and the patriotism, courage and valor of the people, the rebel movement towards Cincinnati has been frustrated and rolled back."[189] This scenario has played out countless times over the course of human history—people coming together to provide mutual protection in times of crisis. This event is a perfect modern-day example of Christian citizenship in action. It should cause citizens, especially those claiming to be Christians, to think about how committed they are to preserving law and order in the area in which they live.

The burning question is, Would you eagerly respond if called upon to defend your local community? Going back to WWII, when the Nazis were rounding up Jews and sending them to concentration camps, would you have risked your life to hide some or smuggle some to safety? This is what it means to truly love your neighbor in times of crisis: challenging an immoral civil government and putting your life on the line. This is biblical citizenship, and we as Christians are called to model this in the communities and nations in which we live.

QUESTIONS AND ANSWERS

A number of questions arise when talking about our citizenship responsibilities here on earth; two are captured below. These are discussed in detail in the Appendix.

- Isn't our citizenship in heaven more important than political engagement here on earth?
- Is it proper to love one's country?

---

* General Lewis "Lew" Wallace wrote the well-known novel *Ben Hur: A Tale of the Christ* in 1880.

SUMMARY

In narrative and principle, the Bible contains a storehouse of timeless information on how to establish and maintain just societies. People of faith must embrace their citizenship duty for a community or nation to honor God and realize these benefits. This includes establishing and maintaining liberty and justice in the home. It also means protecting and defending our national covenant. Failure to embrace our citizenship duty as Christian citizens is not only a violation of the biblical mandate but it will also subject us to encroachments by those who are all too happy to seize control.

Recent history is filled with examples of leaders who capitalized on an ignorant citizenry, manipulating crisis situations to gain control. Such leaders will marginalize their opponents and lead their nations to tyranny or destruction. God calls his people to stand against oppression, always seeking liberty and justice for all. Explaining our citizenship duty is ultimately the responsibility of the church—a topic we will further explore in the next chapter.

SUMMARY POINTS

- The Bible provides Christians with compelling instructions on their citizenship responsibilities.
- Christians should be model citizens, taking primary responsibility for their own well-being and that of their families, serving their church, contributing to their local communities and in the election and accountability of their civil leaders.
- Christians should be informed on the key issues and candidates and prioritize their vote on establishing and maintaining God's blueprint for governance.
- The foundations for the faithful execution of our citizenship responsibilities are biblical virtues, which guide our actions and attitudes.
- Christians are citizens of two kingdoms: God's heavenly kingdom, and the earthly nation in which they live, which means they have duties to both.
- Biblical liberty on earth enables evangelism and protects the pursuit of holy living as individuals are directed by their consciences.
- The American founders modeled the idea of fulfilling their citizenship duty in the years leading up to and through the American founding.
- Christians today have the same responsibility to lead in the civil arena, applying biblical principles to secure "liberty and justice for all."

CHAPTER 10

THE ROLE OF THE CHURCH

Explaining Governing Covenants

Who will rise up for me against the wicked? Who will take a stand for me against evildoers?
—Psalm 94:16

I think you are wrong in trying to be both soldier and preacher together. Be either one or the other. No man can serve two masters.... How different are our ways of thinking!
—Frederick Muhlenberg
In 1776, to his brother, Pastor Peter Muhlenberg

CHAPTER 10

THE ROLE OF THE CHURCH

Explaining Governing Covenants

Who will rise up for me against the wicked? Who will take a stand
for me against evildoers?
—Psalm 94:16

I think you are wrong in trying to be both soldier and preacher
together. Be either one or the other. No man can serve two masters.... How different are our ways of thinking![190]
—Frederick Muhlenberg
In 1776, to his brother, Pastor Peter Muhlenberg

The role the church should play in civil government has
been debated for the last 2,000 years, and this question
was especially pertinent during the founding era. As the
British began exercising more control over the American
colonies, sincere Christians on both ends of the spectrum had deep
convictions on the appropriate level of political engagement. Some
felt submission was the appropriate response and were referred to
as Loyalists. Others felt they had a moral obligation to push back,
claiming the king had exceeded his God-given responsibility as
the civil ruler of the American colonies. Sincere pastors could be
found in both camps. This included two brothers who were both
pastors—one in New York, the other in Virginia. One believed his
pastoral role excluded him from direct involvement in the struggle
for independence; the other saw involvement as an outgrowth of
his Christian duty. They had very different views on the appropriate

level of engagement of pastors in America's struggle for independence.

Peter Muhlenberg pastored a Lutheran church in Virginia. He listened firsthand as Patrick Henry called on Virginians to defend against the British encroachments in his famous "give me liberty or give me death" speech delivered on March 23, 1775. With British hostilities increasing, George Washington asked Muhlenberg to raise a local militia in the fall of 1775. On January 21, 1776, in his home church in Woodstock, Virginia, Pastor Peter Muhlenberg ascended the pulpit of his church to deliver his sermon. The text was from Ecclesiastes 3:1–8:

> There is a time for everything, and a season for every activity under the heavens: a time to be born and a time to die, a time to plant and a time to uproot, a time to kill and a time to heal, a time to tear down and a time to build, a time to weep and a time to laugh, a time to mourn and a time to dance, a time to scatter stones and a time to gather them, a time to embrace and a time to refrain from embracing, a time to search and a time to give up, a time to keep and a time to throw away, a time to tear and a time to mend, a time to be silent and a time to speak, a time to love and a time to hate, a time for war and a time for peace.

Peter's nephew, Henry Augustus Muhlenberg, was in attendance that day and described the end of Peter's sermon:

> [Peter] said "that, in the language of holy writ, there was a time for all things, a time to preach and a time to pray, but those times had passed away;" and in a voice that re-echoed through the church like a trumpet-blast, "that there was a time to fight, and that time had now come!"
>
> The sermon finished, he pronounced the benediction. A breathless stillness brooded over the congregation. Deliberately putting off the gown, which had thus far covered his martial figure, he stood before them a girded warrior; and descending from the pulpit, ordered the drums at the church-door to beat for recruits.

Then followed a scene to which even the American revolution, rich as it is in bright examples of the patriotic devotion of the people, affords no parallel. His audience, excited in the highest degree by the impassioned words which had fallen from his lips, flocked around him, eager to be ranked among his followers.[191]

The next day, Peter Muhlenberg marched with nearly 300 enlistees, forming the 8th Virginia Regiment in the Continental Army. This devoted pastor left his church and led men in battle under General George Washington throughout the war.

Peter's younger brother, Frederick Muhlenberg, pastored a Lutheran congregation in New York. He believed the primary role of the church was to preach the gospel, minister to the needy, and not engage directly in politics. When he heard how his brother had used a sermon to recruit a regiment, he rebuked him, claiming that politics and war were off limits to a man of the cloth. Peter disagreed, surprised that Frederick would refuse to defend his country. He argued that being a clergyman did not relieve him of his duty to his country; it intensified it.[192] Author Dan Fisher captures the more detailed exchange in his book *Bringing Back the Black Robed Regiment*. Their exchange illustrates the same arguments we hear in the church today regarding political engagement:

Peter: "You say as a Clergyman nothing can excuse my Conduct, this excellent Doctrine is certainly a Production of that excellent City N.Y. which must be purged with Fire, before ever it is cleaned from Toryism; may there be none to pity it."
Frederick: "I am convinced the majority here are as strong for the American cause as the Virginians, if not stronger…. Brother, brother, the rough soldier peeps out from behind the black hat… that is contrary to the teaching of Jesus, which you formerly preached."
Peter: "I am a clergyman it is true, but I am a Member of Society as well as the poorest Layman, and my Liberty is as dear to me as to

any Man, shall I then sit still and enjoy myself at Home when the best Blood of the Continent is spilling? Heaven forbid it."

Frederick: "Words, words, words."

Peter: "Seriously Brother, I am afraid you have imbibed bad Principles in N.Y."

Frederick: "How do you make that out? Because I think it wrong for you to be both preacher and soldier in one? Bad logic.... You do not know me—I believe I have always been, and still am, as firm in our American cause as you are, even though I am not a colonel marching to the field."

Peter: "You know that from the Beginning of these Troubles, I have been compelled by Causes to you unknown to have a Hand in public Affairs. I have been Chairman to the Committee and Delegate for this County from the first, do you think then if America should be conquered I should be safe, on the contrary, and would you not sooner fight like a man than die the Death of a dog?"

Frederick: "You would have acted for the best if you had kept out of this business from the beginning. You were impelled by causes to me unknown... I think a needless self-love and ambition, a desire to appear the big man ... were the secret causes.... The Convention could have gotten along whether you were a delegate or not. Die the Death of a Dog... Whoever dies with Christ's image in his heart dies well."

Peter: "I am called by my country in its defense—the cause is just and noble—were I a Bishop, even a Lutheran one I should obey without Hesitation, and so far I am from thinking that I act wrong, I am convinced it is my Duty so to do a Duty I owe to God and my Country."

Frederick: "I now give you my thoughts in brief—I think you are wrong in trying to be both soldier and preacher together. Be either one or the other. No Man can serve two masters. I have long had some doubts of my own.... I incline to think a preacher can with good conscience resign his office and step into another calling. You think a man can be both preacher and colonel at the same time.

How different are our ways of thinking! ... Rest assured I shall always think of you in my prayers."[193]

In this lively exchange, Frederick argues a pastor could not be both a man of the cloth and a man in uniform. More directly, his brother could not remain a pastor and lead troops into battle. He asserted that taking up arms was contrary to the teachings of Jesus, and he suggested Peter might be acting out of self-ambition.

Conversely, Peter perceived military service as an extension of his service to God, wholly appropriate, given the injustices and civil unrest caused by British oppression. He argued it was God who condemned injustice throughout the Bible. To Peter, different situations and seasons in life means different behaviors are appropriate for those who are devoted to God, which is the direct application of Ecclesiastes 3. He believed his involvement in the political arena was of divine origin and wondered why his brother was unable to relate.

Frederick's theology prevented him from validating his brother's position, much less appreciating that military service could be an honorable ministry of God. Still, he affirmed he would pray for Peter. Frederick's position could be summarized like this:

- A committed pastor/preacher cannot also be involved in politics or the military. This would force him to "serve two masters."
- A pastor attempting to be politically or militarily involved is acting contrary to the teachings of Jesus.
- One must choose between political/military service or ministry.
- Ministers who choose political/military service may be motivated by self-ambition instead of spiritual maturity—which prioritizes evangelism, discipleship, and ministering to those in need.

Frederick's position is similar to modern day pastors taking a "New Testament only" view of the faith. This view centers primarily on the life of Christ instead of taking into account the whole counsel of the Bible regarding the purpose of civil government and the duty all

Christians have to support that purpose. In this view, responsibility for civil government is outsourced to the state and separate from the daily sphere of Christian life[194]:

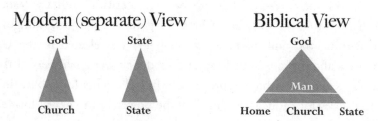

Modern (separate) View

Biblical View

Unfolding events soon challenged Frederick's theology.

A CHANGE IN PERSPECTIVE

In May 1776, Frederick sent his pregnant wife, Cathy, and their two children to her parents in Philadelphia because he was concerned for their safety. He remained with his congregation in New York City. As tensions increased between the colonists and the British during the summer, Frederick fled the city amidst rumors that the British were planning to capture and hang him. The British bolstered the rumors, burning churches from Staten Island to New York City. Frederick's church was among those destroyed.[195]

Exiled to Philadelphia, Frederick rethought his position about political and military involvement and had a change of heart. He joined the patriotic cause and was elected as a delegate to the Continental Congress in 1779. From 1780–1783, he served as Speaker of the Pennsylvania General Assembly and presided over Pennsylvania's Convention to ratify the US Constitution. He was then elected to the first US Congress. The magnitude of this transformation cannot be overstated. Frederick moved from viewing his calling to obey God as pastoral to viewing it as civil. The injustices around him were such that he saw his duty as a Christian shift from the pulpit to confronting injustices from a civil authority with a long train of abuses and no end in sight. He recognized that protecting liberty and justice for all was a Christian duty that merited his consideration and, eventually, his action. This change of heart later positioned him to be a leading national Christian statesman. He became the first Speaker of the House of Representatives and led the charge to protect individual rights.[196]

For his part, Peter Muhlenberg was a critical military leader throughout the Revolutionary War, serving under George Washington and earning the rank of major general. He was elected to the US Congress and Senate. Both Peter and Frederick were members of the first US Congress, which approved the Bill of Rights for submission to the states for ratification, limiting the power of the newly formed federal government. This important legislation bore the signature of Frederick Muhlenberg as the Speaker of the House. It was perhaps the most important bill for the first congress, and both Muhlenberg brothers were involved in its passage.[197]

Originally at odds on the question of political or military service, the Muhlenberg brothers came to see that civil service was a vital part of the Christian faith. Both answered the call and had a significant impact in achieving independence and setting the federal government on the right footing. From the outset, Peter perceived the fight for liberty to be an outgrowth of his commitment to the Lord. Frederick did not. What changed his mind?

We cannot be certain, but the catalyst for his change of heart appears to be because the lives of his family and himself were threatened, forcing his evacuation from New York. The lesson for us is clear: the unalienable right to life, liberty, and the pursuit of happiness empowers us to defend and protect our families. As citizens, this right becomes our duty to protect our communities as well.* This dual responsibility became clear to Frederick through real-life application. Still, many modern-day pastors have not been able to reconcile Jesus's call to evangelize with the idea that Christians have a citizenship duty in the communities in which they live.

---

* Jesus affirmed the right to self-defense in Luke 22:6 when he told his disciples, "But now if you have a purse, take it, and also a bag; and if you don't have a sword, sell your cloak and buy one."

PASTORS' ARGUMENTS FOR INACTION

The debate between the Muhlenberg brothers during the founding era is similar to the debate within the Christian leadership community today. There are a few pastors who, like Peter, believe they have a citizenship duty to ensure there is a just civil authority. But like Frederick, many modern-day pastors take the "pray but submit" approach, regardless of immoral laws thrust upon them. In doing so, they dismiss their God-given responsibility to uphold God's purpose for government, assuming someone else will take care of it. I have talked to many pastors over the years and have found the top reasons they share to justify inaction are the following:

1. The Great Commission calls on believers to evangelize.

We dealt with this question extensively in chapter 4, explaining God's Old Testament strategy for evangelism was for Israel to govern as a just nation (Deut. 4). By doing this, Israel would be a light to the surrounding Gentile nations, who would see this and come to inquire further about their culture and learn about God in the process. The Great Commission from Jesus in Matthew 28 was a key change in strategy. God had to clarify this new evangelistic approach since God sent his Son to die on the cross for the sins of mankind, not yet asserting his role as King reigning on earth, which will occur at his second coming.* Given Jesus was not setting up his kingdom but ushering in a new period where God would reach out to Gentiles with this gospel message, he directed the disciples to go and spread the gospel to the ends of the earth. There is more, however, to the question of what Jesus expects his followers to do.

Jesus affirmed everything in the Old Testament was true and to be followed. He never once suggested civil government, ordained in Gen 9:5–6, was no longer important. Paul's reference to God's purpose for civil government in Romans 13 was a confirmation of Genesis 9; it was not a call to just pray for and unconditionally submit to civil government,

---

* Christians are generally united that Jesus will return again but debate the manner and time when this will occur. This debate, however, is not tied in any way to the argument laid out in this book regarding the citizenship duty all Christians have.

as many modern-day pastors teach. Additionally, Paul gave guidance on gifts critical to establishing a just civil authority, including administration, wisdom, and leadership (Rom. 12, 1 Cor. 12, Eph. 4).* In summary, the Great Commission brought a change in evangelistic strategy and is to be pursued *along with* establishing liberty and justice for all.

2. The 'Separation of Church and State' must be followed.

The phrase "separation of church and state" is often used by both sides to challenge the role the Christian faith had in the founding and ongoing maintenance of civil governments across America. This phrase was invoked in the 1947 SCOTUS ruling regarding the case of *Everson v. Board of Education*. Mentioned in chapters 1 and 8, this case created a new legal principle that biblical principles taught by the church must not be allowed to influence the state-sponsored civil authority:

> In the words of Jefferson, the clause against establishment of religion by law was intended to erect "a wall of separation between church and State".... That wall must be kept high and impregnable. We could not approve the slightest breach.[198]

Many people assume this phrase, "a wall of separation between church and state," is in the Constitution, implying Christians must not seek to incorporate their faith in the public square. But it is not in any of the founding documents or amendments to the Constitution. The phrase comes from a letter from Thomas Jefferson in 1802 to the Danbury Baptist Church, the members of which had written to him expressing concern that the new government could infringe on the church's right to free speech.[199] The established church in Connecticut was the Congregational Church, and this group of Baptists was hoping Jefferson's sentiments, which helped disestablish the Anglican Church in Virginia, might also help disestablish the Congregational Church in Connecticut, ideally influencing all other states which still had an

---

* In the New Testament, a man named Erastus is mentioned as an example of a leading Christian becoming an important city manager, in other words, serving his local community with his gift of administration. He also ministered to and with the apostle Paul (Acts 19:22 and Rom. 16:23).

established state church. This would remove the threat of imprison-
ment many Baptist ministers experienced when preaching in states
with state-sponsored Christian denominations, like the Anglican
Church in Virginia.

Jefferson's reply was to assure them the new federal government
could not pass a law outlawing the Baptist denomination, because
of protections provided by the establishment clause in the First
Amendment:

> I contemplate with sovereign reverence that act of the whole
> American people which declared that their legislature should
> "make no law respecting an establishment of religion, or prohib-
> iting the free exercise thereof," thus building a wall of separation
> between Church & State.[200] (T. Jefferson January 1, 1802, to the
> Danbury Baptist Church)

Jefferson reinforced this view in a letter to Samuel Miller, January
23, 1808:

> I consider the government of the US as interdicted by the constitu-
> tion from intermedling with religious institutions, their doctrines,
> discipline, or exercises. This results not only from the provision
> that no law shall be made respecting the establishment, or free
> exercise, of religion, but from that also which reserves to the states
> the powers not delegated to the US. Certainly no power to pre-
> scribe any religious exercise, or to assume authority in religious dis-
> cipline, has been delegated to the general [federal] government....
> Every religious society has a right to determine for itself the times
> for these exercises & the objects proper for them according to their
> own particular tenets.[201]

Jefferson was stating the exact opposite of the 1947 redefinition
of "separation of church and state." Consider the 1799 opinion of
Supreme Court Associate Justice Samuel Chase, who also signed the

Declaration of Independence, in *Runkel v. Winemiller,* where he declared:

> Religion is of general and public concern, and on its support depend, in great measure, the peace and good order of government, the safety and happiness of the people. By our form of government, the Christian religion is, the established religion, and all sects and denominations of Christians are placed upon the same equal footing and are equally entitled to protection in their religious liberty.[202]

Like the Dred Scott ruling in 1857 that declared slaves were not protected by the Constitution, the 1947 ruling was clearly incorrect. It was contrary to the principles in our founding documents and in legal precedent during the 150 years after our founding.

3. Politics is divisive.

Divisive topics are inherent in conversations about faith, including civil government. But the passion swirling around these topics does not excuse pastors from wrestling with and educating their congregants. Life is full of conflict, and sometimes Christians mistakenly believe they can avoid this conflict by ignoring politics and somehow live in peace. But peace is not the absence of conflict; it is the ability to rest in God in the thick of conflict. This is what Psalm 23 is all about:

> You prepare a table before me in the presence of my enemies. You anoint my head with oil; my cup overflows. Surely your goodness and love will follow me all the days of my life, and I will dwell in the house of the LORD forever. (Ps. 23:5–6)

Unfortunately, many pastors are not providing a clear biblical worldview to their congregations to enable them to calmly reason through political issues and evaluate candidates. The result is a lot of contention and division, with Christians on their own trying to figure things out. Because of the resulting division, it is easier to opt out and focus on something not as contentious that all can agree on, like

CHAPTER 10 : THE ROLE OF THE CHURCH

evangelism. But without Christians actively engaged in the business of governing and educating society as God expects us to, all Americans and the world will suffer the consequences.

It need not be this way for Christians or anyone seeking to live in a society with law and order. Once a person understands the basic principles for governing outlined in earlier chapters and how those principles informed the American founding, he or she can easily respect a neighbor, even when they have disagreements. They will be able to focus on establishing liberty and justice for all, which produces freedom for all. This freedom will continue to inspire and draw people to America from all parts of the globe, as it has since our founding. Any discussion of politics should unite us when we understand God's blueprint for governing. The reality is it is our duty to engage, but we must be informed. The church is called to teach congregants to uphold the moral law and help them understand what a just government looks like.

Why do pastors tend to fall back on these reasons not to engage?

REASONS PASTORS BELIEVE THE WAY THEY DO

As I engage with church leaders, I have found several themes as to why they choose to set aside Christian citizenship as something passive and optional.

1. They have not been taught the full theology behind God's blueprint for governance and the citizenship duty all Christians have.

Many pastors view America's Revolution as a violation of biblical principles to submit to civil authorities rather than seeing it as a bold step to restore biblical justice. They cite Romans 13, claiming the founders never should have resisted the British. They do not recognize God's initial call for justice in Genesis 9, where he demands that all mankind establish justice going forward. Not acknowledging this early call for active citizenship and thousands of verses describing governing principles leads these pastors not to recognize citizenship duties as important work of a faithful Christian. They do not see Romans 13, 1 Timothy 2, and other New Testament passages as an affirmation of the

305

citizenship duty thoroughly described in the Old Testament. Instead, they see Romans 13 as a call for Christians to submit to both "good" and "bad" governing authorities. Given this, they logically conclude the American founding is illegitimate and perceive "following Jesus" is the overriding priority for modern Christians.

The purpose of this book has been to thoroughly explain the whole counsel of God in this area and to provide a thorough biblical defense that Christians are precisely the ones God expects to establish and maintain civil government, not just be submissive to it. Church leaders must revisit this topic.

2. Many in church leadership positions have the gift of evangelism and naturally gravitate to this activity.

While some pastors I talk with are earnestly seeking to teach the whole counsel of God and have simply never heard a biblical argument for active citizenship, others clearly gravitate to and focus almost exclusively on evangelism because it is their spiritual gift and it is a key theme in the New Testament. It is a natural tendency for all Christians to serve where they are most gifted. I would certainly encourage anyone called to evangelism to focus on it, but this is not the same as a person called to church leadership.

Pastors and church leaders are called to teach the whole counsel of God captured in the Bible from cover to cover. It can be a problem when Christians drawn exclusively to evangelism are running the church, because of their singular focus. When people press the need to engage in politics, these leaders use timeless Christian platitudes like "we want to win the lost for Christ" to justify sequestering political discussions. In the end, those concerned and maybe called to the civil arena are often marginalized or even pushed out.*

I want to encourage those reading this book who are concerned about civil affairs and have found themselves marginalized by church leaders. You are correct to care about civil affairs, and I hope this book has helped reassure you how critical your engagement and service is in

---

* I have personally experienced this.

the political arena. It is a vital and legitimate ministry, and there are millions of fellow Christians who feel as you do. Press on, continuing to encourage your church leaders that your church needs to have a change of heart, as Frederick Muhlenberg did.

3. Many in church leadership have accepted the progressive narrative of our country's founding.
Many pastors—especially those born after 1970—grew up on the progressive narrative pressed in public schools and universities.* This narrative rejects any meaningful role Christianity played in America's founding and instead claims the founders intended the church to have no role in civil government. They assert "separation of church and state" as the overriding operative principle.

In addition to claiming Christianity had no role in the founding, progressives blame the founders for much of America's current problems. Progressives insist institutional racism fueled by greed was the founders' true motivation for separation. But they ignore the vision in the Declaration, later expressed in the Pledge as "liberty and justice for all."† They also ignore the fact that most of the founders paid a heavy price for rejecting the immoral rule of King George and pursuing the formation of a new nation. They had nothing to gain and everything to lose—and many lost everything.[203]

Clearly there were issues at the time of the American founding, and some continue to this day. But many problems arose (and continue to arise) from those who *rejected* America's vision—not as a *result* of America's vision. It is true that some took advantage of their power, motivated by greed or discrimination. Any civil leader doing that acted contrary to the original vision outlined in the Declaration of Independence. Their leadership failures serve as examples for us to learn from and guard against, not as evidence that the American vision is a complete failure.

---

* A former US Congressman pointed this out to me years ago. Over time I realized he was correct.

† In his Cooper Union address, Lincoln made the case that the founders believed they had put America on the path to abolish slavery.

Progressive accusations about America's founding cast a misleading and incomplete narrative. Chapter 8, "The Progressive Blueprint for Civil Government," rebuts the error of this revisionist history, and earlier chapters lay out the biblical and historical argument of the impact of the Judeo-Christian faith on the founding. Unfortunately, many pastors have not only accepted this misleading narrative but also use it as a reason to disengage. Many have settled the matter in their minds and are unwilling to even consider a biblical counterargument. This is exactly what progressives hope for—Christians retreating from the political arena en masse. When Christians do this, they are supporting those who are not only enemies of America but also enemies of the Christian faith. This results in their supporting the very forces working against their evangelistic and general ministry objectives.

The clear pattern in history is this: nations that follow this path lose religious and civil liberties and descend into tyranny. When civil liberty erodes, it is not only harder to share the gospel—people also lose their property and the ability to sustain themselves. Some church leaders rationalize this as inevitable oppression we should expect as Christians. It is true Christians should expect persecution in this world, but I believe a strong case can be made that persecution of Christians today in America is due to God's judgment, because we have ignored his direction to establish and maintain the just civil authority our forefathers implemented. All of this is avoidable if church leaders embrace the biblical blueprint for governing, but they must have a change of heart, as Frederick Muhlenberg did.

THE COST OF A DISENGAGED CHURCH

The majority of American churches are in full retreat as a result of the progressive offensive over the last fifty years. This retreat has devasted America morally. Prior to the middle of the twentieth century, it was common for pastors to deliver "election sermons," educating their congregations on the issues of the day and encouraging them to vote according to biblical values. These pastors delivered sermons on the importance of liberty and justice and actively supported those who entered civil service, believing this was a valid and necessary personal ministry.

In the era of seeker-friendly churches, where pastors avoid reinforcing engagement in politics, progressives have moved to redefine America's moral foundation through a series of court rulings. They have successfully removed public displays of the Ten Commandments from most schools, courtrooms, and government buildings. Prior to their removal, the Ten Commandments reminded citizens of the necessary moral foundation of a lawful society, which is the basis of our national founding covenant. The Ten Commandments also provided a context for evangelism, because failure to keep the moral law is what tells us we are sinners in need of a Savior. The loss of this moral compass in America has been devastating.

Several generations have now grown up with little understanding of objective moral truth, sin, and repentance. The churchin-retreat has opened the door to moral chaos and has stripped us of a key evangelism building block. It is ironic that pastors who claim to be focused on evangelism "and want to change the culture for Christ" have remained silent as progressives have recast the moral law as unloving and intolerant.

The silent church has allowed decades of bad policy and has contributed to broken marriages and increasing numbers of children in fatherless homes. In a Father's Day speech in the Apostolic Church of God in Chicago on June 15, 2008, then-Senator Barack Obama described the devastating impact on children who grow up without a father:

> We know the statistics—that children who grow up without a father are five times more likely to live in poverty and commit crime; nine times more likely to drop out of schools and 20 times more likely to end up in prison. They are more likely to have behavioral problems, or run away from home or become teenage parents themselves. And the foundations of our community are weaker because of it.[204]

In this speech Barack Obama acknowledged the problem, a growing population in America not following the biblical template for how to have a happy and fulfilling life. Christians have the ultimate answer to this problem, and they should engage in civil government to promote policies that incentivize kids to get their high school diploma, marry, then have kids. *In that order.* Unfortunately, the church is largely silent and disengaged.*

The disengaged church has impacted the military too. When church leaders embrace the progressive view of the illegitimacy of America's founding, they discredit those in their congregations who serve or have served in the military. The faulty logic follows this path: If America's founding was a sinful act, how can a Christian feel good about serving in the military? And what is honorable about fighting for freedom if America is institutionally racist? Worse, those who served their country may conclude that serving a fundamentally flawed nation with toxic institutional biases and a founding born of a sinful rebellion may have been a waste of their lives. Church leaders seem oblivious to this struggle and do not realize they are contributing to it. Church leaders should honor military personnel for maintaining law and order at home and abroad, carrying out God's plan for government.

The public square is not the only place stripped of symbols. Many sanctuaries are devoid of the American flag, as the stars and stripes are now perceived as offensive. Pastors may drag out the flag on Memorial Day to thank those who served in the past. We might even hear a sermon extolling what Jesus said about sacrifice: "My command is this: Love each other as I have loved you. Greater love has no one than this: to lay down one's life for one's friends..." (John 15:12–13). But the flag disappears with the benediction, and the congregation hears little about citizenship until the next year.

Pastors who refuse to discuss establishing liberty and civil justice

---

* You are highly likely to avoid poverty if you graduate from high school, have a full-time job, wait to get married until after age twenty-one, and do not have children until after you are married. (Jim Hawkins, "There Are Only Three Rules to Avoid Poverty," November 18, 2018, The Wilson Post, https://www.wilsonpost.com/opinion/columns/there-are-only-three-rules-to-avoid-poverty/article_308fc946-eb53-11e8-8adf-6b4a30be1da3.html.)

risk marginalizing gifted congregants and sabotaging their own efforts to energize the congregation. Modern versions of Peter Muhlenberg—men and women who feel called to serve their country—may be sitting idle in the pew instead of getting the encouragement they need to serve in the civil arena.

My own story speaks to this issue. In my twenties, I discovered I loved to teach, and I was encouraged by many people to pursue that calling. If others had not encouraged me and I had not found teaching as a legitimate personal ministry, I would be bored in my faith. Conversely, if my church leaders ignored the way God wired me and plugged me into an evangelism or discipleship team, I would have been uncomfortable—like a fish out of water. Sadly, too many pastors are doing this with people in their congregations who feel called to serve in the civil arena. They may say they support those in politics, but they push programs centered on evangelism and marginalize those interested in politics. They are pushing a "one-size-fits-all" model that alienates a significant portion of believers.

Not including the securing of liberty and justice as part of the Christian faith also creates a narrow and distorted image of the Christian experience. This image is made up of people who go on the mission field, provide spiritual counseling, and work at soup kitchens. These are obviously important and can be aspects of the Christian walk for some people. But what if a Christian wants to be a policeman, lawyer, judge, military servicemember? What might a soldier in the armed forces identify with if the Christian faith gives this narrow image? All Christians are called to follow where the Lord leads them, and he does not always lead them to this narrow image. If believers see themselves as answering God's timeless call to keep evil in check and secure justice for all, then they are honoring him in their civil service. And the church should encourage them however it can if they choose to pursue civil service as their ministry.

BIBLICAL ROLE OF THE CHURCH

God intended the church to function differently. Wherever God raises up a church, he builds a congregation with a range of spiritual gifts that enable the church to thrive and bless the surrounding community. As a church grows, God will draw more people, equipping them to evangelize, disciple, serve, teach, and lead within the walls of the church and in the community at large, *including in the halls of civil government*. The role of church leadership is to develop the congregants' faith and to assist them in discovering their spiritual gifts. Acknowledging all the gifts is critical, which Paul affirms in his first letter to the Corinthian church:

> Just as a body, though one, has many parts, but all its many parts form one body, so it is with Christ. For we were all baptized by one Spirit so as to form one body—whether Jews or Gentiles, slave or free—and we were all given the one Spirit to drink. Even so the body is not made up of one part but of many. Now if the foot should say, "Because I am not a hand, I do not belong to the body," it would not for that reason stop being part of the body. And if the ear should say, "Because I am not an eye, I do not belong to the body," it would not for that reason stop being part of the body. If the whole body were an eye, where would the sense of hearing be? If the whole body were an ear, where would the sense of smell be? But in fact God has placed the parts in the body, every one of them, just as he wanted them to be. If they were all one part, where would the body be? As it is, there are many parts, but one body. The eye cannot say to the hand, "I don't need you!" And the head cannot say to the feet, "I don't need you!" On the contrary, those parts of the body that seem to be weaker are indispensable. (1 Cor. 12:12–22)

Public service is a critical, legitimate, and necessary ministry, and those God calls to engage in it should be supported like all other congregants. When churches focus on helping *all* their congregants discover their gifts, they cannot help but transform the community for Christ.

WHY TWO IRRECONCILABLE POSITIONS?

The conflict between the Muhlenberg brothers has divided the modern church as well. How is it that committed Christians can be diametrically opposed? One side accurately believes that evangelism and discipleship are critical activities that Jesus focused on throughout most of his earthly ministry. The other side agrees with this idea but also believes that Jesus supported the Old Testament, which embeds the Ten Commandments as the foundation of God's blueprint for governance and repeatedly calls for justice. How is it that the first group cannot see this universal call for justice *also* clearly taught in the Bible?

This challenge reminds me of optical illusions that present a clear image upon initial viewing—until someone points out a second image. In the figure below, most people will first see an old woman with a white scarf looking down to the right.[*205] Upon further examination, however, another image can be clearly seen: a younger woman looking back over her left shoulder. Both images are true; it is a matter of perspective. For most of us, we see only one image until someone gives us the information that enlarges our perspective.

This book has been about helping the church see the other perspective. The next question is, "What should the church do, specifically church leaders, with this broader biblical perspective?"

---

*The oldest known image of this type is believed to be from an anonymous German postcard from 1888.

What the Church Should Do Next

Here are some things church leaders should *start* to do right away:

1. Thoroughly research what the Bible teaches about God's blueprint for civil government and a Christian's citizenship duty that grows from that blueprint.

This book provides an overall summary, but more study is needed for church leaders to fully understand and elevate citizenship to a legitimate ministry alongside missions and other typical church ministries.

2. Establish a position statement for your church to declare what you believe and the intention to establish a ministry to engage this aspect of the Christian faith in your church.

Churches are beginning to do this, which is critical to affirm and teach these concepts to their congregations.

3. Appoint a leader who can establish a citizenship ministry in your church.

This leader should be gifted, feel called to this area, and have a position on the church leadership board just as a leader of any other ministry would. Have him or her develop a plan to educate your congregation on the basics of Christian citizenship. This ministry should also support civil servants through education, encouragement, and prayer—much like we do for our missionaries.

Just as there are things church leaders must *start*, there are other things that they must *stop* doing:

1. Stop telling people that voting does not matter.

Pastors must stop downplaying the importance of voting. Boycotting the voting booth dishonors all those Americans who fought and died to protect our right to vote for leaders. It also shirks our most basic citizenship responsibility. Christians cannot afford to surrender their voice in America's future, even when the pool of candidates leaves something to be desired. Christians must evaluate each candidate for how his or her policies compare to the moral law and assess that candidate's character. And remember, supplying good candidates is ultimately the church's responsibility. If you do not like the field you have to choose from, then your church has some work to do.

2. Stop discouraging those whom God has called to serve in civil leadership.

Civil service needs to be recognized and encouraged by church leaders. To keep patriots at bay, the Christian establishment has developed a series of pithy one-liners to undercut any opposition that promotes a more active citizenship responsibility. This language is used to diminish civil service and direct people away from that calling:

"Stop putting your hope in earthly leaders and focus on your relationship with Jesus."

This implies that those fighting for biblical justice are spiritually immature. They put their hope in government, a person, or an old document instead of recognizing God is ultimately in control. These concepts disparage those who fought for freedom in the military, as it implies they, too, put their hope in government or an old document instead of serving the Lord.

"You need to be more concerned about God's heavenly kingdom, not earthly issues."

This also implies those fighting for biblical justice are spiritually immature, not recognizing the significance of our heavenly home and the kingdom that awaits us. It is possible for Christians to love America, *and* to love and yearn for God's kingdom more.

"If you are not supporting evangelism, you are not following the Jesus of the Bible."

This implies a spiritually mature believer would focus only on evangelism.

"Politics is divisive; therefore, we will not allow it to be discussed in our church."

> This implies those fighting for biblical justice are as culpable for the political acrimony as those fighting against biblical justice. While the zeal of some may lack polish, the primary reason for acrimony in the public square is sin in one form or another.

"Jesus didn't talk about politics, so we are not going to talk about politics."

> This implies that serious Christians should never engage with or think about politics. It also does not recognize Jesus affirmed the whole Old Testament, which includes many verses on establishing and maintaining a just civil authority, i.e., politics!

"There is sin in both camps."

> This implies those fighting for justice according to the moral law are acting as sinfully as those who are fighting against justice, subverting it at every opportunity to fundamentally transform America. There is not a moral equivalence between the progressive proponent and the Christian patriot.

3. Stop disparaging the American founding and those individuals who were instrumental in establishing our national covenant and Constitution.

Many modern pastors have embraced the revisionist history that public schools have propagated in recent decades. Rather than present a balanced view of America built on biblical principles with a noble vision and the mistakes made along the way, only a negative one-sided version is reinforced from American evangelical pulpits. I honestly believe Christians affirming this negative narrative do care about truth, but they must do the research and consider the full body of evidence before speaking ill of anyone. Sadly, many are just not interested in doing the research or in reconsidering the position they have held for decades.

By studying the theology and history of America's founders, church leaders will discover a respect for the faith of those who sought to protect the colonists from tyranny. They will discover in personal journals, letters, speeches, and founding documents a glimpse of their motives for founding a free nation. They will not discover a glorified group of revolutionaries or flawless men but instead will be drawn to honor those who came before us as men and women who attempted to live out their faith in an extraordinary way.

Such a study of America's founding requires church leaders to search for balanced truth and operate according to Paul's words to the church at Corinth: "Love is patient, love is kind. It does not envy, it does not boast, it is not proud. It does not dishonor others, it is not self-seeking, it is not easily angered, it keeps no record of wrongs. Love does not delight in evil but rejoices with the truth. It always protects, always trusts, always hopes, always perseveres" (1 Cor. 13:4–7). Studying the founders through this lens, including the mistakes they made, will provide a much different and more accurate perspective than the progressive narrative embraced by many pastors today.

Just as there are things the church should *start* and *stop* doing, there are many good things the evangelical church should *continue* to do with respect to missions, discipleship, and other outreach ministries. The church should continue evangelizing and making disciples, incorporating principles of liberty and justice. The following actions are tangible differences of a more holistic approach to evangelism:

1. Teach God's Old Testament strategy for evangelism, which involves creating a society for establishing and maintaining justice—a community that others are drawn to.

2. Launch advanced discipleship topics that explore God's blueprint for governance for both family and community. Such a study shows that God's design for governing starts in the home and expands to the local, state, and national levels. By beginning with the home, the educational arm of the church can train parents to govern in God-honoring ways while producing the next generation of public servants who love their country.

3. Expand global evangelism efforts to include educating foreign nationals in God's blueprint as part of a discipleship ministry. This discipleship training should recognize the Great Commission's ultimate aim: to make disciples of all *nations*. This implies that Christians should assume leadership positions that will help nations govern in a God-honoring way to encourage evangelism. This means the church should recognize that God will call some to serve in civil leadership and should do what it can to support them. The church should also equip those who engage in the civil arena in principles of governing and Christian integrity.

RESPONSIBILITIES OF THE MODERN CHURCH

The scope of Christian citizenship duty presented in this book is meant to paint a broader ministry vision for church leaders. Each of the following points is critical for churches to fully embrace what the Bible presents as God's blueprint for governance:

1. The theology of governing as an essential part of God's plan for communities and in the home.
Church leaders must rediscover and integrate the theology of governing and acknowledge how Scripture informed America's founders. When we acknowledge that God's governance principles apply in the home, families will understand how those principles apply in their local, state, and national communities as well. This vital part of training "on the way they should go" (Prov. 22:6) will help congregants mature into productive citizens and truly impact the culture for Christ.

2. Teach citizenship as a Christian duty.
Being good citizens means helping to establish and maintain liberty and justice for all. Genesis 9 tells us this is not an option but a duty we all have. Citizenship has many facets, including taking care of ourselves, our families, and our neighbors. Christians should seek to improve the welfare of all in their communities, truly demonstrating the love of Christ to saved and unsaved alike.

3. Teach civil service as a legitimate and vital personal ministry.
Churches must teach *and look for* Christians who are gifted and feel
called to engage in serving in all areas of the public arena. These
are not "second-class" ministry activities; they are vitally important.
Churches should seek to discover who in their midst may have this
calling and create programs led by seasoned Christians to train them
for this ministry, just as they would encourage and train a person for
music ministry or evangelism.

4. Establish citizenship ministries in your church.
Getting serious about citizenship means establishing it as a stand-alone
ministry on the church board. An elder should be assigned to head this
up to provide ongoing citizenship education, help identify and train
those wishing to serve in the public arena, and provide perspective on
key social issues being debated in local, state, and national legislatures.
Some evangelical churches have established ministries like this, and
their programs can serve as templates. There are many Christian organizations looking for opportunities to educate churches who want to
know more about what is happening in the civil arena.

5. Become the moral conscience of society.
God has entrusted the church with the responsibility to set the moral
standard in the community in which it resides. This means calling out
sinful conduct and pressuring civil leaders to govern justly and in harmony with God's moral law. We are not seeking perfection in our civil
leaders and should not constantly put them under a moral microscope,
but blatant immoral behaviors or policies must be confronted. John the
Baptist serves as an example who was willing to challenge Herod for
taking his brother's wife unlawfully. When laws are passed contrary to
God's morality—legalizing abortion or same-sex unions, redistributing
income, closing churches during a pandemic—they must be called out
by Christians. This is how the church becomes "salt and light" in a dark,
sinful, and violent world (Matt. 5:13–16). There are so many verses
that call for people of faith to address injustice (emphases added):

Who will rise up for me against the wicked? Who will take a stand for me against evildoers? (Ps. 94:16)

This is what the LORD says: "*Maintain justice and do what is right*, for my salvation is close at hand and my righteousness will soon be revealed." (Isa. 56:1)

But you must return to your God; *maintain love and justice*, and wait for your God always. (Hosea 12:6)

This is what the LORD Almighty said: "Administer true justice; show mercy and compassion to one another. Do not oppress the widow or the fatherless, the foreigner or the poor. Do not plot evil against each other." (Zech. 7:9–10)

"Does it make you a king to have more and more cedar? Did not your father have food and drink? He did what was right and just, so all went well with him. He defended the cause of the poor and needy, and so all went well. *Is that not what it means to know me?*" declares the LORD. (Jer. 22:15–16)

Woe to you, teachers of the law and Pharisees, you hypocrites! You give a tenth of your spices—mint, dill and cumin. But you have neglected the more important matters of the law—justice, mercy and faithfulness. You should have practiced the latter, without neglecting the former. You blind guides! You strain out a gnat but swallow a camel. (Matt. 23:23–24)

Godly sorrow brings repentance that leads to salvation and leaves no regret, but worldly sorrow brings death. See what this godly sorrow has produced in you: what earnestness, what eagerness to clear yourselves, what indignation, what alarm, what longing, what concern, what *readiness to see justice done*. (2 Cor. 7:10–11)

And what more shall I say? I do not have time to tell about Gideon, Barak, Samson and Jephthah, about David and Samuel and the prophets, who through faith conquered kingdoms, *administered justice*, and gained what was promised. (Heb. 11:32–33)

THE LEGACY OF THE CHURCH

At the time of America's founding, religious leaders spoke out on the need to understand Christian principles for governing, and these principles then had a great influence on the founding of America. The religious leaders talked about our ongoing responsibility to actively participate to preserve liberty—unique to the United States. The British were aware of the role church leaders were playing in the struggle for independence, referring to them as the "Black Robed Regiment." Not only were these leaders preaching biblical principles of liberty and justice but they were also taking up arms and leading troops into battle— as Peter Muhlenberg did. This is the legacy of the church during the founding era, and it sets a high bar for the generations to follow.

The following quotes from prominent leaders inside and outside the church show how important the church has always been in America.

At a celebration of the one-hundredth anniversary of the Declaration of Independence, July 4, 1876, Congressman (and later, President) James Garfield said:

> Now, more than ever before, the people are responsible for the character of their Congress. If that body be ignorant, reckless, and corrupt, it is because the people tolerate ignorance, recklessness, and corruption. If it be intelligent, brave, and pure, it is because the people demand those high qualities to represent them in the national legislature.... If the next centennial does not find us a great nation, with a great and worthy Congress, it will be because those who represent the enterprise, the culture, and the morality of the nation do not aid in controlling the political forces.[206]

In his book *Fear God and Take Your Own Part* (1916), Theodore Roosevelt wrote:

> Christianity is not the creed of Asia and Africa at this moment solely because the seventh century Christians of Asia and Africa … had trained themselves not to fight, whereas the Moslems were trained to fight. Christianity was saved in Europe solely because the peoples of Europe fought. If the peoples of Europe in the seventh and eighth centuries, and on up to and including the seventeenth century, had not possessed a military equality with, and gradually a growing superiority over the Mohammedans who invaded Europe, Europe would at this moment be Mohammedan and the Christian religion would be exterminated.[207]

At the laying of the cornerstone of the New York Avenue Presbyterian Church in Washington, DC, April 3, 1951, President Harry S Truman stated:

> The essential mission of the church is to teach the moral law. We look to our churches, above all other agencies, to teach us the highest moral standards of right and wrong. We rely on the churches particularly to instill into our young people those moral ideals which are the basis of our free institutions. This great Republic is founded on a firm foundation based on those very principles…. [Religion] is a positive force that impels us to affirmative action. We are under divine orders—not only to refrain from doing evil, but also to do good and to make this world a better place in which to live.[208]

At the ceremony where he received the Congressional Gold Medal on May 2, 1996, Reverend Billy Graham reinforced the need for Christians to be active voters, stating:

I believe the fundamental crisis of our time is a crisis of the spirit.... We have lost sight of the moral and spiritual principles on which this nation was established—principles drawn largely from the Judeo-Christian tradition as found in the Bible.... I believe America has gone a long way down the wrong road. We must turn around.... If ever we needed God's help, it is now.[209]

ROADMAP FOR THE CHURCH

The church is ultimately accountable for teaching biblical citizenship to its congregations. But the reality is this: most local churches do not have citizenship on their radar, which makes it especially challenging to get their leadership engaged. If you want to get your church leadership to consider a citizenship ministry, first try to find several others in the congregation who are like-minded. You might review this book together to find points of agreement and where fellow members of the congregation have questions. You might host a Bible study using material from this book or similar videos to begin building a strong base. This may take several cycles to get a critical mass of people to a common level of understanding and level of conviction to engage in this area.

Once you have three or more people aligned and interested in presenting to your church leadership, you might approach a past or current leader to share the ministry idea to get an initial read on how to present your ideas to your church's elder board. Expect resistance; this will be your indicator that more discussion and education is needed. The content of this book will help you.

Once you have a sponsoring elder or supportive member of your church board, there are several things to establish:

- Ongoing education, including training for beginners and for the more advanced. The material in this book overall would be for the more advanced, and the simple model in chapter 9, "Christian Citizenship," would be a good starting point

- Work with your senior pastor on appropriate messages (to be given periodically) that teach governing and citizenship principles from the pulpit.
- Establish a way for your church congregation to be informed on current issues. There are many organizations that provide this kind of information at the local and national level that would love to work with your church. The task is to establish a connection to several of these organizations and create a team of folks from your church who can distill key issues down to a couple of simple paragraphs that others can understand and act on.
- Find out who all the folks are in your church serving in some public capacity (city council, law enforcement, fire department, school board, etc.) and get them together to find out how you can support them as they work through challenging issues. Maybe ask them to share in the main service what they are seeing and how the congregation can pray for them.
- Recruit others in your church who show an interest and may be called to serve in various positions of civil government—they are there! Train and mentor them in how they might develop and use their gifts to serve in this area as a legitimate personal ministry. This is how we fill the pipeline and have a deep bench of high-integrity people willing and ready to serve in civil government at the highest levels.

These are the general things that can be enacted to create a sustainable citizenship ministry. There might be a different order to some of these things, and it may take several years to get all of these in place. The key is to start where you feel you have support. If you are unsuccessful in getting your church leadership to engage, you might do many of the same steps mentioned above, only "off to the side" with like-minded people instead of as an official church ministry.

A LESSON FROM THE MOVIES

Superhero movies enjoy near-universal approval. Who doesn't love a caped crusader saving the day? I remember when the first modern Superman movie came out. The actor, Christopher Reeves, was the caped hero, fighting for justice. Sequels followed, and then the Batman movies took center stage. Spiderman followed, filling theaters. Then the latest series featured my favorite Marvel Comics hero: Captain America. These movies have made billions of dollars. What is it about these stories that seem to resonate with so many people around the globe? In virtually all the storylines, the heroes are ordinary people who do extraordinary things on behalf of a community that is oppressed by some injustice. What appeals to millions of viewers is the ordinary superhero who extends justice and defeats the bad guy.

Securing liberty and justice for all has universal appeal, and this is exactly the citizenship duty all Christians have in the communities in which they live. When ordinary people step forward to defend liberty and justice, they are more than a hero to society; they are stewards of God's timeless call for justice. The role of the church is to prepare and encourage the superhero inside each of us to follow God's blueprint for restoring liberty and justice for all. In doing so, we find a new and exciting dimension to our individual God-given purpose, one that allows us to serve our fellow citizens and honor God. He will bless the individual who stewards this opportunity, and he will bless the nation that benefits from that service.

SUMMARY

Unjust governments are the single biggest source of misery to people throughout the history of the world. God's demand for justice shows why this is a critically important aspect of the Christian faith. But the division in the church today on how to engage politically suggests many Christians do not see the importance of citizenship duties. Sincere pastors and church leaders can believe very different things about the Christian's role in the civil arena. In this book we have laid out the full biblical argument defining active Christian citizenship as a duty, but many earnest believers have not been exposed to it. Those who do see the active-duty position must continue to engage politically while also trying to show their fellow Christians how civil service can be a legitimate and vital ministry.

There are many things the church must start, stop, and continue doing to help reestablish equitable and impartial justice in local communities. Following the roadmap for education and acting on these citizenship responsibilities will set the stage for the one last thing that needs to happen to restore America's founding covenant. This is the subject of the last chapter.

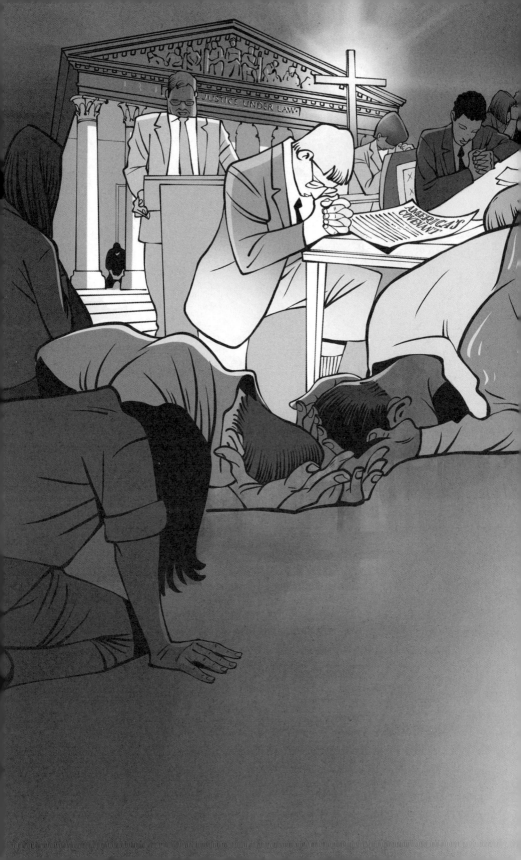

CHAPTER 11

ROADMAP TO RESTORE AMERICA

Recommitting to the American Covenant

> If my people, who are called by my name, will humble themselves
> and pray and seek my face and turn from their wicked ways, then
> I will hear from heaven, and I will forgive their sin and will heal
> their land.
> —2 Chronicles 7:14

CHAPTER 11

ROADMAP TO RESTORE AMERICA

Recommitting to the American Covenant

If my people, who are called by my name, will humble themselves and pray and seek my face and turn from their wicked ways, then I will hear from heaven, and I will forgive their sin and will heal their land.
—2 Chronicles 7:14

We, therefore, the Representatives of the united States of America, in General Congress, Assembled, appealing to the Supreme Judge of the world for the rectitude of our intentions, do, in the Name, and by the Authority of the good People of these Colonies, solemnly publish and declare, That these United Colonies are, and of Right ought to be Free and Independent States.... And for the support of this Declaration, with a firm reliance on the protection of the divine Providence, we mutually pledge to each other our Lives, our Fortunes and our sacred Honor.
—Declaration of Independence

I had an engineering colleague who used to say, "A problem well defined is half solved." In the previous chapters of this book, we defined two parts of the problem: 1) understanding what the Bible teaches regarding civil government, and 2) recognizing what our resulting citizenship responsibilities are. For America to be restored to the governing vision expressed in our nation's founding covenant,

CHAPTER 11 : ROADMAP TO RESTORE AMERICA

these two problems must be addressed. If you believe in God's purpose for civil government and see that his plan served as the founders' blueprint, the remaining question is "What's next?" To answer this question, we must address the last problem: many Americans have rejected our founding covenant and are trying to replace America's founding principles with ideals that have evolved past progressivism and which logically terminate in Marxism.*

The intent of this final chapter is to lay out a clear roadmap to address this problem, which is deepening the division in America today. This is the path for all American patriots—Christian or not—to rekindle the founding vision for America of "liberty and justice for all." The ultimate objective is to *rediscover* and *recommit* to the American founding covenant. This is the only way we can truly restore America to embrace and pursue her founding vision, where every American, regardless of race, sex, or creed, experiences liberty and equal justice. For Christians, this must be seen as a Christian responsibility and a vital part of truly living out our faith. Importantly, this duty must motivate all Christians to reengage in the political process—not only in America but around the world. The goal is not to usher in God's kingdom here on earth but to establish law and order as the Bible clearly instructs the believer to do. This secures justice for all and allows every individual to go on his or her own personal faith journey.

ROADMAP TO RESTORE THE NATION

If American patriots hope to restore America to the principles captured in our founding national covenant, there are several critical things they must do. The first is to acknowledge the true *state of the union*, specifically how far we have deviated from our national founding covenant. This was summarized in chapter 1.

The second is to realize how dire the situation truly is. America has strayed so far into progressive ideology that working harder within the current political system to turn things around will not be enough. The

---

* Many today claim that America's problem is that we are not following the Constitution. It is certainly important that we follow this document, but this is a symptom of the true root cause: a rejection of our national founding covenant.

forces marshalled against America have infiltrated most of America's key institutions. *Turning things around will require divine intervention*—we are going to need God's help. Of course, this assumes God's will is to restore America, and while we do not know if God's will is to intervene for our country, the Bible constantly encourages nations to seek him and to return to him. Seeking to restore "liberty and justice for all" is the only course of action for a sincere believing citizen.

The situation in America today is not that different from the founding era. When the First Continental Congress met in Carpenters' Hall on September 5, 1774, the delegates knew the situation was serious and beyond their control. The colonies were autonomous, having never before met together in person. The global empire of the day was bearing down, and things looked bleak. In desperation, they appealed to God. Reverend Jacob Duché started by reading Psalm 35:

> Plead my cause, O LORD, with them that strive with me: fight against them that fight against me. Take hold of shield and buckler, and stand up for mine help. Draw out also the spear, and stop the way against them that persecute me: say unto my soul, I am thy salvation." (Ps. 35:1–3 KJV)

In a letter to his wife, John Adams put the morning in context:

> You must remember this was the next Morning after we heard the horrible Rumour, of the Cannonade of Boston.—I never saw a greater Effect upon an Audience. It seemed as if Heaven had ordained that Psalm to be read on that Morning. After this Mr. Duche, unexpected to every Body struck out into an extemporary Prayer, which filled the Bosom of every Man present.... It has had an excellent Effect upon every Body here.[210]

Guided by their deep faith, the founders stared down overwhelming odds and declared independence two years later. Their actions changed forever the fate of nations around the globe. The Patriot army was nearly defeated or captured several times during the five-year Revolutionary War. We know how the war turned out, but the outcome was in doubt all the way up to the British surrender at Yorktown. In hindsight, it is clear God showed up numerous times to protect the pursuit of independence.

History has left a clear record of when the founders openly acknowledged God's direct intervention. In *Miracles in American History*, Susie Federer recounts several occasions of divine intervention and the founders acknowledging God's hand in their cause. For example, at the Battle of Brooklyn Heights, on August 27–28, 1776, a spontaneous fog deprived the British of their only opportunity to capture the entire American Army. Major Benjamin Talmadge, Washington's chief of intelligence, wrote:

> As the dawn of the next day approached, those of us who remained in the trenches became very anxious for our own safety, and when the dawn appeared there were several regiments still on duty.
>
> At this time a very dense fog began to rise off the river, and it seemed to settle in a peculiar manner over both encampments.

I recollect this peculiar providential occurrence perfectly well, and so very dense was the atmosphere that I could scarcely discern a man at six yards distance…. We tarried until the sun had risen, but the fog remained as dense as ever.[211]

Federer recounts that later, after the Battle of Cowpens on January 17, 1781, British commander Henry Clinton wrote that at the Yadkin River, "Here the royal army was again stopped by a sudden rise of the waters, which had only just fallen (almost miraculously) to let the enemy over." Two months later, General Washington similarly wrote to William Gordon,

"We have … abundant reasons to thank Providence for its many favorable interpositions in our behalf. It has at times been my only dependence, for all other resources seemed to have failed us."[212]

America's Thanksgiving holiday arose from the founders' gratitude to God for his mercies in the midst of the Revolutionary War, when the Congress of the Confederation passed a resolution on October 11, 1782:

It being the indispensable duty of all nations… to offer up their supplications to Almighty God… the United States in Congress assembled… do hereby recommend it to the inhabitants of these states in general, to observe… the last Thursday… of November next, as a Day of Solemn Thanksgiving to God for all his mercies.[213]

Finally, Federer notes, the Revolutionary War ended with the Treaty of Paris, signed in 1783 by Ben Franklin, John Adams, John Jay, and David Hartley, crediting the treaty to God's favor:

In the name of the Most Holy and Undivided Trinity. It having pleased the Divine Providence to dispose the hearts of the most serene and most potent Prince George the Third, by the Grace of

God, King of Great Britain ... and of the United States of America, to forget all past misunderstandings and differences.... Done at Paris, this third day of September, in the year of our Lord one thousand seven hundred and eighty-three.[214]

These accounts show that the founders believed the odds were stacked against them, yet they also saw how God intervened on their behalf.

What did the founders do that enabled them to defeat the world's global empire at that time? They followed the blueprint of Israel on how to start a nation. This included the following:

- They aligned with each other and with the biblical God on the basic theological vision for a just nation and the moral argument for separation.
- They called out the immoral behavior of the ruling authority, warranting the forfeiture of the God-given governing authority. They documented a "long train of abuses" that spanned years.
- They wrote this all down in their covenant to establish a new nation and then signed it.
- They published and declared to the world their moral and legal rationale to confront, and in their case, to separate from England.
- They implored God several times in the Declaration itself to see the separation through, pledging their lives, fortunes, and sacred honor.
- They prayed and sometimes fasted throughout the revolutionary process and beyond.*

In order for America to return to our founding principles, we need to follow these same steps. To be clear, I am not advocating for

---

* Multiple people observed General Washington praying by himself during the war. When discussions at the Constitutional Convention stalled, Benjamin Franklin reminded the delegates they used to pray routinely—and that those prayers were answered. Presidential prayer proclamations to encourage the nation en masse to turn to God were very common up through the twentieth century, continuing a tradition of America relying on God.

separation but for confronting the litany of immoral activities of our current federal government and returning to America's founding covenant. Recall in chapter 1 the example of a young King Josiah, who ruled about 800 years after Moses received the Law. During the restoration of the temple, the high priest discovered the "Book of the Law." When King Josiah read the Law, he mourned, knowing Israel had gone astray from what God wanted for them. He asked the priests to ask the Lord what he must do for Israel to be restored to God. What the king did is recorded in 2 Kings 23 for the benefit of nations in similar situations of decline—like America. Note the actions he took:

> Then the king called together all the elders of Judah and Jerusalem. He went up to the temple of the LORD with the people of Judah, the inhabitants of Jerusalem, the priests and the prophets—all the people from the least to the greatest. *He read in their hearing all the words of the Book of the Covenant,* which had been found in the temple of the LORD. The king stood by the pillar and *renewed the covenant in the presence of the LORD—to follow the LORD and keep his commands, statutes and decrees with all his heart and all his soul, thus confirming the words of the covenant written in this book.* Then all the people pledged themselves to the covenant. (2 Kings 23:1–3, emphasis added)

This is consistent with what the Lord shared with Solomon during his reign:

> If my people, who are called by my name, will humble themselves and pray and seek my face and turn from their wicked ways, then I will hear from heaven, and I will forgive their sin and will heal their land. (2 Chron. 7:14)

This is also consistent with instruction from Job 36 and Nehemiah 9:

If they obey and serve him, they will spend the rest of their days in prosperity and their years in contentment. But if they do not listen, they will perish by the sword and die without knowledge. (Job 36:11–12)

They stood where they were and read from the Book of the Law of the Lord their God for a quarter of the day, and spent another quarter in confession and in worshiping the Lord their God…. "In view of all this, we are making a binding agreement, putting it in writing, and our leaders, our Levites and our priests are affixing their seals to it." (Neh. 9:3, 38)

The founders followed this same process: seeking out and obeying what God's word says he wants from us as disciples and as citizens, declaring our reliance on God and praying our way through seemingly impossible situations. In 1776 roughly half the population were Patriots—wanting to separate from those loyal to the crown or not eager to take a position either way.* God honored the efforts of the Patriots seeking to establish the biblical vision for governing.

How might this work in America today? What series of events might have to happen for God to forgive and restore our nation? Conditions are different today than during the founding era, but if we were to apply the biblical template the founders followed, it might look something like this:

- Have a gathering of likeminded, nationally recognized spiritual and civil leaders consider the question, "Do we still hold to the American founding covenant, including the Law of Nature and Nature's God, i.e., the moral law, as God's standard?" This group might include current and former government officials who believe in our founding national covenant. It should also include

* It is impossible to know the exact breakdown between supporters of the Revolution, those who opposed it, and those who were indifferent, especially as the war progressed. What is clear is that not everyone was a supporter, which is a similar situation in the biblical accounts of Josiah and Nehemiah.

nationally recognized Judeo-Christian spiritual leaders. They do not need to agree on many doctrinal positions other than the moral law and the basic principles of governing presented in earlier chapters.

- Document a list of immoral offenses pushed by progressive ideology that constitute how America has dishonored God in recent decades. This list would serve as an updated version of a long train of abuses.
- Draft a "Declaration 2.0," affirming the theology and vision of the original, listing the offenses of the current opposing Marxist ideology, and summarizing our collective commitment to restore America to a God-honoring nation by upholding the moral law as the rule of law.
- Recommit to our national founding covenant with a formal signing ceremony, covered in prayer. The updated covenant could be published online for any American to affix his or her signature to, signifying the people's commitment as well. The Bible shows us God will honor this kind of national repentance.
- This should be followed by a week of prayer and fasting by all those Americans, showing commitment and reliance on God to do what is impossible for us to do on our own.

This plan may seem naïve. But do we really think we can turn around America's decline without God's help? And if we agree we need his help, why would we not follow the biblical template so clearly explained? The founders did. And we are a nation today because of their devotion to God's plan for government. The Bible is clear: to garner God's support requires a national intervention by spiritual and civil leaders, where we acknowledge our national sins and plead for his help to restore us to a God-honoring nation. As the founding demonstrated, it does not have to be supported by the entire country, but it does have to be an active, concerted effort by a dedicated critical mass sincerely seeking God's help.

The stakes are high. The future of America and of the world is on the line. When America has operated in harmony with our national covenant and Constitution, she has historically provided the world with significant stabilization, especially for the world's oppressed. If America transforms into a socialist/communist state, oppressed people around the world will lose a main source of their hope for freedom. This is why Abraham Lincoln's statement is still true: America is the last best hope for the world.

In addition to providing a lighthouse to those suffering around the world, America should be doing much more to evangelize the world. This plan affords us the opportunity to explain how biblical principles are the "DNA" behind the American founding that extends "liberty and justice for all" and has led to America's prosperity in the past. This blueprint for governing should be our message to the world, a model available to all nations through which they, too, can receive God's blessing.

CALL TO ACTION

The Bible has laid out a clear path. Christians are not responsible merely *to* civil government (to submit and pray), we are responsible *for* civil government (to establish liberty and justice for all). The founders believed and followed the biblical blueprint in 1776 and gave us the Declaration, our national founding covenant. We must do the same today if we are to restore America to a God-honoring nation. It will not be easy, as a large part of today's citizenry is uninterested or does not see a problem. The few that do step forward will need the spiritual conviction and resolve the founders had when they pledged their lives, fortunes, and sacred honor. I hope this book has equipped you to possess the needed resolve to see this effort through, whether you are Christian or not.

Many quotes from the founding era urged solemn trust in God. They are relevant today as they call to us to act as the founding generation did. You will find them as timely as they are truthful.

Recall Patrick Henry's argument for Virginia in 1775 not only to prepare to fight for its freedom, but also an appeal to God for help:

If we wish to be free—if we mean to preserve inviolate those inestimable privileges for which we have been so long contending—if we mean not basely to abandon the noble struggle in which we have been so long engaged, and which we have pledged ourselves never to abandon until the glorious object of our contest shall be obtained, we must fight! I repeat it, sir, we must fight! An appeal to arms and to the God of Hosts is all that is left us! .... There is a just God who presides over the destinies of nations, and who will raise up friends to fight our battles for us. The battle, sir, is not to the strong alone; it is to the vigilant, the active, the brave.... Is life so dear, or peace so sweet, as to be purchased at the price of chains and slavery? Forbid it, Almighty God! I know not what course others may take; but as for me, give me liberty, or give me death![215]

Three years before his death at the Battle of Bunker Hill, Dr. Joseph Warren also pointed to God to help establish a just nation that would be a haven for the oppressed around the world. On March 5, 1772, he delivered an address in Boston to commemorate the second anniversary of the Boston Massacre:

If you... perform your part, you must have the strongest confidence that THE SAME ALMIGHTY BEING who protected your pious and venerable forefathers, who enabled them to turn a barren wilderness into a fruitful field, who so often made bare his arms for their salvation, will still be mindful of you their offspring...

May we ever be a people favoured of GOD. May our land be a land of liberty, the seat of virtue, the asylum of the oppressed, a name and praise in the whole earth, until the last shock of time shall bury the empires of the world in one common undistinguished ruin![216]

Like our country's founders, we have reason to hope God will direct our nation's steps if we return to following his blueprint for government, the ideals of which the founders applied to America in our national covenant, the Declaration of Independence.

The key to God's blueprint has always been that Christians, educated through the church, take responsibility to establish and maintain a just civil authority. Will Christians today reengage and fulfill our God-given responsibility to seek "liberty and justice for all" in the communities and nation in which we live? Will church leaders today reclaim their role as the moral conscience of society and teach these principles in their churches as part of ongoing discipleship and evangelism efforts?

The question of America's fate stands much as Lincoln framed it in the Gettysburg Address: "whether or not a nation so conceived [in liberty] could long endure." We know that if we abandon our national covenant, we will not endure. But if we collectively rediscover and recommit ourselves to it, relying on God's help, God *may* enable us to restore America. Whether we succeed or not, we who stand will be a testimony for all eternity of what it means to truly live out the Christian faith.

With the blueprint of the Bible laid out before us, the record of history to guide us, and the perils of the modern, Far-Left Marxist movement to warn us, what role will *you* play in the restoration of America?

APPENDIX

Q & A

Q&A for Chapter 3, Learning from Israel: Governing through a Covenant

Question #1–Didn't Jesus Teach That We Should Forgive Instead of Holding to "an Eye for an Eye"?

Some of Jesus's most-quoted teachings come from his Sermon on the Mount, captured in Matthew 5. Jesus describes moral principles that delineate behaviors that are sinful and behaviors that God will bless us for. The Sermon is one of the most challenging discourses he delivered during his earthly ministry, and in many respects, it seems countercultural. Rather than taking vengeance, we are encouraged to be merciful, be peacemakers, and rejoice when persecuted. At one point Jesus even seems to dismiss the clear principle of an "eye for an eye":

> You have heard that it was said, "Eye for eye, and tooth for tooth." But I tell you, do not resist an evil person. If anyone slaps you on the right cheek, turn to them the other cheek also. And if anyone wants to sue you and take your shirt, hand over your coat as well. (Matt. 5:38–40)

This teaching seems to contradict what we learned from Israel on securing civil justice. How do we reconcile these apparent contradictions if Jesus in the New Testament suggests that devout Christians forgive all offenses, yet the Old Testament calls for punitive justice? Is Jesus ushering in a new doctrine of unconditional forgiveness to replace the Old Testament's principles for securing justice?

The key to reconciling this apparent contradiction is to recognize the difference between our personal interactions versus how to deal with those who violate the rights of a person in the community. Without that distinction, one could conclude Jesus is teaching something radically different—that Christians should focus only on forgiveness and are no longer responsible to ensure civil justice in the communities in which they live. But it's not one or the other. People of faith (in the Old and New Testaments) have always been responsible for *both*: forgiving the people who wrong them *and* ensuring justice for their communities. This may seem new to many Christians, but there are several Old Testament passages that clearly condemn revenge and instead encourage kindness:

> Do not testify against your neighbor without cause—would you use your lips to mislead? Do not say, "I'll do to them as they have done to me; I'll pay them back for what they did." (Prov. 24:28–29)

> If your enemy is hungry, give him food to eat; if he is thirsty, give him water to drink. (Prov. 25:21)

Living this out can be very hard for the offended person to do, which is why it is best for other officials to investigate a situation and seek to secure the appropriate measure of justice.* It could be that the target audience for Jesus's teaching was people who were seeking revenge instead of allowing the civil authorities to secure justice. Vigilantism, which this teaching clearly condemns, is a common problem for societies that do not know God.

Jesus's Sermon on the Mount was completely consistent with Old Testament teaching on the need to forgive your neighbor. God's design was never for individuals to take matters into their own hands by exacting "an eye for an eye" retribution when wronged by a neighbor. His design was that we love our fellow man and look to the civil authorities to provide justice. If the civil authorities fail in their responsibility to maintain justice, then believers are to leave it to God, according to Deuteronomy 32:35:

---

* Today this may be secured by an impartial jury.

It is mine to avenge; I will repay. In due time their foot will slip; their day of disaster is near and their doom rushes upon them.

Jesus's teaching of unconditional forgiveness was not a new teaching; it was a reinforcement of what God intended all along, so that instead of being consumed with grudges for wrongs done to us, we can live at peace with one another.

Question #2–What about the Harsh Penalties in the Old Testament?
When Moses gave guidance on civil laws in the Old Testament, he also talked about punishments, including death by stoning. The commandment was that people who committed offenses like adultery, incest, and homosexuality should be stoned to death. This was mentioned in chapter 2 but deserves more discussion, since we are looking to the Old Testament for guidance, and stoning people for these offenses is mentioned.

There are some who believe that these punishments are part of the biblical law code that should be imposed today by nations seeking to govern in a way that honors God. To be clear, I am not advocating for that, but the question remains—why wouldn't these punishments still be relevant if God told Moses to communicate them to the Israelites?

There are several points to make about this. First, the reason God prescribed drastic penalties for some of these crimes was to convey the seriousness of the offense. If God gave a minor penalty for something like adultery, then many would conclude that the offense is not that serious. It would be like getting a parking ticket—a nuisance, but not a big deal. In fact, some may intentionally park in a particular spot, knowing they might get a ticket, because it is more convenient than parking elsewhere. Likewise, if committing adultery were not that serious, many people would be even more tempted to commit it. The problem is that committing adultery not only sins against God, it also destroys families. Since a thriving and safe community must be made up of healthy, thriving families, it is critical that the family unit remain intact. For all these reasons, God commanded a strong penalty for this sin.

The second point to be made is that it is not mandatory that these penalties always be dispensed when these offenses occur. They represent the highest possible level of punishment for an offense but are often not actually dispensed. There is always latitude for the civil authority to grant mercy in the sentencing, especially for a first-time offender. We see this play out in the Bible several times, as when David committed adultery with Bathsheba and had her husband killed on the battlefield to cover up the crime (2 Sam. 11). In this case, God forgave him, and he was not put to death. Jesus also role-modeled this forgiveness when the woman caught in adultery was brought before him (John 8:3–11). He could have endorsed the full punishment, but instead, he extended mercy to her. What we are to learn from these harsh penalties is how serious the offense is to God and, therefore, strive even harder to prevent it in our own lives and in societies where we live.

Q&A for Chapter 4, Evangelism through Justice: How God Uses National Covenants

Question #1—Don't Politically Active Christians Come Across as Unloving and End Up Inhibiting Evangelism?

This is a legitimate concern. I believe the church refusing to educate and equip their congregations to respectfully explain ideas is the root cause of why some politically active Christians can come across as unloving. The first step for Christians who engage in political discussion is to learn biblical principles of civil government and discuss them with fellow believers who serve in this area. Like any other discipline or skill, learning to discuss persuasively but respectfully is something that must be practiced and refined. The goal should be to "let your conversation be always full of grace, *seasoned with salt*, so that you may know how to answer everyone" (Col. 4:6, emphasis added).

Christians must realize, however, that even the most respectful presentation on an issue may be met with outrage from the opposition. Instead of internalizing this outrage, Christians should recognize that criticism is directed at God and his plan, not them personally. Active, ongoing support from the church is critical for public servants, who must maintain the highest level of integrity possible when debating in the public arena. Christians serving today by and large are not getting that support from the local church. That needs to change.

The church also needs to speak with one voice, acting as the moral conscience of society when laws that are clearly immoral are passed. Hobby Lobby's leadership modeled this beautifully when they respectfully objected to providing health insurance that included abortifacients. They took a stand, explaining their objection plainly and respectfully, and God honored their objection with a win in the courts.

Christian civil leaders must also faithfully enforce laws, holding citizens accountable who disregard those laws. If laws are unreasonable, these leaders should change them, balancing justice with mercy. This will be difficult at times, but they must always remember they will ultimately answer to God for how they conduct themselves as God's servants to do good.

Question #2–What If the Candidates Are Immoral and My Conscience Prevents Me from Voting for Any of Them?

Choosing between political candidates will always be a choice between fallen people. However, the Bible is clear. God gave instructions in Genesis 9 for his followers to secure justice with the moral law as the primary guide for all lawmaking. This means we should always do what we can to ensure we select civil leaders who most closely align with biblical principles in securing equal justice for all. We do not have a choice to opt out.

The real issue is how to choose. The logic we should apply must always start with asking "Does the person agree that the moral law is the legal standard from which to judge and govern?" Any leader or party who rejects the moral law as the legal standard is unqualified to govern from a biblical worldview and should not be considered.*

---

* This is the way to choose unless there is no candidate who believes the moral law is the legal standard from which to judge and govern. In that case, it truly is a decision between the lesser of two very flawed people.

If there is a candidate who supports the moral law, he or she should be the one Christians support. The moral law is that important and that determinative. As an illustration of this point, if unborn children could vote, whom would they choose?

It is important to note that God positioned and used rulers even though they had committed idolatry, murder, or adultery. Nebuchadnezzar and David fall into this category; God judged both but blessed their reigns to the benefit of their citizenry.

Given the "lesser-of-two-evils" choice, the church should rethink the failed strategy of civil disengagement. Instead, they should embrace their responsibility of helping those with the gift and calling of civil leadership. This also means actively recruiting and training the next generation of civic leaders, educating, and encouraging them to serve in the public square as ministers of God. If the church does this, there should be many more candidates who both believe in the moral law and live godly lives. The reason there are not more candidates with these traits is squarely the fault of the church.

Question #3–Shouldn't All Christians in Government Roles Use Their Job as a Platform for Evangelism?

Should Christians focus on how to use their jobs to evangelize? Yes and no. I bring this up because pastors ever zealous to push their singular evangelistic agenda may actually do harm by diverting persons serving in civil government away from their primary responsibility based on their actual job. Christians working in government should be focused on doing the best job they can based on governing God's way. That alone is a witness for God. While they should always "be prepared to give an answer to everyone who asks ... the reason for the hope that [they] have" (1 Pet. 3:15), they should focus on doing their job with excellence instead of always looking to have gospel conversations.

As we saw earlier in this chapter, Solomon earned God's blessing by being faithful to his job description: he governed according to God's plan. Solomon's faithful service elevated him in the eyes of his secular neighbors and brought them in droves to his palace. This created countless opportunities for Solomon to talk about God to an unbelieving world. When civil leaders today live by the moral law and do their job well, they earn similar respect, which continues to create new opportunities for evangelism.

Question #4–Shouldn't All Christians Just Seek to Know God?
A common phrase among evangelicals is "I just want to know Jesus." It is a form of spiritual virtue signaling, implying that seeking God should be enough and they shouldn't need to live out their faith in the civil arena. There is an interesting passage in Jeremiah 22, comparing Jehoiakim with his father Josiah, who was a faithful king. God's admonition to Jehoiakim through the prophet Jeremiah was to do justice, as his father did. But notice the last phrase:

> "Does it make you a king to have more and more cedar? Did not your father have food and drink? He did what was right and just, so all went well with him. He defended the cause of the poor and needy, and so all went well. *Is that not what it means to know me?*" declares the Lord. (Jer. 22:15–16) [emphasis added]

If a person claims to know God, he or she must be a strong advocate of equal, fair, and impartial justice for all. This verse and all those in previous chapters regarding God's demand for justice are completely consistent in this regard. Show me a Christian who truly knows God, and I'll show you a Christian who is passionate about defending justice for all.

Q&A for Chapter 5, Starting a Nation: Establishing a Covenant

Introduction
In chapter 2 I described the two basic views of civil government. I declared at that point that this book supports the two-kingdom view, and specifically, its SEPARATE & RESPONSIBLE TO ESTABLISH CIVIL

GOVERNMENT sub-view, with the primary objective of protecting every individual's liberty of conscience. Previous generations struggled to balance a government that honored God and one that did not persecute people because of their opposing faith. Finding this balance is the unique theological contribution of the founding generation, which has a direct connection to evangelism. Thomas Jefferson captured this key theological balance point in his Virginia Statute for Religious Freedom:

> Whereas, Almighty God hath created the mind free;
>
> That all attempts to influence it by temporal punishments or burthens, or by civil incapacitations tend only to beget habits of hypocrisy and meanness, and therefore are a departure from the plan of the holy author of our religion, who being Lord, both of body and mind yet chose not to propagate it by coercions on either, as was in his Almighty power to do,
>
> That the impious presumption of legislators and rulers, civil as well as ecclesiastical, who, being themselves but fallible and uninspired men have assumed dominion over the faith of others, setting up their own opinions and modes of thinking as the only true and infallible, and as such endeavouring to impose them on others, hath established and maintained false religions over the greatest part of the world and through all time;
>
> That to compel a man to furnish contributions of money for the propagation of opinions, which he disbelieves[,] is sinful and tyrannical;
>
> That even the forcing him to support this or that teacher of his own religious persuasion is depriving him of the comfortable liberty of giving his contributions to the particular pastor, whose morals he would make his pattern.

Recognizing the law of nature (conscience), and of nature's God (the moral law), while also recognizing the need to extend liberty, was the theological breakthrough in the American founding. This balance allows everyone to go on his or her own personal faith journey while agreeing on the fundamental rights of life, liberty, and property.

Unfortunately, many Christians are unfamiliar with the theology of the Declaration or how the faith of the founders guided their actions. This has led to many objections in the modern-day church, to which we will now turn.

Question #1–Did the Revolution Violate the Call for Submission in Romans 13?

This is a key stumbling block for many Christians and was the question I wrestled with when I started studying this topic in the early '90s. If Jesus said we should pay our taxes, and the revolution was about "taxation without representation," how could the revolution be biblically justifiable? The first two verses in Romans 13 also seem to imply we should always comply with what our civil leaders direct us to do, or we are rebelling against that which God has established.

> Let everyone be subject to the governing authorities, for there is no authority except that which God has established. The authorities that exist have been established by God. Consequently, whoever rebels against the authority is rebelling against what God has instituted, and those who do so will bring judgment on themselves.

Many interpret these verses to mean we should always submit, especially since Paul wrote them when the Roman government was particularly unjust toward Christians. However, this interpretation fails to account for several important things found elsewhere in the Bible.

The primary duty Christians have related to civil government is to ensure that that government dispenses equal and impartial justice to all citizens. This is the call from Genesis 9, where God first instituted civil government to provide justice. Failing to acknowledge and embrace this duty is what enables today's church leaders to simply say, "We must submit." Yes, we are called to submit, but only to government that is governing justly, which the next two verses in Romans 13 affirm:

For rulers hold no terror for those who do right, but for those who do wrong. Do you want to be free from fear of the one in authority? Then do what is right and you will be commended. For the one in authority is God's servant for your good. But if you do wrong, be afraid, for rulers do not bear the sword for no reason. They are God's servants, agents of wrath to bring punishment on the wrongdoer.

Authorities doing wrong and governing unjustly do not warrant our unconditional, ongoing submission; they warrant our active attention. Many times in the Bible, rulers passed unjust laws and people of faith did not submit, as we will see below. The question is, to what extent should Christians submit, and to what extent should they disobey?

The answer depends first on if their physical safety is imperiled. If a person or community is being attacked unjustly by another group or local civil authority, they have a right to self-defense according to the Bible (Exod. 22:2–3; Esther 8:11; Eccles. 3:1–15).

Second, they should seek redress through legal channels available to them, and if that does not work, they are free to act to restore justice and commit to govern according to biblical principles. In either case, those exercising civil disobedience need to understand they may be punished by the authorities in power. For instance, Shadrach, Meshach, and Abednego knew they could be killed for not kneeling to the Babylonian idol. In the New Testament, Paul was being charged by the Jewish leaders but appealed his case to Caesar—his right as a Roman citizen (Acts 25:1–12). Likewise, the founders knew if they failed to separate from England, they would be hanged for treason. According to Romans 13:5, it is a matter of conscience as to the course of action a person or group may take when they find themselves under an unjust government.

In the case of America, the colonists sought redress for over a decade, and in response, England clamped down even harder. When the British marched on Lexington and Concord to seize munitions, the colonials mounted a defense but committed to not firing the first shot. If there was action, it would be defensive on the part of the colonials. The British did fire the first shot, and a small skirmish ensued.[*] To the founding generation, the American Revolution was a defensive war, and the decision to sign the Declaration was made by men who were responsible for the citizens they represented. They saw no other option but to resist or become slaves of the crown. The founders followed the biblical template and captured all this in the Declaration, including their belief in the purpose of government and their "firm Reliance on the Protection of the divine Providence" to help them see the action through.

Another point to be made about the context for Romans 13 is Paul's intent and organization of this letter. Paul did not found the church in Rome, as he did in other cities to which he wrote letters, so he wrote this letter differently. His letter to the Romans is a "CliffsNotes version" of the Christian faith, explaining man's rebellious nature, the importance of the law, the salvation process, and the call to pursue righteousness by serving Christ.

In chapter 12, based on everything Paul has written up to this point, he explains how we as individuals should live. Then, in chapter 13, he affirms how we should live in community, given the proper role of civil government, first described in Genesis 9, where civil leaders are truly operating as God's servants doing good.

> For the one in authority is God's servant for your good. But if you do wrong, be afraid, for rulers do not bear the sword for no reason. They are God's servants, agents of wrath to bring punishment on the wrongdoer. Therefore, it is necessary to submit to the authorities, not only because of possible punishment but also as a matter of conscience. (Rom. 13:4-5)

---

[*] Some contest who fired the first shot, but a detailed investigation took place with dozens of witnesses. They all affirmed the British fired first, although the specific person was not clear. See Ezra Ripley, *A History of the Fight at Concord on the 19th of April 1775*, 1827, quoted in "Battle of Lexington and Concord – Historical Record Shows Pitcairn Fired The First Shot," The Mike Church Show, accessed August 27, 2021, https://www.mikechurch.com/battle-of-lexington-and-concord-historical-record-shows-pitcairn-fired-the-first-shot/.

Paul is explaining God's design for government and how people should relate to a government operating within that design. He is not telling New Testament Christians to ignore what the Old Testament revealed about God's design for government. As Jesus himself said,

> "For truly I tell you, until heaven and earth disappear, not the smallest letter, not the least stroke of a pen, will by any means disappear from the Law until everything is accomplished" (Matt. 5:18).*

If we do not understand the Christian duty to secure justice given in Genesis 9, then we are more likely to interpret Romans 13 in isolation and conclude Christians must always submit to the government even when injustices occur. This is especially true for the Christian who believes the Great Commission is the primary focus of the Christian life, the filter through which all activities should be measured. If a Christian believes evangelism should be the main focus of life, then he or she will see Romans 13 as a simple statement: "Submit so you can focus on sharing the gospel." This is a narrow New Testament view of the Christian faith, giving believers a way out of their citizenship duty. Pastors taking this view neglect their shepherding responsibility and hope someone else will take care of it. This passive approach fails to recognize commands and narratives throughout the Bible that help us fully understand God's purpose for civil government and our citizenship responsibility.

Both the Old and New Testaments include examples where people of faith do not submit to the civil authority. The Book of Daniel reveals several occasions when disobedience was not only tolerated by God but honored. When civil leaders pass laws commanding people to act in ways that are contrary to God's moral law, opposition is the righteous path. Daniel's fellow countrymen opposed Nebuchadnezzar when the ruler built an idolatrous image and commanded everyone to

---

* Many theologians correctly point out that Jesus fulfilled the requirements of the Law, as only he was able to keep it perfectly and, therefore, be a sufficient sacrifice to atone for the sins of all mankind. Notice the reference to "until heaven and earth disappear," which, clearly, has not happened. This means everything we learn in the Old Testament is still relevant to Christians living today.

bow down in worship (Dan. 3). Shadrach, Meshach, and Abednego refused and were thrown into a fiery furnace. God rescued them because of their faithfulness.

Daniel himself ignored a law King Darius passed—a law which said anyone who prayed to any other god during a thirty-day period would be punished by being thrown into a lions' den (Dan. 6). Daniel defied this order because it violated the moral law—the idea we should be able to worship the one true God. Once again, God honored the choice of civil disobedience.

In the New Testament, Peter and John exercised a path of opposition when the Sanhedrin commanded them to stop proclaiming the resurrection of Jesus. The apostles' response demonstrated their understanding that obedience to God's clear direction and the moral law supersedes obedience to religious leaders, in this case, clearly at odds with God's will:

> "Then they called them in again and commanded them not to speak or teach at all in the name of Jesus. But Peter and John replied, "Which is right in God's eyes: to listen to you, or to him? You be the judges! As for us, we cannot help speaking about what we have seen and heard" (Acts 4:18–20).

People of God are to stand up to their civil or religious leaders when laws contrary to the moral law are passed or they are commanded to act contrary to God's direction for the three major institutions ordained by God: 1) Marriage/Family, 2) Civil Government, and 3) the church. Scripture includes examples of living in both righteous and oppressive regimes, giving believers a proper course of action no matter what time or place they find themselves in. It will always be a matter of conscience whether individuals feel they are being pushed too far, but it is clear that opposition in the face of immoral rule is supported by Scripture.

The path of civil disobedience should never be taken without considerable forethought. In colonial America, the founders reached

consensus after they endured "a long train of abuses" over a thir-
teen-year period. The encroachments from England on the colonists'
right to a just civil authority (and their right to self-government),
began in 1763, when the British levied excessive taxes to fund the
French and Indian War (1754-1763). Various tax burdens increased
into the 1770s. By the spring of 1776, King George had made his
intentions clear: he would not govern the colonists justly as fellow
Englishman, but instead, he was determined to suppress the colonies
in servitude to the crown. With the cards stacked against them, the
colonists concluded they must fight for their God-given rights or be
enslaved by the British government.[217] By the spring of 1776, England
was both passing immoral laws and governing outside of the principles
for God's institution of civil government. The colonists captured all
these offenses in the Declaration and concluded they had no option
but to separate or forfeit their God-given rights.

Given all these reasons, we can see the American founding was
not a violation of Romans 13. History reveals the founders were motivated by their Christian faith and drew justification from biblical principles in separating from England and creating a new nation. They
also acknowledged they needed to explain their actions in the first
paragraph of the Declaration because it could be asserted they were
rebelling for no reason.

Question #2–Was America Founded as a Christian Nation?
A hallmark of the progressive movement is the assertion America was
not founded as a Christian nation. People have challenged this for a
long time, but this claim has picked up momentum in the last fifty
years. The rationale from progressives is that if America was founded
as a secular nation, then adopting policies that veer away from Judeo-
Christian principles is okay. The more people who believe this, the
easier it is to push a secular agenda. This is why we hear this argument
so much in the public arena.

In the preceding chapters I laid out the biblical principles of governing and how quotes from the founding era conclusively show these

principles were applied at the founding. Now let us turn to evidence that proves our nation's Judeo-Christian heritage after the founding:

> And each member, before he takes his seat, shall make and subscribe the following declaration, viz: I do believe in one God, the creator and governor of the universe, the rewarder of the good and the punisher of the wicked. And I do acknowledge the Scriptures of the Old and New Testament to be given by Divine inspiration. And no further or other religious test shall ever hereafter be required of any civil officer or magistrate in this State. [218]
> —Section 10 of Pennsylvania's first Constitution; adopted on September 28, 1776, with Benjamin Franklin as governor

> The general Principles, on which the Fathers Achieved Independence, were the only Principles in which, that beautiful Assembly of young Gentlemen could Unite, and these Principles only could be intended by them in their Address, or by me in my Answer. And what were these general Principles? I answer, the general Principles of Christianity, in which all those Sects were United: And the general Principles of English and American Liberty, in which all those young Men United, and which had United all Parties in America, in Majorities Sufficient to assert and maintain her Independence. Now I will avow, that I then believed, and now believe, that those general Principles of Christianity, are as eternal and immutable, as the Existence and Attributes of God: and that those Principles of Liberty, are as unalterable as human Nature and our terrestrial, mundane System.[219]
> —John Adams in a letter to Thomas Jefferson on June 28, 1813

> The only foundation for ... a republic is to be laid in Religion. Without this there can be no virtue, and without virtue* there can be no liberty, and liberty is the object and life of all republican governments.[220]
> —Benjamin Rush, *Essays, Literary, Moral, and Philosophical* (1798)

---

* Virtue is the pursuit of moral living.

[The Bible] should be read in our schools in preference to all other books from its containing the greatest portion of that kind of knowledge which is calculated to produce private and public temporal happiness.[221]
—Benjamin Rush, *A Defence of the Use of the Bible in Schools*

The hope of a Christian is inseparable from his faith. Whoever believes in the divine inspiration of the Holy Scriptures must hope that the religion of Jesus shall prevail throughout the earth. Never since the foundation of the world have the prospects of mankind been more encouraging to that hope than they appear to be at the present time. And may the associated distribution of the Bible proceed and prosper till the Lord shall have made "bare his holy arm in the eyes of all the nations, and all the ends of the earth shall see the salvation of our God" (Isa. 52:10).[222]

Why is it that, next to the birthday of the Savior of the World, your most joyous and most venerated festival returns on this day. Is it not that, in the chain of human events, the birthday of the nation is indissolubly linked with the birthday of the Savior? That it forms a leading event in the Progress of the Gospel dispensation? Is it not that the Declaration of Independence first organized the social compact on the foundation of the Redeemer's mission upon earth?[223]
—John Quincy Adams on the role the Christian faith played in the founding

From early in our nation's history, the Supreme Court has affirmed the prominent role of Christianity in America's founding. In *Runkel v. Winemiller* (1799), Samuel Chase—Supreme Court justice and signer of the Declaration—declared,

Religion is of general and public concern, and on its support depend, in great measure, the peace and good order of government, the safety and happiness of the people. By our form of government, the Christian religion is, the established religion, and all sects and denominations of Christians are placed upon the same equal footing and are equally entitled to protection in their religious liberty.[224]

One of the most influential Supreme Court justices in the early years of the republic was Joseph Story, who served from 1812 to 1845. He is most remembered for his opinions in the *Amistad* case and *Commentaries on the Constitution of the United States*. In 1829, Story gave a speech at Harvard, in which he stated,

> "There never has been a period of history, in which the Common Law did not recognize Christianity as lying at its foundation."[225]

Bill Federer adds a barrage of support for the prominent role of Christianity in America's founding in an *American Minute* email installment, which I have drawn the next several quotations from.

In 1833, Joseph Story received a pamphlet entitled "The Relation of Christianity to Civil Government in the United States." The pamphlet transmitted a sermon by Rev. Jasper Adams, president of the College of Charleston, South Carolina. In it, Jasper Adams wrote:

> [D]id the people of these States intend to renounce all connection with the Christian religion? Or did they only intend to disclaim all preference of one sect of Christians over another, as far as civil government was concerned; while they still retained the Christian religion as the foundation of all their social, civil and political institutions? ... In our Conventions and Legislative Assemblies, daily Christian worship has been customarily observed. All business proceedings in our Legislative halls and Courts of justice have been

---

* This was an 1841 case about slaves who took control of the Spanish schooner *La Amistad*. They were apprehended, and the case wound up in the Supreme Court. The court ruled in favor of the slaves doing what was needed to regain their freedom. In 1842, thirty-five of them traveled back to Africa along with American Christian missionaries. The case was made popular again by the 1997 film *Amistad*.

suspended by universal consent on Sunday. Christian Ministers have customarily been employed to perform stated religious services in the Army and Navy of the United States.... In administering oaths, the Bible, the standard of Christian truth is used, to give additional weight and solemnity to the transaction.... No nation on earth, is more dependent than our own, for its welfare, on the preservation and general belief and influence of Christianity among us.[226]

After reading Jasper Adams's pamphlet, Joseph Story wrote back to him, saying,

I have read it with uncommon satisfaction. I think its tone and spirit excellent. My own private judgment has long been (and every day's experience more and more confirms me in it) that government cannot long exist without an alliance with religion; and that Christianity is indispensable to the true interests and solid foundations of free government.[227]

In his *Familiar Exposition of the Constitution of the United States*, 1840, Joseph Story affirmed the view the Framers had regarding the role of Christianity in America.

We are not to attribute this prohibition of a national religious establishment to an indifference to religion in general, and especially to Christianity (which none could hold in more reverence than the framers of the Constitution).... At the time of the adoption of the Constitution, and of the Amendment to it now under consideration, the general, if not the universal, sentiment in America was, that Christianity ought to receive encouragement from the state so far as was not incompatible with the private rights of conscience and the freedom of religious worship. An attempt to level all religions, and to make it a matter of state policy to hold all in utter indifference, would have created universal disapprobation, if not universal indignation.... But the duty of supporting religion, and especially the Christian religion, is very different from the right to force the consciences of other men or to punish them for worshiping God in the manner which they believe their accountability to Him requires.... The rights of conscience are, indeed, beyond the just reach of any human power. They are given by God, and cannot be encroached upon by human authority without a criminal disobedience of the precepts of natural as well as of revealed religion.

The real object of the First Amendment was not to countenance (approve), much less to advance Mohammedanism, or Judaism, or infidelity, by prostrating Christianity, but to exclude all rivalry among Christian sects and to prevent any national ecclesiastical establishment which should give to a hierarchy the exclusive patronage of the national government.[228]

In *Vidal v. Girard's Executors*, 1844, Justice Joseph Story offered the following opinion about America as a Christian country.

Christianity ... is not to be maliciously and openly reviled and blasphemed against, to the annoyance of believers or the injury of the public.... It is unnecessary for us, however, to consider the establishment of a school or college, for the propagation of ... Deism, or any other form of infidelity. Such a case is not to be presumed to exist in a Christian country.... Why may not laymen instruct in the general principles of Christianity as well as ecclesiastics.... We cannot overlook the blessings, which such laymen by their conduct, as well as their instructions, may, nay must, impart to their youthful pupils. Why may not the Bible, and especially the New Testament, without note or comment, be read and taught as a Divine Revelation ... its general precepts expounded, its evidences explained and its glorious principles of morality inculcated?[229]

Challenges to the validity of a biblically based American foundation continued through the 1800s. This prompted the US Senate

Judiciary Committee in 1853, and the House Judiciary Committee in 1854, to issue reports clarifying what they felt the founders intended in the American founding:

> SENATE JUDICIARY COMMITTEE: We are Christians, not because the law demands it, not to gain exclusive benefits or to avoid legal disabilities, but from choice and education; and in a land thus universally Christian, what is to be expected – what desired – but that we shall pay a due regard to Christianity?[230]

> HOUSE JUDICIARY COMMITTEE: Had the people, during the Revolution, had a suspicion of any attempt to war against Christianity, that Revolution would have been strangled in its cradle. At the time of the adoption of the Constitution and the amendments, the universal sentiment was that Christianity should be encouraged, not any one sect [denomination].... In this age there can be no substitute for Christianity. That, in its general principles, is the great conservative element on which we must rely for the purity and permanence of free institutions.[231]

In response to this report, the 1854 Congress passed a House resolution, declaring, "The great vital and conservative element in our system is the belief of our people in the pure doctrines and Divine truths of the Gospel of Jesus Christ."[232]

In the 1892 Supreme Court case of *Church of the Holy Trinity v. United States*, the court considered an employment contract between the Church of the Holy Trinity and an English (Anglican) priest. The ruling affirmed that, even though he was a foreigner, the minister was not a foreign laborer under the statute prohibiting foreign labor. Thus, the court validated that Christian principles informed America's founding:

> These, and many other matters which might be noticed, add a volume of unofficial declarations to the mass of organic utterances that

this is a Christian nation…. Shall it be believed that a Congress of
the United States intended to make it a misdemeanor for a church
of this country to contract for the services of a Christian minister
residing in another nation?[233]

On the 150th anniversary of the Declaration of Independence,
President Calvin Coolidge not only affirmed America's Christian heritage but also explained how colonial pastors motivated the founders to
act on their Christian faith:

People at home and abroad consider Independence Hall as hal-
lowed ground and revere the Liberty Bell as a sacred relic. That
pile of bricks and mortar, that mass of metal, might appear to the
uninstructed as only the outgrown meeting place and the shattered
bell of a former time, useless now because of more modern conve-
niences, but to those who know[,] they have become consecrated
by the use which men have made of them. They have long been
identified with a great cause. They are the framework of a spiritual
event. The world looks upon them, because of their associations of
one hundred and fifty years ago, as it looks upon the Holy Land
because of what took place there nineteen hundred years ago.

The American Revolution represented the informed and
mature convictions of a great mass of independent, liberty loving,
God-fearing people who knew their rights, and possessed the courage to dare to maintain them.

In the great outline of its principles the Declaration was the
result of the religious teachings of the preceding period.

The principles of human relationship which went into the
Declaration of Independence…. They are found in the texts, the
sermons, and the writings of the early colonial clergy…. They
preached equality because they believed in the fatherhood of God
and the brotherhood of man. They justified freedom by the text
that we are all created in the divine image, all partakers of the
divine spirit.

Placing every man on a plane where he acknowledged no supe-
riors, where no one possessed any right to rule over him, he must
inevitably choose his own rulers through a system of self-government…. In order that they might have freedom to express these
thoughts and opportunity to put them into action, whole congregations with their pastors had migrated to the Colonies….

In its main features the Declaration of Independence is a great
spiritual document. It is a declaration not of material but of spiritual conceptions. Equality, liberty, popular sovereignty, the rights
of man—these are not elements which we can see and touch. They
are ideals. They have their source and their roots in the religious
convictions. They belong to the unseen world. Unless the faith of
the American people in these religious convictions is to endure, the
principles of our Declaration will perish. We can not continue to
enjoy the result if we neglect and abandon the cause.[234]

Ironically, even President Obama, a progressive, confirmed the
historical view that America was a Christian nation in remarks he gave
on June 28, 2006, when he stated,

Whatever we once were, we are no longer a Christian nation—at least,
not just. We are also a Jewish nation, a Muslim nation, a Buddhist
nation, and a Hindu nation, and a nation of nonbelievers.[235]

This is but a small sample of writings and speeches that affirm
that America was founded on the Judeo-Christian faith with biblical
principles firmly articulated in the Declaration and embedded in the
Constitution. Furthermore, it was evident to the founding generation
and to later generations that God was instrumental in establishing and
preserving the United States.

Question #3–Were the Founders Deists?

A deist is a person who acknowledges God but believes he is not directly
involved in the affairs of mankind. At the time of America's founding,

a deist was as uninterested in God and Christianity as one could be, although he or she may have had respect for natural law applied in the civil arena. The assertion that most of the founders were deists would significantly weaken the argument that America was founded on Christian principles and that those principles are critical to maintain going forward. This is because governing in a way that "honors God" would not matter to the deist, because this person does not believe that God would intervene if he or she governed poorly. This makes the charge that the founders were deists a serious one to investigate.

If the founders were deists, there are two main behaviors we would expect to see consistently throughout the founding era and beyond. First, they would not pray or acknowledge God as directly affecting their lives. Second, they would not worry about God's judgment on the nation. There are hundreds of examples to show that neither of these things was widely true during the founding era. I will start with the Declaration itself:

> *[A]ppealing* to the Supreme Judge of the World for the Rectitude of our Intentions....
> With a *firm Reliance* on the Protection of the divine Providence, we mutually pledge to each other our Lives, our Fortunes, and our sacred Honor.
> —The last portion of the Declaration, emphasizing the signers' reliance on God's protection to see the separation through

> The hand of Providence has been *so conspicuous* in all this, that he must be worse than an infidel that lacks faith, and more than wicked, that has not gratitude enough to acknowledge his obligations.[236]
> —George Washington noting the role God played, in a letter to Brigadier General Thomas Nelson on August 20, 1778 (emphasis mine)

I take a particular Pleasure in acknowleging [sic], that *the interposing Hand of Heaven* in the various Instances of our extensive Preparations for this Operation, has been *most conspicuous* & remarkable.[237]

—George Washington noting the role God played, in a letter to the President of the Continental Congress, Thomas McKean, November 15, 1781 (emphasis mine)

I resign with satisfaction the Appointment I accepted with diffidence—A diffidence in my abilities to accomplish so arduous a task, which however was superseded by a confidence in the rectitude of our Cause, the support of the Supreme Power of the Union, and the patronage of Heaven…. [M]y gratitude for *the interposition of Providence*, and the assistance I have received from my Countrymen, [i]ncreases with every review of the momentous Contest.[238]

—George Washington officially resigning his military commission in Annapolis, Maryland, December 23, 1783 (emphasis mine)

In the beginning of the Contest with G. Britain, when we were sensible of danger, *we had daily prayer in this room for Divine protection.*—Our prayers, Sir, were heard, & *they were graciously answered.* All of us who were engaged in the struggle must have observed frequent instances of *a superintending Providence in our favor.*[239]

—Benjamin Franklin, Constitutional Convention, June 28, 1787 (emphasis mine)

God who gave us life gave us liberty. And can the liberties of a nation be thought secure when we have removed their only firm basis, a conviction in the minds of the people that these liberties are of the Gift of God? That they are not to be violated but with His wrath? Indeed, I tremble for my country when I reflect that God is just; that *His justice cannot sleep forever.*[240]

—Thomas Jefferson making the connection to suffering God's judgment if we were to abandon God. From his *Notes on the State of Virginia*, 1781, also inscribed on the Jefferson Memorial in Washington, DC (emphasis mine)

There are instances of, I would say, an almost astonishing Providence in our favor; our success has staggered our enemies, and almost given faith to infidels; so we may truly say it is not our own arm which has saved us. The hand of Heaven appears to have led us on to be, perhaps, humble instruments and means in the great providential dispensation, which is completing. [241]
—Samuel Adams, August 1, 1776

In addition to this small sampling, there were dozens of Prayer Proclamations with the intended implication that the citizens of the United States pray to God for provision and protection. While those wishing to prove America was founded as a secular nation may find miscellaneous statements to question the faith and motivation of the founders, the full body of evidence clearly shows the founders believed God was directing and blessing their cause, aligning them with Christianity and not with deism. While Europe was swept up in the Enlightenment and deistic thought, there is little evidence the founders were deists. This begs the question, where did this charge of deism come from? The answer was covered in chapter 8, where we walked through the rise of the modern progressive movement.

Question #4–Are Slavery and the Three-Fifths Clause Evidence America Was Founded on Institutional Racism?

The charge from progressives is that the founders believed slaves were worth only three-fifths of a person. Additionally, some progressives assert the founders were primarily motivated to separate from England because they wanted to protect the institution of slavery.* These beliefs have led to a general narrative that America's founding was systemically racist, and we are still suffering from this fundamental

---

* This was partially true in that some in the Southern colonies joined in the conflict because they wanted to protect their institution of slavery. This is an example where progressives take something true in *some* of the colonies and incorrectly ascribe it to *all* of the colonies.

problem today. To address this, I will answer two questions:

1. What was the intent behind the three-fifths clause?
2. What was the founders' intent regarding the institution of slavery?

Let us start with the three-fifths clause, which is found in the Constitution, Article 1, Section 2:

> Representatives and direct Taxes shall be apportioned among the several States which may be included within this Union, according to their respective Numbers, which shall be determined by adding to the whole Number of free Persons, including those bound to Service for a Term of Years, and excluding Indians not taxed, three fifths of all other Persons.... The Number of Representatives shall not exceed one for every thirty Thousand....

The question being discussed was representation, and it was agreed that a representative would be assigned to every 30,000 persons. Abolitionists saw a problem, however, with counting slaves at the same ratio as free persons. The same ratio would give pro-slavery states greater representation in the new federal government, making the abolition of slavery much more difficult. There was also the moral problem of telling slaves they would have representation, when those representing them would undoubtedly push to maintain their enslavement. Slaves were obviously whole people, and abolitionists sought to do whatever they could to end the horrific practice of slavery. The problem at the time, though, was that if slaves were counted with the same ratio as free people, their numbers would become a legislative advantage for the pro-slavery South.

James Wilson and Roger Sherman, both abolitionists, were the ones who proposed that instead of one representative for every 30,000 slaves, the ratio should be one representative for every 50,000 slaves, which is where "three-fifths" comes from. This ratio had been discussed previously in 1783 for property taxes, so the proposal easily passed. With this ratio, slave-holding states would be incented to abolish slavery, because if they did so, they would immediately pick up additional representation in the new federal Congress.

So, how did this three-fifths strategy play out? Below is the table showing how many representatives the North and South had with the three-fifths ratio applied. With this approach, the North had about 55% representation, a significant political advantage. What people don't realize when they say "the slaves should have been counted at the same ratio as free persons" is that this would have given the South about nine more representatives in Congress, equally splitting political power between free and slave-holding states. Would this have been good for the abolitionist movement? Absolutely not.

One could argue that slave-holding states should have gotten no representatives for their slaves, which would have significantly curbed their political power. (The South's ratio in Congress would have dropped to 36%.) Southern states would have rejected this uncompromising proposal. This would have killed the Constitution in its cradle, dooming the country to collapse under the Articles of Confederation, the inadequacy of which prompted the Constitutional Convention in the first place.

Table A.1

Scenario	Three-Fifths	100%	0%
North # representatives	58	58	58
South # representatives	47	56	33
Total # representatives	105	114	91
Southern %	45%	49%	36%

In short, the three-fifths clause had nothing to do with evaluating the worth of the slave. It was an approach endorsed by abolitionists to count slaves but limit the power of the pro-slavery South in Congress. Some I share this with have trouble acknowledging the true motive of the three-fifths clause because it is so different from the progressive narrative we have heard for decades, but the effect of the three-fifths clause proves the case. This clause resulted in less political power in the pro-slavery South.

As further evidence this is the true meaning behind this fraction in the Constitution, consider the testimony of Frederick Douglass. He was born a slave around 1820 and was treated harshly growing up. He fled to the North to secure his freedom as a young man and became a successful businessman and spokesman for the abolitionist movement. In a speech he gave in Glasgow, Scotland, on March 26, 1860, he explained his view of the three-fifths clause:

> It is a downright disability laid upon the slaveholding States; one which deprives those States of two-fifths of their natural basis of representation. A black man in a free State is worth just two-fifths more than a black man in a slave State, as a basis of political power under the Constitution. Therefore, instead of encouraging slavery, the Constitution encourages freedom by giving an increase of "two-fifths" of political power to free over slave States. So much for the three-fifths clause; taking it at is worst, it still leans to freedom, not slavery; for, be it remembered that the Constitution nowhere forbids a coloured man to vote.[242]

Contradicting Frederick Douglass, the narrative that the founders believed slaves were three-fifths of a person leads people to believe that the founders were all racists, wanting to maintain the institution of slavery. But the majority of the founders openly expressed concerns with slavery but were not sure how to end it, especially with the strong political will in the South to continue it.[243]

Now that you understand the intent behind the three-fifths clause, the next question to consider is this: Was the founders' objective in separating from England to institutionalize slavery? Naturally, to answer this question, we'll explore what the founders did, if anything, to end slavery.

Two key assumptions of the progressive argument are that nothing was done to end slavery in the founding era and that any meaning-ful action to end slavery must occur at the federal level. Progressives assert that the new national government should have ended the prac-tice right from the start. This point of view fails to recognize one of the most important realities of the new national government—that it had very little power by design. The states were highly suspicious that the new federal government would impose tyranny on them, so the founders strictly limited the federal government's power. If slavery was to be dealt with at all, it would have to be addressed at the state level. So, did the states do anything to address slavery?

It turns out the states did a *lot* to end the institution of slavery, and their actions started even before the Declaration was signed. In 1775 the Pennsylvania Society for Promoting the Abolition of Slavery was founded, dedicated to the abolition of slavery.[244] This early push was in large part due to Quaker influence, which started way back in 1688 with the "German Petition Against Slavery." At the time, this petition had little effect, but it is evidence there were early colonials who believed slavery needed to be abolished.

With the writing of the Declaration, we see the next attempt to call out slavery as an example of the immoral rule of the king. Jefferson's first draft included twenty-eight examples of illegitimate rule on the part of King George, with the slave trade listed as one of the examples. Jefferson included this, *as a slave owner*, as an example of why the col-onies needed to separate from England, as slavery was a legal practice across the British empire at that time,*

> [H]e has waged cruel war against human nature itself, violating
> [its] most sacred rights of life & liberty in the persons of a distant
> people who never offended him, captivating & carrying them into
> slavery in another hemisphere, or to incur miserable death in their
> transportation thither. this piratical warfare, the opprobrium of *infi-del* powers, is the warfare of the CHRISTIAN king of Great Britain.

---

* Jefferson's approach to slavery was complicated, as he inherited slaves and owned slaves through-out his life. His initial draft of the Declaration shows he believed the practice to be immoral, even though he participated in it.

Determined to keep open a market where MEN should be bought & sold, he has prostituted his negative for suppressing every legislative attempt to prohibit or to restrain this execrable commerce: and that this assemblage of horrors might want no fact of distinguished die, he is now exciting those very people to rise in arms among us, and to purchase that liberty of which *he* has deprived them, by murdering the people upon whom he also obtruded them; thus paying off former crimes committed against the *liberties* of one people, with crimes which he urges them to commit against the lives of another.[245]

Unfortunately, the Southern states could not accept this language, and it was removed in the final draft. What this writing reflects, however, is a growing concern about the lawfulness of the institution, even among slaveholders like Jefferson.

SELECTIVE BIBLIOGRAPHY

The books I chose for this bibliography are ones I feel are particularly important to understanding how history, theology, politics, and citizenship intersect to reveal the broader and more complete picture of America. I recommend them to anyone interested in digging deeper into these topics.

Alinsky, Saul. *Rules For Radicals: A Practical Primer for Realistic Radicals.* New York: Vintage Books, 1989. (Discrepancy between the front cover and the title page: front cover says "Pragmatic"; title page says "Practical." This book is the only one of its kind on this list; I include it to give insight into the progressive mind. Saul Alinsky lived his life and wrote this book to incite unrest and mayhem in civilized society in order to bring about change. In a statement near the beginning, Alinsky views Lucifer [Satan] as the first successful radical. The book and its author have been greatly influential in the life of Hillary Rodham Clinton.)

Anderson, Bruce, Mark Beliles, and Stephen McDowell. *Watchmen on the Walls: Pastors Equipping Christians for Their Civil Duties.* Charlottesville, VA: Providence Foundation, 1995.

Arnn, Larry P. *The Founders' Key: The Divine and Natural Connection Between the Declaration and the Constitution and What We Risk by Losing It.* Nashville: Thomas Nelson Inc., 2012.

Barton, David. *The Jefferson Lies: Exposing the Myths You've Always Believed About Thomas Jefferson.* Nashville: Thomas Nelson, 2012.

Barton, David, and Tim Barton. *The American Story: The Beginnings.* 2nd ed. Aledo, TX: WallBuilder Press, 2021.

Beliles, Mark A., and Jerry Newcombe. *Doubting Thomas: The Religious Life and Legacy of Thomas Jefferson.* New York: Morgan James Publishing, 2015.

Beliles, Mark A., and Stephen K. McDowell. *America's Providential History.* 3rd ed. Charlottesville, VA: The Providence Foundation, 2010.

Budziszewski, J. *Written on the Heart: The Case for Natural Law.* Westmont, IL: IVP Academic, 1997.

Cobin, John M. *Christian Theology of Public Policy: Highlighting the American Experience.* Greenville, SC: Alertness Ltd., 2006.

Colson, Charles. *God and Government: An Insider's View on the Boundaries Between Faith and Politics.* Grand Rapids, MI: Zondervan, 2007.

Engeman, Thomas S., and Michael P. Zuckert, eds. *Protestantism and the American Founding.* Notre Dame, IN: University of Notre Dame Press, 2004.

Fisher, Dan. *Bringing Back the Black Robed Regiment: A Call for Preachers Who Will Fight.* 2 vols. Mustang, OK: Tate Publishing and Enterprises, 2013.

Franklin, Benjamin. *The Autobiography of Benjamin Franklin.* 1791. Reprint, New York: Dover, 1996.

Garlow, James L. *Well Versed: Biblical Answers to Today's Tough Issues.* Washington, DC: Salem Books, 2016.

Gingrich, Newt. *Rediscovering God in America.* Nashville: Thomas Nelson, 2009.

Grudem, Wayne. *Politics According to the Bible: A Comprehensive Resource for Understanding Modern Political Issues in Light of Scripture.* Grand Rapids: Zondervan, 2010.

Grudem, Wayne. *Voting as a Christian: The Social Issues.* Grand Rapids: Zondervan, 2012.

Hall, Mark David. *Did America Have a Christian Founding?* Nashville: Thomas Nelson, 2019.

Hill, Jason D. *What Do White Americans Owe Black People? Racial Justice in the Age of Post-Oppression.* New York: Emancipation Books, 2021.

Homes, Jr., Oliver Wendell. *The Common Law.* Boston: Little, Brown, and Company, 1881. Reprinted with introduction by Sheldon M. Novick. New York: Dover, 1991.

Howard, Kevin, and Marvin Rosenthal. *The Feasts of the Lord: God's Prophetic Calendar from Calvary to the Kingdom.* Nashville: Thomas Nelson, 1997.

Isaacson, Walter. *Ben Franklin: An American Life.* New York: Simon & Schuster, 2003.

Lossing, Benson J. *Lives of the Signers of the Declaration of Independence*. 1848. Reprint with foreword by David Barton. Aledo, TX: WallBuilder Press, 2010.

Marshall, Peter, and David Manuel. *The Light and the Glory*. Grand Rapids, MI: Revell, 1977.

McCullough, David. *1776*. New York: Simon & Schuster, 2005.

Millard, Catherine. *The Rewriting of America's History*. Camp Hill, PA: Horizon House Publishers, 1991.

Mowery, David L. *Cincinnati in the Civil War: The Union's Queen City*. Charleston, SC: The History Press, 2021.

Newcombe, Jerry. *The Book That Made America: How the Bible Formed Our Nation*. Ventura, CA: Nordskog Publishing, 2009.

Ostrowski, James. *Progressivism: A Primer on the Idea Destroying America*. Buffalo, NY: Cazenovia Books, 2014.

Ryrie, Charles C. *Basic Theology: A Popular Systematic Guide to Understanding Biblical Truth*. Wheaton, IL: Victor Books, 1986.

Ryrie, Charles C. *Dispensationalism Today*. Chicago: Moody Press, 1996.

Shelley, Bruce L. *Church History in Plain Language*. Dallas: W Publishing Group, 1982.

Skousen, W. Cleon. *The Five Thousand Year Leap: 28 Great Ideas That Changed the World*. Malta, ID: National Center for Constitutional Studies, 1981.

Smith, K. Carl. *Frederick Douglass Republicans: The Movement to Re-Ignite America's Passion for Liberty*. Bloomington, IN: AuthorHouse, 2011.

Swanson, Mary-Elaine. *John Locke: Philosopher of American Liberty*. Ventura, CA: Nordskog Publishing, 2012.

West, Thomas G. *Vindicating the Founders: Race, Sex, Class, and Justice in the Origins of America*. New York: Rowman & Littlefield Publishers, Inc., 1997.

Wise, John. *Vindication of the Government of New England Churches*. 1717. Reprint, Whitefish, MT: Kessinger Publishing, 2003.

ENDNOTES

1   Joe Pierre, "Why Has America Become So Divided?," Psychology Today, September 5, 2018, https://www.psychologytoday.com/us/blog/psych-unseen/201809/why-has-america-become-so-divided.

2   The Virginia Declaration of Rights, June 12, 1776, online at National Archives, https://www.archives.gov/founding-d.

3   S.C. Const. of 1778, art. XIII and XXXVIII, accessed at https://avalon.law.yale.edu/18th_century/sc02.asp.

4   Charter of Rhode Island and Providence Plantations, July 15, 1663, The Avalon Project, https://avalon.law.yale.edu/17th_century/ri04.asp#1.

5   Charter of Connecticut, 1662, The Avalon Project, https://avalon.law.yale.edu/17th_century/ct03.asp.

6   N.H. Const. of 1784, art. VI, accessed at https://lonang.com/library/organic/1784-nhr/.

7   "God in Our Nation's Capital," Probe, last modified January 29, 2007, https://probe.org/god-in-our-nations-capital/.

8   "God in Our Nation's Capital."

9   Newt Gingrich, *Rediscovering God in America: Reflections on the Role of Faith in Our Nation's History and Future* (Nashville: Integrity House, 2006), 70–71.

10   Gingrich, *Rediscovering God in America*, 71.

11   William Howard Taft, Proclamation 1223—Thanksgiving Day, November 7, 1912, online by Gerhard Peters and John T. Woolley, The American Presidency Project, https://www.presidency.ucsb.edu/node/207574.

12   Calvin Coolidge, Address at the Unveiling of the Equestrian Statue of Bishop Francis Asbury, Washington, DC, October 15, 1924, online by Gerhard Peters and John T. Woolley, The American Presidency Project, https://www.presidency.ucsb.edu/node/268893.

13   Harry S. Truman, Address Before the Attorney General's Conference on Law Enforcement Problems, February 15, 1950, online by Gerhard Peters and John T. Woolley, The American Presidency Project, https://www.presidency.ucsb.edu/node/230655.

14   Ronald Reagan, Remarks to Chinese Community Leaders in Beijing, China, April 27, 1984, online by Gerhard Peters and John T. Woolley, The American Presidency Project, https://www.presidency.ucsb.edu/node/260682.

15   Ronald Reagan, Message to the Congress Transmitting a Proposed Constitutional Amendment on Prayer in School, May 17, 1982, online by Gerhard Peters and John T. Woolley, The American Presidency Project, https://www.presidency.ucsb.edu/node/245829.

16   Ronald Reagan, Proclamation 5018—Year of the Bible, 1983, February 3, 1983, online by Gerhard Peters and John T. Woolley, The American Presidency Project, https://www.presidency.ucsb.edu/node/262128.

17   Bill Federer, "Jefferson Opposed Censorship of Opinions: Virginia Statute of Religious Freedom & How Courts have taken Freedom away!" American Minute, https://americanminute.com/blogs/todays-american-minute/jefferson-opposed-censorship-of-opinions-virginia-statute-of-religious-freedom-how-courts-have-taken-freedom-away-american-miute-with-bill-federer?_pos=2&_sid=a263dd0e7&_ss=r.

18   "'Old Ironsides' USS Constitution - Oliver Wendell Holmes, Sr., & His Dissenting Son - American Minute with Bill Federer," American Minute,10https://americanminute.com/blogs/todays-american-minute/olwendell-holmes-sr-his-dissenting-son-american-minute-with-bill-federer?_pos=1&_sid=eccde944b&_ss=r.

19   Liva Baker, *The Justice from Beacon Hill: The Life and Times of Oliver Wendell Holmes* (New York: Harpercollins, 1991), quoted in "'Old Ironsides,'" American Minute.

20   Bradley C. S. Watson, "The Curious Constitution of Oliver Wendell Holmes Jr.," National Review, December 17, 2009, https://www.nationalreview.com/magazine/2009/12/31/curious-constitution-oliver-wendell-holmes-jr/, quoted in "'Old Ironsides,'" American Minute.

21   Federer, "Jefferson Opposed Censorship."

22   Abraham Lincoln, Address at the Illinois State Republican Convention in Springfield, Illinois, June 17, 1858, online by Gerhard Peters and John T. Woolley, The American Presidency Project, https://www.presidency.ucsb.edu/node/342161.

23   Ted Tuttle, "Christian Pollster Sheds New Light on What Church-goers Want Preached from the Pulpit," Glenn, accessed September 30, 2021, https://

www.glennbeck.com/2015/09/23/christian-pollster-sheds-new-light-on-what-church-goers-want-preached-from-the-pulpit/.

24   Alexis de Tocqueville, *Democracy in America*, quoted in William J. Federer, *America's God and Country Encyclopedia of Quotations* (St. Louis: Amerisearch, Inc., 2000), 205.

25   "The Great World Wide Flood: Genesis Six," Bible Truth Bible Studies, accessed September 13, 2021, https://www.bible-truth.org/gen6.htm.

26   See Jay Nordlinger, *Children of Monsters* (New York: Encounter Books, 2015).

27   John Jay, *The Correspondence and Public Papers of John Jay*, ed. Henry P. Johnston (New York: Burt Franklin, 1970), 4:383, quoted in William J. Federer, *America's God and Country Encyclopedia of Quotations* (St. Louis: Amerisearch, Inc., 2000), 318.

28   John Adams, *The Works of John Adams – Second President of the United States: with a Life of the Author, Notes, and Illustration*, ed. Charles Francis Adams (Boston: Little, Brown, & Co., 1854), 9:228–229, quoted in William J. Federer, *America's God and Country Encyclopedia of Quotations* (St. Louis: Amerisearch, Inc., 2000), 10–11.

29   Abigail Adams, *The Quotable Abigail Adams*, ed. John P. Kaminski (Cambridge: Belknap Press, 2009), 66.

30   Alexis de Tocqueville, *Democracy in America*.

31   Charles Ryrie, *Basic Theology: A Popular Systematic Guide to Understanding Biblical Truth* (Chicago: Moody Publishers, 1986), 444.

32   Thomas Jefferson, Act for Establishing Religious Freedom, January 16, 1786, online at Encyclopedia Virginia, https://encyclopediavirginia.org/entries/an-act-for-establishing-religious-freedom-1786/.

33   John M. Cobin, *Christian Theology of Public Policy* (Greenville, SC: Alertness Ltd., 2006), 60. I have added content to the table.

34   "Divine right of kings," Wikipedia, last modified August 22, 2021, https://en.wikipedia.org/wiki/Divine_right_of_kings.

35   Charles Ryrie, *Basic Theology*, 441, 444.

36   Luke 22:29–30; John 14:2; Acts 22:22–29; Eph. 2:9; Phil. 3:20–21; Heb. 13:14; 1 Pet. 1:4; Rev. 21:2, 27, 22:3–5.

37   John Adams, Letter to F.A. Van der Kemp, December 27, 1816, quoted in Michael Novak, "Meacham Nods," National Review, December 13, 2007, https://www.nationalreview.com/2007/12/meacham-nods-michael-novak/.

38   Thomas Jefferson, *Notes on the State of Virginia*, Query XVIII, 237, quoted in William J. Federer, *America's God and Country Encyclopedia of Quotations* (St. Louis: Amerisearch, Inc., 2000).

39   James Madison, *Notes of Debates in the Federal Convention of 1787* (NY: W.W. Morton & Co., Original 1787 reprinted 1987), 1:504, quoted in William J. Federer, *America's God and Country Encyclopedia of Quotations* (St. Louis: Amerisearch, Inc., 2000), 248–249.

40   George Washington, First Inaugural Address, April 30, 1789, National Archives and Records Administration, https://www.archives.gov/exhibits/american_originals/inaugtxt.html.

41   John Jay, *The Correspondence and Public Papers of John Jay*, ed. Henry Johnston (New York: G. P. Punam's Sons, 1893), 4:391-393, quoted in "John Jay on the Biblical View of War," WallBuilders, December 29, 2016, https://wallbuilders.com/john-jay-biblical-view-war/.

42   Thomas Hooker, The Fundamental Orders of Connecticut, January 14, 1639, online at American History from Revolution to Reconstruction and Beyond, www.let.rug.nl/usa/documents/1600-1650/the-fundamental-orders-of-connecticut-1639.php.

43   Verna M. Hall, ed., *The Christian History of the Constitution of the United States of America* (San Francisco, 1980), 252, quoted in Mark A. Beliles and Stephen K. McDowell, *America's Providential History*, 3rd ed. (Charlottesville: The Providence Foundation, 2010), 86.

44   John Locke, *The Works of John Locke in Nine Volumes*, 12th ed., vol. 6, (London: Rivington, 1824), online at https://oll.libertyfund.org/title/locke-the-works-vol-6-the-reasonableness-of-christianity.

45   Lisa Gold, "Books the Founders Read: Commentaries on the Laws of England," Bauman Rare Books, April 21, 2015, https://www.baumanrarebooks.com/blog/blackstones-commentaries-books-founders-read/#:~:text=The%20Founding%20Fathers%E2%80%99%20most%20important%20and%20widely-owned%20law,editions%20and%20frequently%20cited%20it%20in%20their%20writings. See also David A. Lockmiller, *Sir William Blackstone* (1938, 1970), https://www.biblio.com/book/sir-william-blackstone-david-lockmiller-llb/d/1263629945.

46   William Blackstone, *Commentaries on the Laws of England*, 1765, online at The Avalon Project, https://avalon.law.yale.edu/18th_century/blackstone_intro.asp#2.

47   John Adams, Letter to F.A. Van der Kemp.

48   Lord Acton, Letter to Bishop Creighton, 1887, online at Online Library of Liberty, oll.libertyfund.org/quotes/214.

49   Ben Jacobs, "'Love Is Love': Obama Lauds Gay Marriage Activists in Hailing 'a Victory for America,'" The Guardian, June 26, 2015, https://www.theguardian.com/us-news/2015/jun/26/obama-gay-marriage-speech-victory-for-america.

50   George Washington, Farewell Address, September 19, 1796, online at National Archives, https://founders.archives.gov/documents/Washington/05-20-02-0440-0002.

51   Marvin Rosenthal and Kevin Howard, *The Feasts of the Lord: God's Prophetic Calendar from Calvary to the Kingdom* (Winter Garden, FL: Zion's Hope Inc., 1997), 44. Bible references added.

52   John Adams, *Letters of John Adams – Addressed to His Wife*, ed. Charles Francis Adams (Boston: Charles C. Little and James Brown, 1841), 1:128, quoted in William J. Federer, *America's God and Country Encyclopedia of Quotations* (St. Louis: Amerisearch, Inc., 2000), 9.

53   *Journals of the Continental Congress 1774–1789* (Washington, DC: Government Printing Office, 1905), 9:854–855, quoted in William J. Federer, *America's God and Country Encyclopedia of Quotations* (St. Louis: Amerisearch, Inc., 2000), 147.

54   Abraham Lincoln, Proclamation 106—Thanksgiving Day, 1863, October 3, 1863, online by Gerhard Peters and John T. Woolley, The American Presidency Project, https://www.presidency.ucsb.edu/node/203180.

55   John Winthrop, "A Model of Christian Charity," *Winthrop Papers, 1623–1630* (Boston: Massachusetts Historical Society, 1931), 2:292–295, quoted in William J. Federer, *America's God and Country Encyclopedia of Quotations* (St. Louis: Amerisearch, Inc., 2000), 700.

56   John Winthrop, "A Model of Christian Charity."

57   Emma Lazarus, "Not Like the Brazen Giant of Greek Fame," online at The LiederNet Archive, October 8, 2009, https://www.lieder.net/lieder/get_text.html?TextId=54619.

58   Charles G. Finney, "The Decay of Conscience," December 4, 1873, online at The Independent of New York, https://www.gospeltruth. net/1868_75Independent/731204_conscience.htm.

59   Samuel Adams, Speech about the Declaration of Independence, August 1, 1776, online at Samuel Adams Heritage Society, http://www.samuel-adams-heritage.com/documents/speech-about-declaration-of-independence.html.

60   David R. Reagan, "The Bibles of the Reformation: A History of English Translations of the Bible," Lamb & Lion Ministries, accessed September 15, 2021, https://christinprophecy.org/articles/the-bibles-of-the-reformation/.

61   Reagan, "The Bibles of the Reformation."

62   Ted Chaney, Ken Cohen, and Lee Pelham Cotton, "The Virginia Company of London," National Park Service, last modified February 26, 2015, https://www.nps.gov/jame/learn/historyculture/the-virginia-company-of-london.htm.

63   "Jamestown Colony," HISTORY, last modified September 10, 2021, https://www.history.com/topics/colonial-america/jamestown.

64   "Jamestown Colony," HISTORY.

65   Walter Opinde, "1619: The First African Slaves Arrive in a Ship into What Would then Become the United States," Black Then, last modified April 23, 2019, https://blackthen. com/1619-first-african-slaves-arrive-ship-become-united-states/.

66   Chaney, Cohen, and Cotton, "The Virginia Company of London."

67   Chaney, Cohen, and Cotton, "The Virginia Company of London."

68   Opinde, "1619."

69   Opinde, "1619."

70   David Barton and Tim Barton, The American Story (Aledo: WallBuilder Press, 2020), 50.

71   Verna M. Hall, ed., The Christian History of the Constitution of the United States of America (Chesapeake, VA: Foundation for American Christian Education, 2006), 205–206.

72   Barton and Barton, The American Story, 50.

73   Hall, The Christian History, 205–206.

74　Hall, *The Christian History*, 212–213.

75　"The Fundamental Orders of Connecticut," The Historical Marker Database, last modified February 16, 2021, https://www.hmdb.org/m.asp?m=52695.

76　Thomas Hooker, The Fundamental Orders of Connecticut, January 14, 1639, online at American History from Revolution to Reconstruction and Beyond, www.let.rug.nl/usa/documents/1600-1650/the-fundamental-orders-of-connecticut-1639.php.

77　Marshall E. Foster and Mary E. Swanson, *The American Covenant: The Untold Story* (Moorpark, CA: Mayflower Institute, 1982), 95, quoted in Beliles and McDowell, *America's Providential History*, 86–87.

78　Barton and Barton, *The American Story*, 80.

79　Thomas G. West, "The Transformation of Protestant Theology as a Condition of the American Revolution," in Thomas S. Engeman and Michael P. Zuckert, eds., *Protestantism and the American Founding* (Notre Dame: University of Notre Dame Press, 2004), 198–201.

80　West, "Transformation," 199.

81　Edmund S. Morgan, ed., *Puritan Political Ideas* (Indianapolis: Bobbs-Merrill, 1965), 226–233, quoted in West, "Transformation," 199.

82　West, "Transformation," 199.

83　Samuel Nowell, *Abraham in Arms* (1678), quoted in West, "Transformation," 200.

84　West, "Transformation," 201.

85　John Locke, *Two Treatises on Government: A Translation into Modern English*, trans. Lewis F. Abbott, (Manchester, UK: Industrial Systems Research, 2009), 76.

86　John Wise, *Vindication of the Government of New England Churches* (Whitefish, MT: Kessinger Publishing, LLC, 2010), 35–39.

87　Ben Franklin, *The Autobiography of Benjamin Franklin* (New York: New York Books, Inc., 1791), 146, quoted in William J. Federer, *America's God and Country Encyclopedia of Quotations* (St. Louis: Amerisearch, Inc., 2000), 245.

88　Clinton Rossiter, *Seedtime of the Republic* (New York: Harcourt, Brace & World, Inc., 1953), 241, quoted in William J. Federer, *America's God and*

Country Encyclopedia of Quotations (St. Louis: Amerisearch, Inc., 2000), 436.

89   Dan Fisher, *Bringing Back the Black Robed Regiment* (Mustang, OK: Tate Publishing & Enterprises, LLC, 2013), 1:15.

90   This table was influenced by Bill Federer, "Government Intolerable Acts, Dr. Joseph Warren, & the Suffolk Resolves - American Minute with Bill Federer," American Minute, June 11, 2021, https://americanminute.com/blogs/todays-american-minute/intolerable-acts-dr-joseph-warrens-suffolk-resolves-american-minute-with-bill-federer.

91   Patrick Henry, Speech to the Virginia House of Burgesses, Richmond, Virginia, March 23, 1775, online at Lit2Go, https://etc.usf.edu/lit2go/133/historic-american-documents/4956/patrick-henrys-speech-to-the-virginia-house-of-burgesses-richmond-virginia-march-23-1775/.

92   *An American Dictionary of the English Language* (1828), s.v. "solemnly."

93   Dr. Larry P. Arnn, *The Founders' Key: The Divine and Natural Connection Between the Declaration and the Constitution and What We Risk by Losing It* (Nashville: Thomas Nelson, 2012), 5.

94   Walter Isaacson, *Benjamin Franklin: An American Life* (New York: Simon & Schuster, 2006), 309.

95   Calvin Coolidge, Address at the Celebration of the 150th Anniversary of the Declaration of Independence in Philadelphia, Pennsylvania, July 5, 1926, online by Gerhard Peters and John T. Woolley, The American Presidency Project, https://www.presidency.ucsb.edu/node/267359.

96   Abraham Lincoln, "Fragment on the Constitution and the Union," *The U.S. Constitution: A Reader* (Hillsdale: Hillsdale College, 2012), 67–68.

97   Adams, Speech about the Declaration.

98   George Washington, *The Writings of George Washington*, ed. Jared Sparks (Boston: American Stationer's Company, 1837; New York: F. Andrew's, 1834–1847), 6:36, quoted in William J. Federer, *America's God and Country Encyclopedia of Quotations* (St. Louis: Amerisearch, Inc., 2000), 643.

99   Washington, *The Writings of George Washington*, 10:222.

100   John Quincy Adams, Executive Order [on the deaths of Thomas Jefferson and John Adams], July 11, 1826, online by Gerhard Peters and John T. Woolley, The American Presidency Project, https://www.presidency.ucsb.edu/node/200526.

101 *An American Dictionary of the English Language* (1828), s.v. "freedom."

102 *An American Dictionary of the English Language* (1828), s.v. "liberty."

103 *An American Dictionary of the English Language* (1828), s.v. "liberty."

104 "Roger Williams," Wikipedia, last modified August 24, 2021, https://en.wikipedia.org/wiki/Roger_Williams.

105 Thomas Jefferson, Act for Establishing Religious Freedom, January 16, 1786, online at Encyclopedia Virginia, https://encyclopediavirginia.org/entries/an-act-for-establishing-religious-freedom-1786/.

106 George Washington, Letter to Johann Daniel Gros, November 27, 1783, online at Founders Early Access, rotunda.upress.virginia.edu/founders/default.xqy?keys=FOEA-print-01-02-02-6105.

107 *An American Dictionary of the English Language* (1828), s.v. "justice."

108 *An American Dictionary of the English Language* (1828), s.v. "justice."

109 Pallitto, Robert. "The Legacy of the Magna Carta in Recent Supreme Court Decisions on Detainees' Rights." *PS: Political Science and Politics* 43, no. 3 (2010): 483–86. http://www.jstor.org/stable/25699355.

110 John Locke, *The Works of John Locke in Nine Volumes*, 12th ed., vol. 6, (London: Rivington, 1824), online at https://oll.libertyfund.org/title/locke-the-works-vol-6-the-reasonableness-of-christianity.

111 John Locke, *Two Treatises of Government*, ed. Peter Laslett, stud. ed. (Cambridge: Cambridge University Press, 1988), 358.

112 James Otis, *The Rights of the British Colonies Asserted and Proved*, 1763, online at https://oll.libertyfund.org/page/1763-otis-rights-of-british-colonies-asserted-pamphlet.

113 John Adams, Letter to Massachusetts Militia, October 11, 1798, online at National Archives, https://founders.archives.gov/documents/Adams/99-02-02-3102.

114 Harry S. Truman, Address Before the Attorney General's Conference on Law Enforcement Problems, February 15, 1950, online by Gerhard Peters and John T. Woolley, The American Presidency Project, https://www.presidency.ucsb.edu/node/230655.

115 *An American Dictionary of the English Language* (1828), s.v. "politic."

116 *An American Dictionary of the English Language* (1828), s.v. "politics."

117 *An American Dictionary of the English Language* (1828), s.v. "virtue."

118 George Washington, Farewell Address, September 19, 1796, online at National Archives, https://founders.archives.gov/documents/ Washington/05-20-02-0440-0002.

119 John Adams, *The Works of John Adams – Second President of the United States*, ed. Charles Francis Adams (Boston: Little, Brown & Co., 1854), 9:401, quoted in William J. Federer, America's God and Country Encyclopedia of Quotations (St. Louis: Amerisearch, Inc., 2000), 8.

120 John Jay, *The Correspondence and Public Papers of John Jay, 1794-1826*, ed. Henry P. Johnston (New York: G.P. Putnam's Sons, 1893), 4:365, quoted in "John Jay," Blow the Trumpet, accessed September 15, 2021, https://www. blowthetrumpet.org/JohnJay.htm.

121 John Jay, *The Correspondence and Public Papers of John Jay*, ed. Henry P. Johnston (NY: Burt Franklin, 1970), 4:393, quoted in William J. Federer, America's God and Country Encyclopedia of Quotations (St. Louis: Amerisearch, Inc., 2000), 318.

122 Ronald Reagan, "Encroaching Control," March 30, 1961, Phoenix Chamber of Commerce, transcript and audio, 42:51, https://archive.org/ details/RonaldReagan-EncroachingControl.

123 John Jay, *The Correspondence and Public Papers of John Jay*, ed. Henry Johnston (New York: G. P. Punam's Sons, 1893), 4:391-393, quoted in "John Jay on the Biblical View of War," WallBuilders, December 29, 2016, https:// wallbuilders.com/john-jay-biblical-view-war/.

124 David Jeremiah, "Life Outside the Amusement Park," August 7, 2020, Turning Point, audio, 1:05, https://www.truthnetwork.com/show/turn- ing-point-david-jeremiah/14799/st with David Jeremiah (truthnetwork.com).

125 Malcolm Muggeridge, *Conversion: A Spiritual Journey* (Eugene: Wipf & Stock, 1988), 55.

126 *An American Dictionary of the English Language* (1828), s.v. "happiness."

127 *An American Dictionary of the English Language* (1828), s.v. "happy." Emphasis added.

128 William Blackstone, *Commentaries on the Laws of England*, online at The Avalon Project, https://avalon.law.yale.edu/18th_century/blackstone_intro.asp#2.

129 David C. Gibbs, *One Nation Under God*, 2nd ed. (Seminole, FL: Christian Law Association, 2006), 279.

130 Mark David Hall, *Did America Have A Christian Founding? Separating Modern Myth from Historical Truth* (Nashville: Nelson Books, 2019), 106.

131 US Congress, Congressional Resolution Recommending the Promotion of Morals, October 12, 1778, quoted in Hall, *Did America?*, 106.

132 Hall, *Did America?*, 92.

133 Hall, *Did America?*, 93.

134 Hall, *Did America?*, 117.

135 Hall, *Did America?*, 117.

136 Hall, *Did America?*, 100.

137 Abraham Baldwin, "For the Regular Establishment and Support of the Public Duties of Religion," quoted in Hall, *Did America?*, 100.

138 Ordinance of 1787: The Northwest Territorial Government, July 13, 1787, online at https://uscode.house.gov/static/1787ordinance.pdf. Emphasis added.

139 Petition from the Pennsylvania Society for the Abolition of Slavery, February 3, 1790, online at UShistory.org, https://www.ushistory.org/documents/antislavery.htm.

140 Thomas Jefferson, Letter to John Manners, June 12, 1817, online at National Archives, https://founders.archives.gov/documents/Jefferson/03-11-02-0360.

141 James Madison, Letter to Frederick Beasley, November 20, 1825, online at National Archives, https://founders.archives.gov/documents/Madison/04-03-02-0663. Emphasis added.

142 John Marshall, Letter to Jasper Adams, May 9, 1833, online at The Constitution Principle: Separation of Church and State, http://www.members.tripod.com/~candst/jaspltrs.htm. Emphasis added.

143 William Henry Harrison, Inaugural Address, March 4, 1841, online by Gerhard Peters and John T. Woolley, The American Presidency Project, https://www.presidency.ucsb.edu/node/200391. Emphasis added.

144 Holy Trinity Church v. United States, 143 U.S. 457 (1892).

145 Woodrow Wilson, "The Bible is the word of life," 1917, online at Museum of the Bible, https://collections.museumofthebible.org/artifacts/34440-typewritten-statement-by-woodrow-wilson-on-the-bible-framed?&tab=description#/. Emphasis added.

146 John Locke, *Two Treatises of Government*, ed. Peter Laslett, stud. ed. (Cambridge: Cambridge University Press, 1988), 271.

147 The Virginia Declaration of Rights, June 12, 1776, online at National Archives, https://www.archives.gov/founding-docs/virginia-declaration-of-rights.

148 Aleksandr Solzhenitsyn, Templeton Address, May 10, 1983, online at Templeton Prize, https://www.templetonprize.org/laureate-sub/solzhenitsyn-acceptance-speech/.

149 Democratic National Convention, "2020 Democratic Party Platform," August 18, 2020, 32, online at https://democrats.org/wp-content/uploads/sites/2/2020/08/2020-Democratic-Party-Platform.pdf.

150 Alexandra DeSanctis, "Biden Spends First 100 Days Expanding Abortion on Demand," National Review, April 30, 2021, https://www.nationalreview.com/2021/04/biden-spends-first-100-days-expanding-abortion-on-demand/;

Angie Leventis Lourgos, "Illinois Democrats Propose Laws Expanding Abortion Access—Including Repeal of Parental Notification for Minors," Chicago Tribune, February 14, 2019, https://www.chicagotribune.com/news/ct-met-illinois-abortion-bills-20190214-story.html;

Jill Hopke, "Protect Abortion Access This Election Year," The Progressive, January 14, 2008, https://progressive.org/op-eds/protect-abortion-access-election-year/;

"Where 2020 Democrats Stand on Abortion," PBS, June 7, 2019, https://www.pbs.org/newshour/politics/where-2020-democrats-stand-on-abortion.

151 Mark A. Beliles and Stephen K. McDowell, *America's Providential History*, 3rd ed. (Charlottesville: The Providence Foundation, 2010), 30.

152 Glenn Beck, *Arguing with Socialists* (n.p.: Threshold Editions, 2020). My source is an unpublished draft of this work, the contents of which may differ from the published version.

153 Daniel Di Martino, "How Socialism Destroyed Venezuela," E21, March 21, 2019, https://economics21.org/how-socialism-destroyed-venezuela.

154 Di Martino, "How Socialism Destroyed Venezuela."

155 "What Caused Venezuela's Collapse Is No Mystery — Except To Economically Illiterate Journalists," Investor Business Daily, May 4, 2017, https://www.investors.com/politics/editorials/what-caused-venezuelas-collapse-is-no-mystery-except-to-economically-illiterate-journalists/.

156 Solzhenitsyn, Templeton Address.

157 John Adams, The Works of John Adams – Second President of the United States: with a Life of the Author, Notes, and Illustration, ed. Charles Francis Adams (Boston: Little, Brown, & Co., 1854), 9:228–229, quoted in William J. Federer, America's God and Country Encyclopedia of Quotations (St. Louis: Amerisearch, Inc., 2000), 10–11.

158 Paul Harvey, "Paul Harvey and The Declaration of Independence," YouTube video, July 16, 2014, https://www.youtube.com/watch?v=b2qCOZOJ4p4.

159 Mark A. Beliles and Jerry Newcombe, Doubting Thomas (New York: Morgan James Publishing, 2014), 289.

160 David Barton, The Jefferson Lies (Nashville: Thomas Nelson, 2012), xvi–xxiii.

161 Barton, The Jefferson Lies, xvi–xxiii.

162 Woodrow Wilson, The New Freedom: A Call for the Emancipation of the Generous Energies of a People, (New York and Garden City: Doubleday, Page and Company, 1918), 3–4.

163 George Washington, Farewell Address, September 17, 1796, online by Gerhard Peters and John T. Woolley, The American Presidency Project, https://www.presidency.ucsb.edu/node/200675.

164 Sahil Kapur, "Democrats to Introduce Bill to Expand Supreme Court from 9 to 13 Justices," NBC News, April 14, 2021, https://www.nbcnews.com/politics/supreme-court/democrats-introduce-bill-expand-supreme-court-9-13-justices-n1264132.

165 Saul Alinsky, Rules for Radicals (New York: Vintage Books, 1989), 127–130.

166 Masterpiece Cakeshop, Ltd. v. Colorado Civil Rights Comm'n, 584 U.S. ___ (2018).

167 "Arlene's Flowers v. State of Washington," Alliance Defending Freedom, accessed on October 6, 2021, http://www.adflegal.org/detailspages/case-details/state-of-washington-v.-arlene-s-flowers-inc.-and-barronelle-stutzman.

168 "Social Justice," Wikipedia, last modified October 6, 2021, https://en.wikipedia.org/wiki/Social_justice.

169 Jason D Hill, *What Do White Americans Owe Black People?* (New York: Post Hill Press, 2021), 131.

170 Hill, *White Americans*, 130.

171 Hill, *White Americans*, 133.

172 George Washington, General Orders, July 2, 1776, online at National Archives, https://founders.archives.gov/documents/Washington/03-05-02-0117.

173 James Monroe, Inaugural Address, March 4, 1817, online by Gerhard Peters and John T. Woolley, The American Presidency Project, https://www.presidency.ucsb.edu/node/206322.

174 *An American Dictionary of the English Language* (1828), s.v. "citizen."

175 *An American Dictionary of the English Language*, s.v. "citizenship."

176 *An American Dictionary of the English Language*, s.v. "patriot."

177 *An American Dictionary of the English Language*, s.v. "patriotism."

178 George Washington, General Orders, July 9, 1776, online at National Archives, https://founders.archives.gov/documents/Washington/03-05-02-0176#GEWN-03-05-02-0176-fn-0002.

179 *An American Dictionary of the English Language*, s.v. "virtue."

180 Timothy Dwight, *Theology; Explained and Defended in a Series of Sermons*, 4th ed. (New-Haven: S. Converse, 1825), 3:478.

181 George Washington, Farewell Address, September 19, 1796, online at National Archives, https://founders.archives.gov/documents/Washington/05-20-02-0440-0002.

182 William John Bennett, *The Book of Virtues: A Treasury of Great Moral Stories* (New York: Simon & Schuster, 1993).

183 Roe v. Wade, 410 U.S. 113 (1973).

184 "Abortion Regulations by State," Ballotpedia, accessed September 20, 2021, https://ballotpedia.org/Abortion_regulations_by_state.

185 Dietrich Bonhoeffer, quoted in Eric Metaxas, *Bonhoeffer: Pastor, Martyr, Prophet, Spy* (Nashville: Thomas Nelson, 2010), back flap.

186 "Martin Niemöller: 'First They Came for the Socialists,'" United States Holocaust Memorial Museum, last edited March 30, 2012, https://encyclopedia.ushmm.org/content/en/article/ martin-niemoeller-first-they-came-for-the-socialists.

187 The Council of the Protestant Church of Germany, The Stuttgart Declaration of Guilt, October 19, 1945, trans. Harold Marcuse, https://mar-cuse.faculty.history.ucsb.edu/projects/niem/StuttgartDeclaration.htm.

188 David L. Mowery, *Cincinnati in the Civil War: The Union's Queen City* (Charleston, SC: History Press, 2021), 66–73.

189 The Cincinnati Gazette, September 14, quoted in Mowery, *Cincinnati in the Civil War*, 73.

190 Dan Fisher, *Bringing Back the Black Robed Regiment* (Mustang, OK: Tate Publishing & Enterprises, LLC, 2013), 1:50.

191 Henry Augustus Muhlenberg, *The Life of Major-General Peter Muhlenberg of the Revolutionary Army* (Philadelphia: Carey and Hart, 1849), 50–54, online at Internet Archive, https://archive.org/details/lifemajorgenera02muhlgoog/page/n60/mode/2up?view=theater.

192 Dan Fisher, *Bringing Back the Black Robed Regiment* (Mustang, OK: Tate Publishing & Enterprises, LLC, 2013), 1:49.

193 Paul A. W. Wallace, *The Muhlenbergs of Pennsylvania* (Philadelphia: Philadelphia University Press, 1950), 120–121, quoted in Dan Fisher, *Bringing Back the Black Robed Regiment* (Mustang, OK: Tate Publishing & Enterprises, LLC, 2013), 1:48–50.

194 Mark A. Beliles and Stephen K. McDowell, *America's Providential History*, 3rd ed. (Charlottesville: The Providence Foundation, 2010), 30.

195 Dan Fisher, *Bringing Back the Black Robed Regiment* (Mustang, OK: Tate Publishing & Enterprises, LLC, 2013), 2:312.

196 Fisher, *Bringing Back the Black*, 2:312–313.

197 Fisher, *Bringing Back the Black*, 1:37–66, 2:311–313.

198 Everson v. Board of Education, 330 U.S. 1 (1947).

199 Gary Scott Smith, "Thomas Jefferson and the Separation of Church and State," The Institute for Faith and Freedom, October 27, 2006, https://www.faithandfreedom.com/thomas-jefferson-and-the-separation-of-church-and-state/.

200 Thomas Jefferson, Letter to Danbury Baptists, January 1, 1802, online at Library of Congress, https://www.loc.gov/loc/lcib/9806/danpre.html.

201 Thomas Jefferson, Letter to Samuel Miller, January 23, 1808, online at National Archives, https://founders.archives.gov/documents/Jefferson/99-01-02-7257.

202 Runkel v. Winemiller, 4 H. & McH. 429 (1799).

203 Paul Harvey, "Paul Harvey and The Declaration of Independence," YouTube video, July 16, 2014, https://www.youtube.com/watch?v=b2qCOZOJ4p4.

204 Barack Obama, Father's Day Speech to the Apostolic Church of God in Chicago, June 15, 2008, online at Politico, https://www.politico.com/story/2008/06/text-of-obamas-fatherhood-speech-011094.

205 William Ely Hill, *My Wife and My Mother-in-Law*, November 6, 1915, Puck Magazine, online at https://brainycounty.com/young-or-old-woman.

206 James A. Garfield, Centennial Address, July 4, 1876, online at The Atlantic, https://www.theatlantic.com/magazine/archive/1877/04/a-century-of-congress/519708/.

207 Theodore Roosevelt, *Fear God and Take Your Own Part: Roosevelt and His View on World War One* (George H. Doran Company, 1916, repr. 2016), 85.

208 Harry S. Truman, Address at the Cornerstone Laying of the New York Avenue Presbyterian Church, April 3, 1951, online by Gerhard Peters and John T. Woolley, The American Presidency Project, https://www.presidency.ucsb.edu/node/230367.

209 Billy Graham, "Congressional Gold Medal," May 2, 1996, C-SPAN, video, 55:39–56:13, 58:38–58:52, https://www.c-span.org/video/?71572-1/congressional-gold-medal.

210 John Adams, Letter to Abigail Adams, September 16, 1774, online at National Archives, https://founders.archives.gov/documents/Adams/04-01-02-0101.

211 Benjamin Talmadge, quoted in Susie Federer, *Miracles in American History* (St. Louis: Amerisearch, Inc., 2012), 48.

212   Henry Clinton, quoted in Federer, *Miracles*, 70.

213   Congress of the Confederation, quoted in Federer, *Miracles*, 72.

214   Treaty of Paris, quoted in Federer, *Miracles*, 72–73.

215   Patrick Henry, Speech to the Virginia House of Burgesses, Richmond, Virginia, March 23, 1775, online at Lit2Go, https://etc.usf.edu/lit2go/133/historic-american-documents/4956/patrick-henrys-speech-to-the-virginia-house-of-burgesses-richmond-virginia-march-23-1775/.

216   Joseph Warren, Boston Massacre Oration, March 5, 1772, online at http://www.drjosephwarren.com/2014/02/boston-massacre-oration-highlights/.

217   For extensive, granular treatment of the crown's abuses of the colonies in the context of the 1760s and 1770s, see John Ferling, *A Leap in the Dark* (Oxford: Oxford University Press, 2004).

218   Constitution of Pennsylvania, 1776, online at The Avalon Project, https://avalon.law.yale.edu/18th_century/pa08.asp#1.

219   John Adams, Letter to Thomas Jefferson, June 28, 1813, online at National Archives, https://founders.archives.gov/documents/Jefferson/03-06-02-0208.

220   Benjamin Rush, Essays, Literary, Moral, and Philosophical (1798, 2nd edition, 1806), quoted in William J. Federer, *America's God and Country Encyclopedia of Quotations* (St. Louis: Amerisearch, Inc., 2000), 543.

221   Benjamin Rush, *A Defence of the Use of the Bible in Schools* (repr. American Tract Society, 1830), online at Bible Believers, https://www.biblebelievers.com/Bible_in_schools.html.

222   John Quincy Adams, *Life of John Quincy Adams*, 248, quoted in "The Hope of a Christian," America's Founding Fathers, November 26, 2010, https://americasfoundingfathers.wordpress.com/2010/11/26/the-hope-of-a-christian/.

223   John Quincy Adams, An Oration Delivered Before the Inhabitants of the Town of Newburyport at their Request on the Sixty-First Anniversary of the Declaration of Independence (Newburyport: Charles Whipple, 1837), quoted in William J. Federer, America's God and Country Encyclopedia of Quotations (St. Louis: Amerisearch, Inc., 2000), 18.

224   Runkel v. Winemiller, 4 H. & McH. 429 (1799).

225 Joseph Story, *Life and Letters of Joseph Story*, William W. Story, editor (Boston: Charles C. Little and James Brown, 1851), Vol. II, 8, 92, quoted in "The Bible in Public Schools," Vine & Fig Tree's, accessed October 18, 2021, http://vftonline.org/EndTheWall/Educ_Bible.htm.

226 Jasper Adams, *Religion and Politics in the Early Republic*, Daniel L. Dreisbach, ed. (Lexington, KY: The University Press of Kentucky, 1996), 39–50, quoted in David Hall, "The Relation of Christianity to Civil Government in the United States," Place for Truth, May 17, 2016, https://www.placefortruth.org/blog/the-relation-of-christianity-to-civil-government-in-the-united-states.

227 Quoted in Bill Federer, "Imagine a Supreme Court Justice like THIS!" American Minute with Bill Federer, accessed October 22, 2021, https://myemail.constantcontact.com/Imagine-a-Supreme-Court-Justice-like-THIS---Justice-Joseph-Story--The-real-object-of-the-FIRST-AMENDMENT-was-not-to---advance-Mo.html?soid=1108762609255&aid=Q-I4IggdGXs.

228 Quoted in Federer, "Imagine."

229 Quoted in Federer, "Imagine."

230 *Reports... of the Senate* (1853), 3, "Rep. Com. No. 376," January 21, 1853, quoted in Barton, *The American Story*, 260.

231 *Reports... of the Thirty-Third Congress* (1854), 6, 8, "Rep. No. 124," March 27, 1854, quoted in David Barton and Tim Barton, *The American Story* (Aledo: WallBuilder Press, 2020), 260.

232 Journal of the House of Representatives of the United States: Being the First Session of the Thirty-Fourth Congress (Washington DC: Cornelius Wendell, 1855 [sic]), 354, January 23, 1856, quoted in Barton, The American Story, 260.

233 Church of the Holy Trinity v. United States, 143 U.S. 457 (1892).

234 Calvin Coolidge, Address at the Celebration of the 150th Anniversary of the Declaration of Independence in Philadelphia, Pennsylvania, July 5, 1926, online by Gerhard Peters and John T. Woolley, The American Presidency Project, https://www.presidency.ucsb.edu/node/267359.

235 Barack Obama, "10 Questions: Religion in America," 1:03–1:19, https://www.youtube.com/watch?v=35sGJrWKcmY.

236 George Washington, Letter to Brigadier General Thomas Nelson, August 20, 1778, online at National Archives, https://founders.archives.gov/documents/Washington/03-16-02-0373.

237 George Washington, Letter to Thomas McKean, November 15, 1781, online at National Archives, https://founders.archives.gov/documents/Washington/99-01-02-07409.

238 George Washington, Speech to United States Congress, December 23, 1783, online at National Archives, https://founders.archives.gov/documents/Washington/99-01-02-12223.

239 James Madison, Notes of Debates in the Federal Convention of 1787 (NY: W.W. Morton & Co., Original 1787 reprinted 1987), 1:504, quoted in William J. Federer, America's God and Country Encyclopedia of Quotations (St. Louis: Amerisearch, Inc., 2000), 248–249.

240 Thomas Jefferson, Notes on the State of Virginia, Query XVIII, 237, quoted in William J. Federer, America's God and Country Encyclopedia of Quotations (St. Louis: Amerisearch, Inc., 2000).

241 Samuel Adams, Speech about the Declaration of Independence, August 1, 1776, online at Samuel Adams Heritage Society, http://www.samuel-adams-heritage.com/documents/speech-about-declaration-of-independence.html.

242 "(1860) Frederick Douglass, 'The Constitution of the United States: Is It Pro-Slavery or Anti-Slavery?,'" BlackPast, March 15, 2012, https://www.blackpast.org/global-african-history/1860-frederick-douglass-constitution-united-states-it-pro-slavery-or-anti-slavery/.

243 Barton, *The American Story*, 291.

244 "The Pennsylvania Abolition Society," Pennsylvania Abolition Society, accessed October 22, 2021, http://paabolition.org/.

245 "Jefferson's 'original Rough draught' of the Declaration of Independence," The Papers of Thomas Jefferson, accessed October 19, 2021, https://jeffersonpapers.princeton.edu/selected-documents/jefferson%E2%80%99s-%E2%80%9Coriginal-rough-draught%E2%80%9D-declaration-independence.